Boundaries of the Wind

BOUNDARIES OF THE WIND
A MEMOIR

Keywords: arranged marriage, aum, bindi, dowry, ghar-grahasthi, immigration, karma, memoir, Michigan, pediatrician, Punjabi wedding, Urmilla Khanna

iUniverse books may be ordered through booksellers or by contacting:

iUniverse
1663 Liberty Drive
Bloomington, IN 47403
www.iuniverse.com
1-800-Authors (1-800-288-4677)

Cover photo by Martha J Padgette

ISBN: 978-1-4917-5982-0 (sc)
ISBN: 978-1-4917-5981-3 (e)

Library of Congress Control Number: 2015901673

Print information available on the last page.

iUniverse rev. date: 05/01/2015

Author's Note

This book is an autobiographical narrative of a slice of my life. Although it is written in chronological order, covering about thirteen years of my life, the compilation of events is sometimes approximate and at other times compressed. Events are presented as I perceived them. Scenes and dialogues have been recreated from memory. Some life situations that may have taken days or weeks to resolve have been condensed into single scenes in order to keep the story moving forward. Names of some individuals have been changed to preserve anonymity. A few dates have been mentioned in order to keep the reader focused on the period at which the events occurred.

To Miranda

My dear friend who taught me to use the note-pad on my iphone effectively

Boundaries of the Wind

A Memoir

Urmilla

9/11/17.

Urmilla Khanna

urmilla.khanna@gmail.com

Just like the wind,

knowledge

has no fences, no boundaries.

—Kris Khanna (1933–2003)

In memory of

my husband, Kris,

and

to

Pita-ji,

the force behind the wind

Advance praise for Boundaries of the Wind

Boundaries of the Wind introduces us to situations and cultures that may seem foreign to the world we know, but the stories are really about all of us because they *are* us, in the persona of a bright Indian woman.

Christine F. Chaisson, PhD, Founding Director, The LifeLine Group

In her memoir, Dr. Khanna narrates the life of a foreign born physician who comes to America in the sixties in order to live out her dreams. Her stories resonate with me as they will with other physicians and immigrants of her generation. A must read memoir. I look forward to her sequel.

Narendra Desai MD, FACP, Affordable Primary Care, LLC

I opened Dr. Khanna's completed manuscript early one evening, planning to skim through it quickly so I could write an endorsement. Several hours later, I found that I had read the entire book cover to cover, leaving my husband to fend for his own dinner. A compelling book.

Margaret Placentra Johnston, Author, Faith Beyond Belief: Stories of Good People Who Left Their Church Behind.

Dr. Urmilla Khanna's remarkable autobiographical account of emigrating from India to the United States captures the emotional struggles and paradoxes of balancing Indian customs against assimilation, and striving to succeed in an arranged marriage against pursuing educational and professional goals.

Lisa Lipkind Leibow, Author of Double Out and Back

Acknowledgments

AUM GURU BRAHMA GURU VISHNU

GURU DEVO MAHESHVARAH

GURU SAAKSHAAT, PARAM BRAHMA

TASMAI SHREE GURAVE NAMAH

This shloka, the first verse in a Sanskrit hymn called "Guru Stotrum," keeps coming back to me again and again as I try to pen my words of acknowledgment. I had heard the hymn being chanted on and off through my growing years, and its essence was given to me by my mother in simple Hindi language. Every morning, as I put on my blue-and-white uniform, braided my hair in two pigtails, and hurriedly gathered my schoolbag to catch the bus, Mother followed me around, saying, "No matter which classes you are in, what subjects you will study today, and who your teacher will be, you must be thankful to her, for knowledge can come only when you respect your teacher from the bottom of your heart and listen to what she is about to disclose to you." Now, with her words ringing in my ears, I would like to offer this book to you, my readers, with this humble prayer and with heartfelt thanks to my teacher and mentor, Joanne Lozar Glenn. She has taught me and mentored me through the long process of becoming a committed writer and being able to put my innermost thoughts on paper, clear and decipherable.

I would also like to thank Mary Alice Beard, who has sat hours on end with me trying to keep me focused and not drifting away from my story. Her words "This is a good story, well told; I hate to see you let it go, but it does not belong here" are only too familiar to me.

I would like to thank all the members of my writing groups, the Circle, the Round Table, the Unitarian Memoirs Writers Group, and many others who have helped me bring my story to fruition. I hope you will pardon me for not listing each one of you individually.

And many thanks to you, Tishya Soni-Chopra, for taking me back to my root language, Sanskrit, and helping me with the precise meaning of the Hindi and Sanskrit words used in my manuscript; and to Ramesha and Poonam for helping me in the final stages of compiling this book. I could not have done this alone.

Going to writers' retreats has also helped me with my writing, and I would like to thank the members of Write Time, Write Place, Write Now [WTWPWN] writers' retreat for their trust and support.

When I look at the substance of my book, I feel I owe many thanks to the teachers and authorities mentioned in my text. Some may have appeared harsh and inconsiderate at the time, but they were also instrumental in keeping me focused as I accepted their challenges and continued to aspire toward my goal. Thanks to all of you, the Good Samaritans in my life's path.

Foreword

A woman has many loads to carry—the expectations that are thrust upon her by her parents, her in-laws, and her husband; those that the society expects her to carry—being a mother and caregiver to the family; and finally those that she puts upon herself—a career, success, happiness, and lots more. Urmilla has chronicled these beautifully in her memoir, *Boundaries of the Wind*. The emotions that arise from reading her account are only awe and respect.

In her book, she just tells us exactly how laden her life was with all the loads she carried so gracefully throughout her life. Her words are economical, her emotions even more carefully measured on the page. Her meaning is always clear and poignant. She does not belabor a point or make it speak.

She has successfully shown how a woman can have the force of a gale, yet the tenderness of a gentle breeze on a hot weary brow. She has done this not relying on fiction or fantasy but simply narrating her life as an example. Her words ring true and are solid of conviction. From Japan to Turkey and indeed in pockets of the Western world, women will know and understand her story like their own.

Urmilla has given us a glimpse of postindependence India when it made sense for fathers to empower their daughters with education while still keeping them domesticated and tame. She so beautifully brings to life the Indian philosophy of karma in every chapter of her constantly changing life and its inevitable ups and downs. Her writing will go a long way in audiences to finally appreciate that karma is not meekly submitting to fate but understanding and accepting and indeed embracing your circumstances with faith, stoicism, and guts. I love the fact that she has written this account in the final *ashrama* of her life—*sanyasa ashrama*—the last post of earthly life when you close accounts, settle debts, and make all things square. She has indeed achieved closure by penning down significant events of her life and saying to the world and to herself, "This was it, and I'm happy I did it all."

As a woman, a cowriter, and her niece, I owe a debt to Urmilla *bua-ji* for writing this book and making our own jumbled lives so much clearer in our mind's eye.

Mohyna Srinivasan, author of *House on Mall Road*

Introduction

Library shelves are filled with stories from immigrants. Why, then, would someone want to read another memoir about immigration? *Boundaries of the Wind* is not merely an account of how I came to America. It is about a journey. It is about how the everyday experiences of my early upbringing helped me shape my life. Questions about women's education, arranged marriages, dowry systems, career choices, parenting, and the feminist revolution confronted me head-on along the way.

I was born in India during the glory days of the British Raj. It ended when I was in my early teens, leaving behind a hybrid culture that had elements of modern England blended with the heritage and traditions of ancient India. In the glory days of the Raj, intelligent boys like my father were being handpicked by the Brits and offered college educations followed by excellent jobs. Girls, on the other hand, were left behind. They never stepped into a classroom. They studied at the feet of their mothers by borrowing their brothers' books. Women yearned to see their daughters educated.

Women's education was becoming a passport for finding a better husband. A girl who could speak English with a British accent, set the table in style, and make beautiful flower arrangements was in high demand. Mother, who had never had formal schooling, believed that my convent education would be enough to fetch me a good husband. My father, on the other hand, had his dreams soaring high. He was observing what Indira Nehru—later Indira Gandhi—was able to achieve. She was studying at the University of Oxford in London. He wanted his daughter also to be like her.

"What will my dearest little baby girl be when she grows up?" he would ask me at our lazy Sunday morning breakfasts.

"A doctor," I answered dutifully on cue.

"And the best ever," he added to complete our dialogue ritual.

In school, I was absorbing the Western way of life. As the British were exiting the country one by one, they were leaving behind not only their customs but also a vast population of Anglo-Indians. I was surrounded by them. They wore short dresses, they read dirty novels, and they had boyfriends at an early age. I wanted to be like them. After school, however, I was expected to change into Indian attire, sit beside Mother, learn the fine stitchery that she taught me so eagerly, and silently absorb her mantra of being a good daughter, wife, and homemaker—always obedient, always subservient to elders.

Growing up in that milieu, I was developing a mind of my own—a mind that was impenetrable. This book is about the unfolding of that mind. It is about how I managed to navigate my life through the convoluted messages that came from my parents that were further compounded by the mixed-up societal expectations of our times, finally achieving my stubborn and lofty dreams. Looking back, it is what I learned from my mother and from my father by sheer osmosis that has seen me through all the joys as well as the hiccups of my life.

Places of interest to the reader

Cities shown as reference points

PART 1

Bhilai, Madhya Pradesh, India

Chapter 1

The rickshaw came to a halt in front of a small rambler on Street 15 in sector 10 in Bhilai. I paid the *rickshaw-wala* with some loose change as he unloaded my trunk and holdall. Standing beside my luggage, I breathed deeply to take it all in. Home at last. The dry, earthy smell enveloped me. The garden was neatly manicured, and the fragrance of jasmine permeated the heavy air. Marigolds in hues of vibrant gold and saffron stood upright in rows, challenging the heat of the October sun. Living in dormitories for the past ten years and coming home for short intermittent breaks, I had felt as if I were a guest in my own home. Now that I had completed my studies, I looked forward to spending a few idle days with my family, enjoying Mother's home cooking and thinking about my future.

In a few weeks, or maybe a few months, I would leave again to enter the next stage of my life, that of *ghar-grahasthi*, the stage that encompasses marriage, career, and family. Dreams and visions of my new life were endless—a perfect husband, a small home with café curtains in the kitchen, two little children, and a career in medicine. I was twenty-five, and the year was 1961.

As I walked toward the house, the door opened, and Mother met me on the narrow brick walkway. "My, my, don't you look good. Come on in," she said. "Aren't you glad your studies are finally over? You are now a full-fledged doctor—and on top of that, a child specialist." Her words were generous, but there was something missing. Her voice lacked the enthusiasm I was expecting. She also looked older than where my memory of her had locked.

"Yes, I love it," I said, my own voice falling several octaves to fit in with hers. "It seems as though a large stone has been lifted off my shoulders." I smiled meekly, gave her a hug, and looked at my older sister, Pramilla, who stood behind her, waiting for her turn to welcome me. I saw no spark in those otherwise bright eyes, either. As I gave her a hug, she whispered, "Life is never easy, is it?"

I did not understand what she meant. Having completed my studies, I was feeling exuberant and quite accomplished. I was looking forward to my life ahead.

When I walked into the two-bedroom rambler that was allotted to my sister by the authorities of the Bhilai Steel Plant where she was employed, the place appeared cramped and overcrowded. *Pita-ji*—that is how I addressed my father—had recently retired from his job as a chief engineer in the Public Works Department, surrendering his huge, government-allotted bungalow. He, Mother, and their dog, Jackie, had moved in with my sister on a temporary basis. The furniture they had brought with them was oversized and out of proportion for the size of the house, and the atmosphere was morose and lifeless. The vase on the living room table was unattended, the roses in it wilted, their petals shed. I knew immediately that there must be more to this gloom than Pita-ji's adjustments to his retirement.

♦♦♦♦♦♦

When my sister and I were alone in her bedroom that night, chatting and catching up on all the news, I asked her, "What is it? Why is everybody so … so gloomy?"

Her countenance changed, and her chatter stopped. She gently shut the door to the bedroom. Reclining on her bed, she said in a low tone, "Parents are very concerned about our future. They have been looking for a groom for me since I graduated from college and seem to have hit a roadblock everywhere."

"I do not understand what you are saying," I said as I changed into my pajamas. "You mean they have not been able to settle your affairs in all these years? It's been almost four years since you graduated." Sitting across from her on the bed, I continued, "What became of Rajan? Did they not like him? Did they meet him?"

"No, they refused."

"Why? What is their problem?"

I had met Rajan. I thought Pramilla and he were so perfect together. Just like Pramilla he was an engineer and a Punjabi too.

Pramilla saw the look of utter shock and disbelief on my face. "You truly do not understand the complexity of all this," she said as she pulled herself to a sitting position and aimlessly traced the outline of a paisley print on the bedspread. Hot tears rolled down her cheeks. "It has taken me all this time to understand and accept their views. I am sure you will too, by and by. You have always been the baby in this house and have led such a sheltered life."

Tears still streaming down her face, she blew her nose into the hem of her nightgown and continued, "They have their own parameters, and there is no way on earth that anyone we propose will ever meet their standards. They feel strongly that they are the only ones capable of selecting our partners. They are very rigid about their views, and it has been difficult for me to have a meaningful conversation with them on this subject." Her lips quivered as words tumbled out of her mouth. "I want you to know this because I am sure you will also be approached on this matter. I just want you to be prepared. Soon you will be put in situations of meeting prospective grooms—choosing, rejecting, or being rejected and dealing with all the melodrama that goes with it."

Composing herself, she said, "I have gone through it all. We are their daughters and must respect them, no matter what their views."

I gave my sister a hug as I listened, my own eyes welling with tears.

"Surely Pita-ji would understand? He has always been so supportive about our education. He has fought all odds to see us educated. What now?" I asked.

"That is what I cannot understand. He had given us complete freedom when it came to our education. But now, when it has come to our marriages, he has a solid wall in his head that separates intellectual progress from cultural beliefs. If we have been acquainted with a boy, he categorizes it as a love-marriage. Then, all I get from him is '*samaj kya kahega*' (what will the society say)?"

That night, sitting beside Pramilla on her bed, I learned a lot more about Pita-ji's convictions. He believed that the entire community would look down upon him if we were to choose our own partners in marriage. Society would reproach him for not having fulfilled the one major responsibility of his life—that of personally placing his daughters in proper homes.

Pramilla and I continued to talk for a long while without resolution. The clock struck two, and the fatigue of my long journey home finally got to me. I slid under the covers and fell asleep, my arm wrapped around my sister's waist. I slept fitfully, troubled by thoughts about her uncertain future—and of course, how it would affect mine. I took solace in the fact that she was my older sister. She would have to get married first. Whatever happened with her life would determine mine. She was, after all, the role model.

♦♦♦♦♦♦

I was awakened the next morning by a thin beam of sunlight making its way through the slightly parted curtains on the window. I drew the curtains apart and let the yellow sunshine flood the bedroom. Lavender buds of morning glory on the vines outside the window were still moist from the night's dew and were starting to turn toward the sun and pop open.

I walked through the adjacent room, the one being used by my parents as their bedroom, and went to the dining room. There were papers and photos spread all over the table. I concluded that Pita-ji must have been working late into the night. He was up again, sitting at the table. I greeted him as usual with "*Namaste,* Pita-ji." He nodded without looking up, his eyes intensely focused on whatever he was reading. The folder from which the papers were spilling out was labeled "Matrimonial Matters." My eyes traveled from one photo to the next. Any one of those black-and-white images could be my future husband. I cringed. Without making a conversation, I poured two cups of tea, added milk and sugar, and brought the cups to our bedroom.

I handed Pramilla her tea. "I see what you mean," I said. "But where is all this correspondence coming from?"

"Pita-ji puts an ad in the matrimonial column of *Hindustan Times* every few months. Now he has advertised for you as well."

"That is disgusting."

"I know."

I could not make sense of what I had seen and heard. Whatever was going on in the minds of my parents was hidden behind their tense frowns and hard faces. The absurdity of their approach toward getting their educated daughters married bothered me, yet I saw no way out of it. Pramilla had been dealing with the issue for so many years.

♦♦♦♦♦♦

Every day, Pita-ji fervently opened stacks of mail, looking for the perfect match for Pramilla—and in some ways, for me as well, since I was just a year younger. The correspondence formerly contained in a single folder was now separated into two—one for me and the other for my sister. My opinion was neither sought nor deemed necessary. If Pita-ji needed an opinion on a proposal, he talked to Pramilla. She had always been the pivot of the family. I was indeed the baby. Uneasy about what I perceived, I settled into a quiet routine, sharing my sister's bedroom. I spoke little, slept a lot, and avoided any eye contact with Pita-ji's restive, fiery eyes. Mother, as always, tried to keep the turbulence at bay, maintaining a surface calm.

While Pita-ji restlessly shuffled papers in his files, Mother continued to pamper me with her cooking—*poori-aloo* for breakfast and *gobhi-paratha* with *dahi* for lunch. With Pramilla at work all day, Mother and I began to spend a lot of time together, making small talk, working on embroidery or crocheting tablecloths. "This will go in your trousseau," she would say dreamily as she displayed the beautiful patterns of her crotchet. On occasions when I accompanied her to the bazaar and she saw a young couple stooping over a vendor's basket selecting vegetables or fruit, she sighed. "Someday, with God's grace, my daughters will also go to the market hand in hand with their grooms." However, the subjects I really yearned to discuss with her could never be brought up. Discussing intimate matters of love or sex was never an option. What should go into choosing our marriage partners was not an acceptable conversation. That was to be left as the responsibility of the elders.

The ills and taboo of marrying someone of your choice were alluded to only indirectly in our conversations. "Did you see today's paper?" Mother said one day as she dropped the small, four-page local newspaper that she was reading, picked up her crotchet, and wrapped the fine silk thread around her finger. "I feel sorry for the parents. Imagine being written up like this in the newspaper? They must feel so humiliated. They let their daughter marry a boy that she claimed she was in love with. Now see what has happened? A year later, not only has he left her, he has filed for a divorce." She rested her work on her lap and looked at me, seeking my approval. Her eyes appeared absurdly large through the magnification of her thick bifocal glasses. I looked at her vaguely. "Tsk-tsk," she clucked her tongue. "What has life come to, a sacred matter like a marriage being contested in court? This is what I call *kal-yug*—the dark millennium."

We were living under the same roof, Mother and I, and yet we were on two different planets. I felt suffocated. I needed to get away from those constant taxing undercurrents in the home. I joined the Bhilai Social Club. Its year-round outdoor swimming pool, a rare facility in clubs in those days, was my diversion.

Chapter 2

I had been home for over two months and had not seen a single "showing the bride-to-be" activity. Pramilla continued to go to work daily, and Pita-ji worked at his task of groom hunting. My life seemed purposeless, dull, and monotonous. Boredom began to set in, and I decided to pursue my career. *They have not found a mate for Pramilla in all these years. Who knows—they may never find one for me either. I may be destined to follow the path of such women who spend their lives as lonely spinsters. In that case, at least I will have a career to fall back on.*

I learned about a vacancy for the position of junior pediatrician at the hospital that served the needs of the Bhilai Steel Plant employees and their families. I called up the chief medical officer, a family friend, and mentioned my availability. With my qualifications of an MBBS (bachelor of medicine and bachelor of surgery) from Nagpur University and a DCH (diploma in child health) from the Christian Medical College and Hospital, Vellore—two well-known universities—I was a welcome candidate. Everyone in town was acquainted with Pramilla's accomplishments as an engineer in the company. That was another testament that served as a recommendation for me. I was offered the job without a screening or a formal interview. I accepted the offer.

I was introduced to Dr. Joshi, the senior pediatrician, who would be my boss. Not much older than I, he had recently joined the steel plant after completing his studies in the United States. He welcomed me and looked forward to my sharing the heavy workload. This was my first job as a qualified doctor, and I was excited about putting my recently acquired knowledge to use. In just a few weeks, Dr. Joshi began to rely on my clinical acumen and judgment. He could now relax with frequent and longer tea breaks. I, on the other hand, enjoyed the privilege of working independently, taking charge of admissions, discharges, and treatment plans. It was quite challenging to manage a forty-bed children's ward where we generally housed sixty-some patients, doubling the space by tucking the less sick children in the floor space under the cots and the older convalescents on the veranda. I felt comfortable working under Dr. Joshi's guidance, and the job setting gave me immense satisfaction. I became engrossed in my work and spent long hours at the hospital.

In contrast to my professional life as a trusted young doctor, my life at home was dismal. I smelled the pent-up anger and frustration as soon as I got off the bus. The two folders labeled "Matrimonial Matters" never escaped my eye. While proposals for Pramilla were beginning to dwindle, my folder was bursting at its seams. Now my parents' entire focus rested on me. There was new fury, new burning energy for finding me a mate. Shuffling back and forth through the files, my parents talked to each other in hushed tones. Their plan was to screen every prospective groom for his age, caste, education, family background, and even his physical and mental health. Too short, too tall, too fat, or too thin were immediately eliminated. Only after they saw some prospects did they arrange for a meeting. Matching the horoscope was the last thing. It could be used as a trump card. If, at the last minute, they uncovered something in the boy or his family that did not appeal to them, they could always use the nonmatching of the horoscopes as an excuse for breaking the alliance. If, on the other hand, all seemed well and *Purohit-ji*, our family priest, informed them that the horoscopes did not match, that could be remedied with a little extra donation to the temple or even by a couple of extra fasts by Mother.

The thought of accepting such a marriage and leaving my sister behind made me nervous. She was, after all, my role model, my strength. I could not see myself plunging into such a blind arrangement without Pramilla setting the example. I yearned to have a sensible conversation with my parents. The way it was, it was best for me to just stay in my own cocoon. Time would tell.

♦♦♦♦♦♦

One evening, returning from work, I got off the bus and took the short walk home. My parents were sitting on the veranda having their tea. Kapildas, one of our old and trusted servants who had returned to his village after retirement, had come over for a courtesy visit. He sat at my parents' feet, paying his respects to my father for engineering the waterways and irrigation systems in his village. "Because of your greatness, *Sahib-ji,* we do not have to depend on the rains for sowing our crops," he was saying. "Oh, *choti-baby,*" he said, addressing me as I walked by. The creases of toil and poverty on his otherwise peaceful face deepened as he smiled to greet me. "Look how you have grown. God willing, you will now marry and have many children. Sahib-ji says you have become a doctor."

They were obviously on the subject of my degrees and my marriage. I greeted him fondly and went to my room. Their conversation filtered through the open door.

"See what I mean," Pita-ji was saying. "Both girls are big now. With God's grace, they will be married soon, and we will be relieved of our duty. We can then withdraw from all our worldly attachments and make our journeys to holy places. And if God is gracious, he will take us from the sufferings of this earth during one of our pilgrimages."

I heard the clink as Pita-ji placed his cup in its saucer.

"It is such bad omen to have grown unmarried daughters living at home. Is it not, Kapildas?" he continued.

I saw Kapildas's turbaned head nod in agreement.

Parents believed that they could not achieve *moksha*—deliverance of the soul from rebirth and restless transmigration—and would have to live their next life in *papum*—sin—if they failed to complete their duties in their present life. Getting us married and settled in our new homes was a prime prerequisite for them to complete their life of ghar-grahasthi and enter the next stage—the life of renunciation—and seek peace and moksha.

I was aware of such views being prevalent in the lay society, Kapildas's society. My father was an educated man, a successful engineer. I began to realize that the barrier that separated Pita-ji's intellectual reasoning from his fear of going against the *samaj*, the cultural beliefs of the society, was indeed rigid and immutable.

We, his two beloved daughters, were now his burden.

I swallowed, shed some silent tears. Changing into comfortable clothes, I went to the kitchen to see what Mother had prepared for supper.

♦♦♦♦♦♦

I had been working for about six months and had become comfortable with my life of dichotomy. As soon as I left home, I could shed my thoughts of despondency and immerse into a different world, the exciting world of medicine and healing. In spite of my strong academic training, there was much to learn. For one thing, I needed to improve my speed of examining patients. Dr. Joshi and I were expected to finish inpatient rounds and then see eighty-some patients in the outpatient clinic, all in about four hours.

In the clinic, we were assigned a single room. We shared a desk, sitting across from each other. Unlike at a teaching hospital, we did not have a nurse or an aide to assist us. An orderly stood at the door guarding the flow of traffic and maintaining order amid the long queue in the corridor, some patients having been in line since the crack of dawn.

I marveled at how Dr. Joshi could clear a dozen or more patients in a half hour. I was a fresh graduate, trained to take detailed histories and follow that with full physical exams.

"What is your secret?" I asked him.

"There is no secret," he said. "Be practical. This is not academia. Don't spend your time focusing on details. The diagnosis is usually obvious. It is glaring at you as the patient walks in—upper respiratory infection, infected sores, dysentery, worms, malaria, tuberculosis. Pick up the presenting symptom, and make your assessment. Place your stethoscope here and there on the child's chest with confidence, and then hand the parent a prescription. Those are the secrets: confidence and a prescription. Most likely, the child will improve. If he doesn't, he will return, and then we will consider further testing. Our labs are limited, and so is our pharmacopeia. Write your scripts from the ten or twelve items available in our pharmacy so they never go home without filling their bottle with a syrup of some sort. They have waited long hours with their empty bottles in hand."

Dr. Joshi laid down his stethoscope and looked at me as I went through my long and protracted routine. His intense stare made me aware of my movements as I dug into the child's belly to look for an enlarged liver or spleen. I blushed and hurried with my examination, dispensing the patient quickly and asking for the next one to be sent in.

There was always a pressure on me to finish my assigned work on time. The transportation provided for the hospital staff departed at one. If I was not done, I would have to wait long hours until an emergency vehicle became available to take me home. One day, Dr. Joshi offered to give me a ride.

"You don't have to do that," I said to him. "It is too much trouble for you."

"My pleasure," he said, and he retired to the doctor's lounge to wait for me. When he was dropping me off, he said, "I did not know you lived here. I drive this route every day. I can pick you up in the morning, as well."

I took him up on his offer and began to ride with him whenever our schedules coincided, thus avoiding the long and cumbersome bus rides.

Mother often stood at the drawing room window awaiting my return after the evening rounds. When she saw Dr. Joshi stepping out of his sleek new Ambassador and coming around to open the door for me, she came to the front porch and said, "It is teatime. Why don't you invite your brother for a cup of tea?" All my male friends and acquaintances were "brothers," just as all my parents' friends were "aunties" and "uncles."

Hot freshly made snacks were usually served with the evening tea. Dr. Joshi was a bachelor and began to enjoy his stopovers. One day, wrapped in matrimonial thoughts, as Mother usually was, she watched Dr. Joshi intently as he wriggled out of his chair and rose to say good-bye. After he left, she said, "Such a nice fellow, so polite. Hope he finds a good Gujarati wife." With a sigh, she continued, "He will have trouble, though. He is so short and *gol-matol*, chub-chub-fat."

Chapter 3

It had been a busy day at work. After lunch, I had returned to the hospital for evening rounds and had also taken care of some pending administrative work. Satisfied with my day's accomplishments, I took a seat in the bus going home. As we were about to take off, a nurse from the emergency department came running up to the bus. She sought me out and said, "We could use your help. A sick baby has just arrived." I stepped off the bus to attend to the emergency. The mother was sitting on a stack of hay in a bullock cart, caressing her eight-month-old baby and coaxing him to suckle on her sagging, dried-up breast. Teary-eyed, the father was standing beside the cart, his palms folded in front of his chest. "We will be ever so grateful …" he started to say to me, begging for help. The ashen-gray baby was severely dehydrated, his breath intermittent, shallow, and smelling of acetone. There was no time to talk to the parents or to listen to their woes. I grabbed the infant, who weighed no more than ten pounds, and strapped him on a papoose board on the gurney. The nurse brought an IV kit. Standing beside the bullock cart, I gave a small nick on the baby's tibial vein, inserted a cannula, and pushed a bolus of 5 percent glucose in saline. The baby's color improved. The struggle for breath subsided. There was hope. This baby might make it. I regulated the flow of the IV fluids and observed his vital signs and waited. When stable, the baby was transferred to the pediatric ward. Leaving him in the care of the night nurse, I took the emergency transport home. It was around eight o'clock in the evening.

When I walked in the door, there was a strong aroma of deep frying and an extraordinary hustle and bustle in the kitchen. The good china had been retrieved from the upper shelves. Tea was brewing in a teapot covered with a fancy embroidered tea-cozy. "What's going on?" I asked. My sister quietly held me by my arm and took me to the bedroom. "Hurry up and change. The Bajaj family has sent a message that they are coming over to see you."

I was baffled.

"Will the boy be here too?" I asked anxiously.

"No, I don't think so. This is just a preliminary look-see. I think his sisters, two of them, and an aunt will come."

A soft, rose-colored sari had been ironed and made ready for me. I undid my cotton sari and put on the silk one. "This is how it is going to be," my sister said as she stood behind me and worked on the clasp of the heavy gold necklace. I heard it snap. My sister gave me a gentle pat on my back. "This is your first time. You will get used to it. Just try to be yourself," she said.

Be myself? Not only was I to deck myself in silk and gold, I was also expected to instantly transform myself into an innocent, cute, shy, beautiful, marriageable daughter. My thoughts were on the skin-and-bones marasmic baby and the outcome of my treatment.

The boy did come. All I remember about him is his round face, large nostrils, and a halo of black, bushy hair as he slumped on the living room chair. Mother served tea with hot, freshly fried *pakorras* and mint chutney. In an hour or so, they left, and Mother commented, "This was a lost cause, wasn't it?" She scrubbed the bloodstain on the upholstery of our sofa and sanitized it with phenol. One of the girls was obviously not prepared for her period. I was quite amused by the whole thing.

♦♦♦♦♦♦

Several suitors followed in the months to come. The process was always the same. So was the outcome. When presented to a prospective groom, I sat quietly, wearing a persona of innocence and cuteness. I had no clue as to what they were judging me by and what I was to gain from that visit.

I remember meeting a young man who was stationed in Darjeeling. *If I do get betrothed to him, I would be the mem-sahib of a tea plantation,* I thought. I pictured my life in that capacity, supervising thirty or forty women picking and sorting tea leaves. "It rains too much in Darjeeling," Mother commented after he left. "My *beti,* dear daughter, will always be wet and moldy." I was glad to get rid of him so easily.

Another person went off our consideration merely because he worked for the Indian Foreign Service. In theory, he would have been a perfect catch, bright and well educated. "But what about her profession?" Pita-ji said after he left. "Multiple transfers to different countries will interfere with her career."

The Germany-returned engineer was considered too flirtatious. On our first meeting, he asked if he and I could go for a walk so we could talk. Pita-ji hesitated and then gave permission. As we strolled through the dimly lit neighborhood streets on that moonlit night, he reached for my hand, squeezing it gently and pulling me closer to him with a remote gesture of a kiss. When I told my sister about it, she said, "He certainly is not good husband material." I must admit, he was the most handsome of all the suitors I had met, at least so I thought at the time.

Thus, I kept presenting myself to prospective grooms, and the file labeled "Rejected" kept building up.

There were times when I was on the other side of the playing field—I was the one being rejected. The way I learned about this was by overhearing my parents' conversation.

"They have not contacted us after our last encounter."

"They must not be interested in her."

These remarks were hurtful in the beginning. I stood before the mirror and hated what I saw. Such ordinary features further obscured by the thick plastic frame of my eyeglasses. "It could just as well be the attitude of my parents," I said to the taunting mirror.

Whatever it was, I learned to deal with that as well. Each encounter became just another event in my life, no emotions attached. Fearful of the unknown, I would feel relieved when things did not materialize. Today, I can wonder and chuckle as to what my life would have been if fate had thrown me in the hands of any one of the multiple suitors I had met so begrudgingly. The reasons for their rejections, as presented to me at the time, now seem so petty and sometimes amusing. But as I look back, I am sure there must have been deeper reasons that my parents alone were able to perceive. As for me, it was the inexperienced youth in me—fearful, timid, rebellious, and proud all at the same time. Which of these emotions was dominant at any single encounter is hard to pinpoint and seems inconsequential now.

♦♦♦♦♦♦

One day, Pita-ji picked out a letter from the piles of mail and brought it to the breakfast table. He read aloud, "We have received your inquiry about our son in regard to a matrimonial alliance with your daughter. We have great regard for you and your family. However, we see a small problem in moving this case forward. We do not want the women in our family to be wearing the pants, if you understand what we mean. You mention in your letter that you have another daughter who has finished her medical studies. If you would like to consider her instead, we would be very interested in moving the case forward."

Turning to the next page, he said, "The biodata of the young man looks promising."

"And you are willing to negotiate with them?" I said. "I don't care how promising the young man appears to you; I will not deal with him or his family." I surprised myself at my courage of having talked back to my revered father.

"I don't see anything wrong," he said. "You are just being difficult."

I was being traded over my older sister merely because of my field of education, and Pita-ji did not see anything wrong. He was beginning to treat us as commodities to be unloaded so he could attain moksha, and Mother was in agreement. They were blinded by their frustration. I walked away in silence, my *alloo-paratha* and scrambled eggs untouched.

My sister followed me. "I have gone through such humiliations a million times. You have to get used it. We are indeed commodities to be unloaded," she said softly, her voice tremulous.

I hated the thought of being so angry with my parents. I hated myself for who I was—a doctor, the younger sister of an accomplished woman engineer.

I despised the samaj.

Sitting beside each other in our bedroom, we both wept.

Chapter 4

It was April 1963, almost eighteen months since I had been living at home, when something happened that changed my life. It was like a rumbling thunder on that hot, sunny Sunday afternoon. Pramilla, my father's precious older daughter, the apple of his eye, his life's hopes and aspirations, announced that she would go her own way in marriage.

The drama on the front porch was like a stage play. I remember that day, that very moment, so clearly. I remember it all.

I was in the courtyard in the back of our house, standing on the third rung of a spindly stepladder, stretching my hand up to reach for a large yellow papaya, ready for consumption. The front and back doors of the rambler were open to allow for cross ventilation. The warm breeze carried with it every sound, every word of the conversation from the front veranda. I heard it all. I trembled, and the ladder shook. I slowly got off the ladder and walked in. I stood behind the half-open door of the bedroom, shuddering. Jackie, our dog, had been at my feet, giving me company, helping me pick the best papaya. He followed me, his tail tucked between his legs. He disappeared under the bed and remained there a long, long while.

Pita-ji stood at one end of the veranda and Pramilla at the other.

"I have waited long enough," I heard Pramilla say. "I am twenty-eight, and no one you seek seems to be good enough for me or I for him. You come close to making an alliance, and then it all fizzles out. All I hear is that I am too educated or I am too old for matrimony, or they fear that I might wear the pants in their family. The bottom line is that I am rejected by every prospective groom." Her voice was soft but firm. There were no tears in her eyes. "Now I would like to take matters into my own hands. I would like you to meet Mr. Balachandran. He will be the man I will marry."

She said no more.

"Am I hearing what I am hearing? Are these words coming from that same daughter for whom I have sacrificed my life, poured my sweat and blood? Now you tell me you are going to go your own way?"

The grip on his cane tightened, and his face flushed as he fumbled for words. Then his words came in a stream. "You will commit a sin not only for yourself but put me into a graver sin. Don't you know that it is my godly duty and responsibility to give your hand in marriage to a worthy man? What will I answer to God? And what will I tell the society? That I failed in my duty? I am the one who has to answer to God and to the society, not you. Don't you see that it is sinful for me to give you away to someone who is not from our community and is in a caste lower than ours?"

He walked closer to her, his voice now loud and hoarse. "I educated you to be an engineer, not a whore. I sent you out into the workforce to shine as a woman engineer and bring respect and fame to our family and not for you to go around picking your life partner. That has to be left to me. Mr. Balachandran is your workmate, not your soul mate, someone with whom you are to talk business matters. How could you ever marry someone like that?"

He put down his cane.

"I do not think you mean to do this. I don't think it is you who is speaking. It is the voice of a devil, a devil implanted in your head by that bastard who claims to be in love with you. No love ever starts before marriage. Don't you know that? What you are talking about is lust. Pure love can come only when you first sit before the sacred fire and make the promise to God about your sincerity toward the man, and in return, God gives you his blessings to start on that journey. Don't you understand?"

Then he fell into silence. His red, angry eyes looked smaller as tears trickled down his cheeks. He slumped on the bamboo chair, and, leaning on his cane, he wept.

Mother comforted him, bringing him a glass of cold water. He took a sip and leaned back in his chair. She wiped the beads of sweat building up on his brow with a cool, moist rag. "Calm down, calm down," she said, and I saw a piece of Pita-ji die.

I shriveled behind the door, listening. My legs became limp. I wished the earth would crack open and swallow me. I wanted to have nothing to do with my sister, my parents, my marriage, or with life itself.

Chapter 5

"Why, why, why?" I asked my sister later that afternoon, pouring salt over her open and bleeding wounds. "Why did you not tell me your plans? I have been subjecting myself to the humiliation of presenting myself to this one and that, and you have walked out on me."

I threw myself on her bed and sobbed.

She came and sat beside me. "I am hurting inside and out, believe me," she said. "I would not have taken this path if I had another option. I have none. I had been introduced to many young men before you arrived, and nothing had gelled. Now, as you see, my prospects are virtually nil."

Placing her hand on my heaving shoulder, she begged that I stop crying. "I know I have made the right decision for myself. As for you, I would never, not for a moment, suggest that you go through what I am going through. It is very painful. You still have many suitors. Grab the best proposal that comes your way and leave. You will be very happy."

She wiped my tears with the *palloo* of her sari and encouraged me to smile. "You will give our parents some comfort, as well. They are hurting bad."

Nothing that Pramilla said was of any comfort to me. I felt that she had betrayed me. I felt lonely and forlorn and had an intense desire to be alone. I wanted to go away somewhere, anywhere.

I left the room. I took a bath, pouring cold water over my face and shoulders. I picked up my swim bag and walked away.

♦♦♦♦♦♦

When I arrived at the clubhouse, the water in the swimming pool was tranquil, tepid from the day's heat. I climbed up to the diving board, jumped in, and began to swim. I swam for a long while. With each lap, my rhythm improved, my nerves relaxed, and my temper subsided. After my swim, I sat at a table beside the pool listening to the songs being played on the overhead PA system, allowing my hair to dry in the cool evening breeze. My thoughts were floating this way and that. Now I understood why my sister had been so distant from me in the past weeks. She'd had a lot on her mind. I dwelled on my own uncertain future.

I ordered a lemon squash. "Put it on my bill," I said to the bearer when Dr. Joshi came along.

"Make it two, and put it on my bill," he said. Turning to me, he asked, "May I join you?"

"Good evening, sir," I said as he pulled up his chair. He was my boss, so I greeted him courteously with the expected "sir." We talked about a couple of patients in the hospital. Then, looking right at me and meeting my gaze, he said, "I love to watch you swim."

"I don't swim too well," I said a bit embarrassed, and I covered my neck and shoulders with my towel.

"I know," he said. "But I still love to watch you."

In the dim evening light, I saw again that glitter in his eyes that I had seen time and again as he sat across the table from me examining patients in the clinic. At times, his patient flow would stop for a minute or two as he drummed his fingers on the table and stared at me, his gaze intense and uninterrupted. I had always thought he was assessing my clinical performance. Now, I was certain that he was falling in love with me.

We sat for a while, talking. Then I left. I was not going to unload my troubles on to him or let my vulnerable heart slip away.

Walking home, I could hear the music slowly fading in the distance. I heard the popular tune "Love Is a Many Splendored Thing." I tried to understand the complexity that surrounded me, the innumerable facets of love … and marriage.

Chapter 6

Long and tenuous discussions continued at home. Every day, Pita-ji was pleading with Pramilla to change her mind. She in turn was insisting that he not only accept her proposal but also agree to give her away in marriage with his own hands. She was firm and unyielding.

While Pramilla was going her own way in marriage, I was left to myself to decide the path that would be best for me. I could not afford to be the baby of the house anymore. I needed to grow up. I needed to think. And for this, I needed time. I needed space.

Days were getting longer in the hot, dry months of May and June. With the sun rising as early as four thirty, I had time to go to the clubhouse and get a swim in the wee hours of the morning before I started my workday. Except for the twitter of a few sparrows and the familiar throaty cough of the *chaukidar,* the night watchman, the place was quiet and deserted, giving me the opportunity to distance myself from everyone and spend time with myself, alone. I began to go to the pool daily. Each visit to the pool brought new meanings to my life.

Floating in the pool and gazing at the azure-blue sky above, my mind churned over the events of the past months and then years. I saw everything written clearly on that panoramic screen called karma. Was I not fighting against karma, my destiny? Something that had been stamped with indelible ink on an invisible screen the day I was born?

I was born to parents with strong convictions, driven to education, the first act of karma.

I had a sister sixteen months older than I who would be instrumental in shaping my life, another act of karma. During our toddler days, preschool years, and early life, my sister and I were playmates, the two older siblings being boys. We needed to band together, because our brothers teased and bullied us all the time.

As a child, my sister was chubby with baby curls framing her round face. She was prettier than I, more outgoing. I was slender, skin and bones, and had straight black hair. I learned to adore my sister. She did everything right. She sheltered me from my parents' wrath. "Mum is going to yell anyway," she would say when we were an hour late coming home. "You just go in by the back door. I see no reason for both of us to listen to her music." She protected me from everything noxious, even from the bullying that was so freely hurled at me from the boys. She was my *badhi-behen,* the big sister.

This pattern became permanently etched in our lives.

When Pita-ji was transferred to Jabalpur and we were admitted to Saint Joseph's Convent, an English school, I fell almost four grades behind my sister. She had the benefit of having had one year of English in Durg. She qualified for second grade. Although I could read and write in Hindi and recite tables up to twelve, I had had no exposure to the English language. I was placed in prekindergarten. At the age of seven, I sat amid the four-year-olds with a pictorial primer, *A* is for apple, *B* is for boy. Pita-ji bought me many books in English and encouraged me to study the language at home. In three months, he asked Mother Superior to test my skills and promote me to kindergarten. In the following years, I jumped two and even three grades in a year. I was in third grade for a few months when Pita-ji thought it would be great if I could catch up with my sister. It would save on the cost of books, rides to school events, and private tuitions. So I did. My sister and I finished fourth grade together. From here on, we became twins, Siamese twins. We were always together. We rarely argued or fought over anything. We studied with just one set of books, taking turns to do our homework. When we talked or laughed, we could not be differentiated. My sister shared all her clothes with me, her size being ever so slightly larger than mine. Thus she gave, and I took. That also became etched in our lives.

She still remained the prettier, the more outgoing, and the more capable older sister. I depended on her for everything except my grades. When I told her I envied her looks, she said, "But you have the brains. You always outdo me in your grades." Thus, another aspect of our being was etched in our relationship. She was prettier; I was smarter.

Then it was time for us to choose our careers. I had my heart set on medicine since I was a little girl—and she on engineering. Though our careers set us apart, she moving to Jabalpur Engineering College and I to Government Medical College and Hospital in Nagpur, our relationship did not change. During summer and Christmas breaks, I had to continue living in my dorm, completing one clinical posting or another, plus cramming for the next exam. Instead of going home to my parents' town, Pramilla often spent her break in my dorm, helping me with meals and giving me courage to carry on. Sometimes she studied a whole chapter in pathology, made a synopsis, and highlighted the salient points, thus making it easier for me to memorize.

When she fell in love with her classmate Rajan, we had to somehow be in equal partnership, so she sent a boy my way. She had met him casually. He was a lieutenant in the army, posted in Dehradun. He began to woo me as he passed through Nagpur on home leave once or twice a year. A train journey from Dehradun to Hyderabad, his hometown, could take well over three days, and a break at the midpoint for a day or two was always welcome. When in town, he took me to the movies, to nice places to eat, and even to army dances, which I enjoyed very much. He took to my charm instantly. When he was gone, I concentrated on my studies, exchanging childish letters of love. He remained my boyfriend in absentia.

The thought that my sister and I would have to eventually go our own ways was a faraway idea. We were too preoccupied in our happy lives moving so parallel and yet together. Now I could see that the time had come when our paths were turning, and I needed to find my own identity. I had turned twenty-six. Whereas my sister had decided what she wanted for her future, I was still seeking.

Sometimes I awoke in the middle of the night, unwilling to accept my fate. I pictured being married off to someone, just anyone that my parents would pick from nowhere. What if things went wrong? What would my parents do besides taking the blame? Maybe they would not do that, either. They would just push the blame right back at me for not having tried hard enough. I would end up lonely and destitute. Distraught and frightened, I awakened my sister and rested my head on her lap, sobbing.

"It is all written in our karmas," my sister comforted me, sitting up in bed and running her fingers across her forehead. Tapping the center of her forehead, the *bindu,* she continued, "Right here, it is all written right here."

"Maybe," I said, and I fell sound asleep.

♦♦♦♦♦♦

I began to realize that my parents were neither inconsiderate nor self-centered. On the contrary, they had sacrificed much of their lives for their daughters. Pita-ji had stood firm when family and friends had criticized him for sending his girls to professional schools.

My train of thought went to the time I was three. When I threw a tantrum, wanting to be in school with my siblings, he fudged my age as being four, the required age for school entry. Being precocious in education, I was fifteen when I graduated from Senior Cambridge. When my age worked against me, declaring me underage to enroll in medical school, my father had no qualms in taking the blame, saying that he had messed up my birth date in his memory. "With so many children, it's not easy to remember each one's birth date," he said to the clerk. We were five siblings and three or more that had not survived. Born at home, we had no birth records. He gave me a new date of birth, making me a year older.

He cared for Pramilla as well. He used extremely circuitous ways to get her admitted to an all-male engineering school. Her college application had no column for identifying the gender of the student. Her merit got her the admission. Then when she appeared for her interview, the dean was shocked to see a female appear at his office. "This is an all-male college," he said to Pita-ji, fuming in anger. "We absolutely cannot have your daughter here." Pita-ji gently asked if he could see the prospectus and review the article barring admission to females. Much to the dean's dismay, there was no such clause. All students were assumed to be males. The dean tried to find other legitimate reasons. He expressed a concern that in an all-male college, the solitary female could be a victim of harassment. "Leave that to my daughter," Pita-ji said. "She is strong and will fend for herself."

Now she was fending for herself, and Pita-ji was hurting as a result. He was not being selfish, just being driven by his convictions and hurting. I, on the other hand, was seeking strength to comfort him. My unhappiness came from within me. It was neither the system nor my parents that were to blame. It was the rebelliousness in me to challenge an age-old system. The system had worked, not once or twice, but innumerable times. My own parents stood as a testament to a happy and contented relationship.

♦♦♦♦♦♦

Alone at the pool when it was neither night nor day, just a dim, milky haze that announced the passing of the night and the beginning of a new day, I found my precious moments to think. One morning, I got an urge to revisit a story that I used to listen to over and over when I was a child. I recalled sitting beside my mother, learning from her the crafts she had perfected so well—knitting, crocheting, embroidery. As I practiced my stitches, she entertained me with her story.

Mother was born in Chak 59, a small village nine miles from the town of Sargodha, where Pita-ji grew up. At an early age, she had been promised to Pita-ji in marriage by her parents, because they knew of his high intellect and a potential for an excellent future. He went on to Roorkee College of Engineering, one of the best-known institutes for engineering in those times. The young couple had never met, but their future was secured by their parents.

Mother was fifteen, and Father was eighteen when they were married. When the groom and his wedding party, the *baratis,* came to Chak 59, they were housed in the outskirts of the village in large tents and shelters. It was a big wedding, the ceremonies and festivities going on for several days. During the celebrations, Mother had to stay in the inner sanctum of her house, lest the groom steal a glimpse of her. On the day of the wedding, she was led to the *mandapam,* the wedding canopy, with her veil, the *dupatta*, drawn over her head and face. According to the customs of those days, Mother did not set eyes on her husband even after the wedding vows, and he was not given a chance to see her face. After the wedding, the groom and his family returned to Sargodha.

In my childhood, this story came across to me like a fairy tale. I used to listen to it wrapped in thoughts of romanticism. Latching on to the passion with which Mother told her story, I would ask impatiently, "Then what happened?" as though I were hearing it for the first time. Mother continued.

Three months later, Father returned to Chak 59 for the final ceremony, *bidai,* where the bride leaves her parents' home and proceeds to her new home, that of her in-laws. His younger brother had accompanied him for this ceremony. They were on their bicycles and had lost their sense of direction in the crisscross walkways between the farms. Mother was in the fields collecting mustard greens that her mother wanted to cook for the evening guests.

Father hailed her and asked for directions. She trotted across the fields on her pony, bags of greens straddled across the pony's back.

Here, Mother would lay her knitting on her lap and stop her narrative for a second or two, as though there was a block in the linking of her thoughts. Her lips curled up in a faint smile, exaggerating her dimples. Her brown skin turned pinkish purple. Then she started again where she had left off.

"He looked so handsome. He was fair and tall, his face flushed red from riding in the sun, his shirt soaked with sweat. I blushed inside of me, looking right into the face of this handsome young man. I did not know I was looking at my own husband. I thought he was a traveler, a passerby. 'Come, follow me,' I said."

When she reached home with the travelers in tow, her parents met the visitors at the door and greeted them with great pomp and honor.

"I immediately realized my blunder, and my mother reprimanded me, saying, 'You should have at least covered your head with your dupatta and kept your eyes to the ground, you shameless girl.'" Mother blushed again as she recited her story. "That's the way it used to be in those days. I felt so embarrassed. I retreated into my little bedroom and refused to come out for the rest of the day."

Next morning, her parents gave a ceremonious send-off to the young couple.

"When we were departing, I felt so awkward sitting on the backseat of your father's bicycle with my arm around his waist. I felt like all eyes were on me. As my friends hailed me good-bye, they teased me that they had already seen me flirting with my husband in the open fields the previous day, and I had no reason to feel so embarrassed now," she narrated.

Listening to this story again and again as a child, I would become an integral part of it. When I grow up, I will meet the love of my life somewhere in a paddy field. We will exchange glances, and I will fall in love. We will marry. Life was going to be that simple.

Now, seated at the edge of the pool, at the brink of my life's decisions, memories of the same story played out differently. Mother had accepted her marriage blindfolded, determined that she could make it work. She had trusted her parents, and they had trusted their instincts. I must pick up courage. I must do the same.

With passage of time, the crevice that had formed between my parents and me began to appear less formidable. I could perceive their worries. If it was not my fault that I was still single at the age of twenty-six, it was not their fault, either. Pursuing my education, I had passed the desirable age for marriage. Girls who did not take to higher education were generally married off by the time they were twenty-two. However, neither Pita-ji nor I would have traded my education for anything in life. Now we had to deal with the consequences. Additionally, our original homeland, Punjab, had been lost to us after the Indo-Pakistan partition. When the Hindus fled from Pakistan, they scattered all over India, making it difficult for Pita-ji to locate his old Punjabi contacts. His frustration was understandable.

As I let my thoughts mellow and ripen, I was more and more willing to gamble with an arranged marriage. That is my karma. I should not fight it. I should embrace it. I will just have to bend and shape my karma according to my needs.

♦♦♦♦♦♦

A small stream of suitors kept trickling in. My parents were emotionally exhausted, recovering from the trauma of their older daughter's wishes in marriage. They wanted to see me married to a Punjabi boy, and they were running out of time.

Their impatience took the form of Dr. Monga, a Punjabi and an internist working at the Bhilai Steel Plant. They met his family and brought the proposal back to me.

"I can't understand why you do not consent to this," Pita-ji said in frustration. "He is a physician. He works right here. You will not even have to move out of the area."

"I have told you a thousand times, I will never marry a physician." I stood firm on my convictions, though my heart was trembling at the thought of voicing my opinion and opposing my father.

"And that is because?"

I could not formulate proper words to answer him, but my head was clear. By marrying a physician, I could see the possibility of ruining our marital relationship by being competitive with each other. I did not want to take that chance. "A household with two physicians can get monotonously boring," I managed to say. "And then if we are both so busy professionally, who will take care of the children?"

"That is an excuse, *beta*," Mother said in a pleading voice. "You will have enough money to hire ayahs and servants for everything."

I had seen the ratio of eight servants to four family members during Pita-ji's glory days in the civil service. How could I say to Mother that I resented that?

"All these are petty excuses." Pita-ji's voice was loud and threatening. "Why don't you come straight out and tell us if you also have someone in mind like your sister? Tell us now, and spare us the agony. One blow is hard enough. If we have to take another, it will not be any harder."

"No," I said, "there is no one in my life that I would marry. However, I will not say yes unless I feel comfortable."

Chapter 7

One afternoon in the summer of 1963, I was surprised to see Pramilla at home when I returned from the hospital. Whereas we, the medical staff, worked two shifts with a midday siesta break, she normally worked a straight eight-hour day.

"What's the matter? You did not go to work today?" I asked.

"No, I took a day off."

"Why?"

"Oh, it's a long story."

"Like what?"

"We'll talk about it in the evening when we have more time."

She wore a faint smile as she spoke, and I did not question her any further. From her placid countenance and the contented looks on the faces of my parents, I suspected that it must have something to do with a new marriage proposal for me. I did not wish to second-guess what they had on their minds. *Proposals come and go,* I thought. Discussions about them had become quite a routine in my life.

In a few hours, I left for the hospital for evening rounds. However, the advice Pramilla had given me earlier kept reverberating in my head and distracting me from attending to my patients. "Grab the best proposal that comes your way and leave. You will be very happy."

By the time I returned from the hospital, the sun had set, and the intolerable heat of the day had given way to a subtle, cooler breeze. Pramilla and I set out for a walk, and she broached the subject.

"Karma does work in mysterious ways," she started.

"Come on, don't beat around the bush. Tell me what's going on."

"Well, it all dates back to several months ago when Pita-ji had put a new ad in the paper for you. Right around that time, this person—a boy named Krishan Khanna—was finishing his PhD in America and was corresponding with his family in Amritsar, expressing his desire to take a three-month break, come to India, choose a bride, and get married. Upon seeing your ad, his father had communicated with Pita-ji, and your photo and bio and so on had been sent to him."

"And then?"

"Then there was silence. Since Pita-ji did not hear anymore from Amritsar, he closed that file, assuming they were not interested in you. Last Monday, all of a sudden, we received a call from a person named Mr. Mehra. He wanted to talk to us about a possible alliance between the two of you."

"What triggered that?"

"Krishan's having arrived in India."

"And who is this Mr. Mehra?"

"He is Krishan's distant cousin and works as a private contractor in Bhilai."

"Oh, so we are now going to deal with a middleman, a matchmaker," I said. "What the hell is he getting out of this? He will say good things about his cousin and get us hooked up. And then what?"

"No, it does not work that way." Pramilla and I continued to stroll at a relaxed pace, and she continued, "Middlemen are actually very useful in making matrimonial connections. They are not biased and do a lot of the groundwork. Mummy, Pita-ji, and I visited Mr. Mehra this morning and spent good two or three hours in his home. We learned a great deal about Krishan."

Pramilla was eager to tell me everything. I was eager to listen.

"Mr. Mehra knows Krishan well and spoke highly about him, mostly his serene temperament. He told us that Krishan has just finished his PhD in pharmacy and pharmacology. He will be in India for three months, after which he has to return to America for his postdoctoral fellowship. Mr. Mehra also said that he had gone to the hospital to get a glimpse of you and make some sort of an assessment about your compatibility with Krishan. He observed you for quite awhile."

"So is that how a middleman works?"

"That is one way. But, don't worry. Mr. Mehra had a lot of good things to say about you. He talked about the grace with which you were moving about in the corridors and interacting with your staff and patients."

"I am glad I was wearing a pretty sari," I giggled, interrupting Pramilla's thoughts.

"He came back with the feeling that the two of you are well suited to each other and will make a good match."

"So …?" Now I was keen to know more.

"The boy is in Amritsar at the moment and is looking actively. He has had proposals from two or three local families but has expressed a desire to see you before he sees anyone else. Pita-ji and I have come away with positive vibes about the whole thing. He appears to be a nice fellow."

When we were near a streetlight, Pramilla stopped, opened her pocketbook, took out an envelope, and pulled out a photo.

"Isn't he handsome?" she said, handing me the photo.

The small three-by-five-inch photo was signed *Kris.*

"Oh, that is his Americanized name," Pramilla said.

In the gray-yellow light, I liked what I saw, and I wanted to know everything about Kris. We walked another small block and squatted on a patch of weathered grassland under a lamppost. Pramilla took out the papers in the envelope and read the contents. I liked what I heard. Although the thought of another tableau of my being decked up and presenting myself in a persona of cuteness irked me, I was willing to put up with it to meet this boy.

"Everything has to be done in a hurry. All we have is three months. Pita-ji has suggested that you meet him in Dehradun, in Brother Satish's house. That will cut down on his travel time and hasten things a bit. He has also emphasized that he wants to take his bride back with him. He does not believe in getting married and leaving the bride behind to come later and all that rigmarole," Pramilla said.

My long-standing desire for going to the States resurfaced in my mind. When in college, I had asked my parents' permission to go abroad for graduate studies. The answer was, yes, you can go, but only with your husband. My excitement about this proposal became apparent.

"I don't want you to get too excited, for you will get another heartbreak if things don't work out," Pramilla said. "Just take it as a small holiday and an adventure. I will come with you to Dehradun."

♦♦♦♦♦♦

The following week, Pramilla and I left on our holiday and adventure.

Dehradun is a small town nestled in the foothills of the Himalayas, home to an army base. My brother Satish, then a colonel in the army, and his wife, Sita, were living in a spacious bungalow allotted to them by the military. After welcoming us to their home, Sita-*bhabhi* got busy organizing for the event. She scurried around commanding her servants to bring out the bone china and the silver tea servers. She wanted to impress our guest not just with our riches but also with our Western upbringing, our convent education, the pseudosophisticated elite society of which we were a part. "He must be very rich and sophisticated since he is coming from America," she said. "We should not fall below the standards of this 'America-returned gentleman.'"

I was now being indoctrinated not just by my sister but also by Sita-bhabhi. Having gone through an arranged marriage herself at a tender age of twenty-two, she now played a maternal role. "Be yourself. Stay relaxed. Do not talk too much. Be polite. Keep your eyes down. If he asks you a question, be brief, and play shy. Girls should be seen and not heard." She pitter-pattered all day long as she moved from room to room supervising the servants.

Finally, it was 5:00 p.m., the time for his arrival. I was doing exactly as I was instructed. Decked in a turmeric-yellow silk sari, I waited in the bedroom. Sitting at the edge of the bed, I kept raising my eyes and glancing at the window. I got my first glimpse. The America-returned gentleman was not as rich as we had imagined. He had not come by a taxi or a limousine. He took a rickshaw, dispensed the rickshaw-wala at the bottom of the hill, and was walking up the long driveway, an umbrella in hand. His older brother accompanied him.

I kept looking. Short in stature! There goes my dream of tall, dark, and handsome. Fair complexion, that's good, a much-desired quality in the Punjabi community. I was already making judgments. I had to remind myself to pull back, no emotions to be attached.

While I waited inside, the rest of the family went to the front porch to receive the guests. There were handshakes between the men, gestures of namaste, and then loud bursts of laughter. My heart was racing and my mind wandering. Here is my chance to "marry and leave." I will go away to America and distance myself from the tumultuous raging fires at home. I will be able to start a new life in a distant land. I will be happy.

Do not leap so far ahead, I reminded myself again. *Do not make emotional attachments. Isn't that what Pramilla had instructed you?*

After a very long half hour of sitting and waiting, I was led to the drawing room by my sister. There were formal introductions again and more namastes. I took the chair closest to the entrance from the dining room, a rehearsed arrangement. The chatter that was going on went above my head. I was not listening. I was concentrating on my own personal needs in life. If those were met, will this marriage still come through? There is such a long chain of events for an arranged marriage to work. My liking him, his liking me. My family liking him and his family. His family liking me and my family. Then, finally, the priest's input and the matching of horoscopes. Anything could go wrong. Again a reminder to myself—*don't waste your energy. Don't get attached.* So I sat quietly musing and tracing the intricate patterns on the silk kashmir carpet and the delicate carvings on the legs of the octagonal center table. As my mind was wandering, I could not help but look at his shoes. The brown shoes were an awkward contrast to the well-tailored pinstriped black suit. Can he be my dream man, an America-returned hero?

Sita-bhabhi's request stirred me from my reverie. I got up and poured the tea, taking the first cup to him. Not in the least bit shy, he stared right into my face as I handed him the cup. There was a penetrating tenderness in those eyes. My heart thumped so loudly that I was afraid my sari-palloo would fall off my shoulder. At the thought of such embarrassment, a smile escaped from the corners of my lips. He smiled back, and our eyes locked. I saw that he was very relaxed, not at all conscious of his shoes. I returned to my seat and rested my eyes blankly on those shoes. The desire to have another look at him surfaced again, and I raised my eyelids. He was still staring at me, and our gaze met once more.

After the short visit, Kris and his brother left. A chatter of excitement resonated in the drawing room. I left the room, returned to the bedroom, and undid my sari. I sat staring into the void and … found myself in a pool of tears. I had finally met the man I cared for both from my heart and from my head. His smile stayed with me. No one that I had met so far had smiled as he had. They had all looked at me as though I was a specimen in a zoo. *This is the man I would like to marry,* I thought. *That is, if he will marry me.*

Pramilla walked in with bubbling enthusiasm. "He is so nice. Did you see his face? No worry wrinkles; no creases whatsoever. Mr. Mehra is right. This is the man for you," she said. Then, seeing the kohl of my eyes smudged all over my face, she said, "What's the matter? Why are you crying? You have reservations?"

I looked at her, saying nothing. My tears were private, too complex to explain.

She asked again, "Do you have reservations?"

I had to say something. I ended up saying, "He does not even know how to match his shoes to his suit."

The joke of the sophisticated America-returned prospective groom presenting himself in a black suit and light brown shoes—and more importantly, the prospective bride picking up on it—stayed with us for a long time. As the story developed over the years, we learned that in the two-hour bus journey from Amritsar to Dehradun, Kris's black Florsheims had been stolen. He had taken them off in the bus and dozed off. When he reached Dehradun, the shoes were gone. He had to rush to Bata Shoes, the only shoe store in town, and buy whatever was available in his size.

"We can fix that." My sister's laughter was hearty and all embracing. "I know it has all come about too abruptly. It will take some time for the whole thing to sink in."

The following day, Pramilla walked to a nearby pay phone and rang up my parents. I accompanied her and waited in the booth with her while the operator connected the phone lines. In an hour or so, the call came through. "Hello, Mummy, I have good news," Pramilla started. "Everything went off very well." Then, in hurried fragments, "Yes, Pita-ji, he seems very nice, self-made man. Yes, hardworking. Paid his own way to America. Yes, Mother, down to earth, not arrogant. Handsome, Mummy,

I am telling you, handsome." The allotted three minutes were over, and the call ended.

We walked back to Sita-bhabhi's in silence. Pramilla's phone conversation with my parents echoed in my mind: *self-made, hardworking, down to earth.* The only thing that had stayed with me was his brown shoes. Whatever it was, I felt the tension in my shoulders melting.

♦♦♦♦♦♦

Two days later, when my sister and I returned home from Dehradun, Pita-ji had already received a telegram from Kris's father asking for my hand in marriage.

Pita-ji, of course, had to leave no stone unturned. His tenacious and persistent nature brought him to Amritsar. He and Mother met Kris and his family and gave my prospective in-laws a basket of fruits and a large platter of sweets. In return, my in-laws-to-be sent me a sari and some jewelry as their token of acceptance. When my parents returned from Amritsar, they were at peace with themselves, pleased with their selection. Mother told me that I had been well accepted by his family. I began to realize that marriage was not just a romantic assignation between a girl and a boy but a bond between two families.

A long and protracted journey was over. Kris and I were engaged.

Chapter 8

Preparations for my wedding started with a new thrust of energy.

Purohit-ji, our family priest, had settled comfortably in our home since he was first summoned to come and match up Kris's stars with mine for lifelong compatibility. Having given his approval, he had waited on the sidelines while the final negotiations were in progress. Now he was in the limelight again.

"*Pundit-ji*"—this is how Mother fondly addressed Purohit-ji—"you have brought nothing but good luck to this family. We are very grateful to you for the blessings you have bestowed upon us. The young boy that we consulted you about has turned out to be a gem. He comes from an honorable family, and we have accepted their offer."

"*Ashirwad,* beti, may God bless you, my daughter." Pundit-ji placed his prone hand on Mother's head, giving her blessings as she bowed to him in a gesture of grace. "This is all the doings of God, not me," he said.

Mother sat beside him on the veranda and offered him a plate of freshly made *motichoor-ke-laddoo,* a sweet made from chickpea flour, sugar syrup, ghee, and cardamom, along with a glass of hot creamy milk.

"Now, Pundit-ji, please look at their *janam-patris,* the horoscopes, and give us the auspicious date and time that they should wed," she said.

"Do find us a good date, Pundit-ji," Pita-ji interjected. "Make sure the date you give us will not interfere with the boy's plans. He has come on a holiday from America and needs to return in just about two months. He holds a very important position there." A postdoctoral fellowship in America was indeed looked upon as a very high position in the eyes of my parents and the priest. It was, after all, in a faraway land, a land that none of them had visited.

Purohit-ji spread the scrolls of our horoscopes in the courtyard and studied them, seeking the most auspicious day for us to wed. After two days of intent study and tallying the positions of the stars with the dates of our births, he announced that the wedding must be performed in the wee hours of the eighteenth of October, all rituals to be completed before seven in the morning. Thus, the time to start the ceremony was set for 4:00 a.m., giving sufficient leeway to complete the ceremony on time.

♦♦♦♦♦♦

Although a date and time was set for my wedding, I had not had any personal note or correspondence from my husband-to-be. I knew him from his photo and from our brief encounter in Dehradun, my only lingering memories of him his brown shoes and a ready smile. Every day, I awaited the postman's arrival, looking for that first letter of love. When nothing came, I buried my apprehensions in my work. I spent more and more time in the clinic and focused on my patients, hoping to get away from the unfolding chaos of wedding preparations that were starting up at home.

In a week, which seemed like a very long time, I received my first letter from Kris. I held it in my hands, nervous and excited. *Is he in love with me at all? What will the letter say? How will he address me?* I opened it and quickly read the two short pages. I felt rather disappointed. It was not much of a love letter, after all. It read like notes that a college professor might make in preparation for a lecture to a classroom full of students. It contained, in bullet form, a list of papers and documents that I would have to collect in order to travel abroad. I read it again and again, hoping to find a tinge of romantic love encrypted somewhere in those smudges of ink on the crisp blue paper. I finally did. He had concluded the short two-page note by saying, "There is no way I am leaving the country without you. If there are glitches in obtaining the necessary documents, I will just extend my leave, but we must travel back together." I harvested the words *must* and *together* and pivoted my life on them.

We continued to correspond, exchanging letters every two or three days. He expressed no passion. He asked no questions. The contents of his letters pertained to nothing but our upcoming travel. He gave me instructions on how to apply for my passport, get a medical certificate, obtain a tax clearance, and so on. "And don't forget, you need to bring the actual X-ray film with you, not just the radiologist's report. The American consulate is sometimes sticky about that," he wrote. I learned to take refuge in the clarity of the contents, the attention to detail and the straight, upright configuration of his handwriting. I read between his lines and replaced my disappointments with hope. With the exchange of each letter, I slowly began to feel a sense of devotion, a loyalty that no words of passion can describe. I felt more confident with the choice my parents had made for me and hoped that no unforeseen obstacles would separate us now. In one of my letters, I asked him why he could not be working on getting my visa while I was trying to obtain my passport. He replied to my naive question with a brief but clear answer, and I admired his patience. This was going to be my first international flight, and I fantasized about it. Methodically and systematically, I worked on the necessary paperwork.

♦♦♦♦♦♦

Pita-ji was all files and lists again, and preparations for my wedding were in full swing. From dawn to dusk, he carried around his red diary and made notes on everything he needed to do in order to organize this marriage to his utmost satisfaction, and Kapildas was back, offering his services and running errands. This was going to be the wedding of his dreams—a daughter's full-fledged Punjabi wedding. Since my sister was marrying someone who was not from our community, and moreover she was not going away to America like I was, it gave my parents great fervor to arrange my wedding.

Mother's eyes would get misty every time she spoke about my trousseau. She opened the big trunk where she had been storing her collections. Aroma of camphor and incense filled the air as she showed me the saris she had purchased over the years. "I bought this one in Calcutta," she said as she held a package still wrapped in its original wrapping of white tissue. "I thought this color would look good on you." It was a delicate peacock blue embroidered in pastel pinks and muted gold. "You were just about five or six at the time." Mother had obviously been making imaginary filmstrips of my wedding and my wedded life from the day I was born. I carefully removed the mass of silk from its wrappings and draped it around myself in front of the mirror, my own eyes becoming misty with tears of hope.

♦♦♦♦♦♦

One day, as Mother was piling up the items for my trousseau in the corner of her bedroom, she said to me, "You know what?" She appeared perplexed.

"What is it, Mother? What worries you now?" I asked as I sat down on the small stool beside the dresser.

"We have visited with your in-laws-to-be. They seemed kind and respectful of us, but they made no mention whatsoever of their dowry expectations."

The letter I had received from Kris that day had touched on the subject of dowry. It was as though there had been a telepathic communication. I unfolded the letter, laid it on the dresser, and read aloud, "Tell your parents that a dowry is not necessary. It will make me very unhappy if your father brings up the subject. I am marrying you for who you are and not for your riches. I know we won't have much to start with. You will just have to do with what I can provide."

What he wrote next, I chose not to read aloud. "If any hurdles come up now," he wrote, "you and I may have to just elope and get married on our own. I will not return to America without you."

Mother was hung up on the subject of dowry. She immediately interpreted the words that she had heard to her advantage. "Oh, good," she said. "That is good. They don't have any demands or expectations. We can therefore follow our customs and give you whatever we please."

I knew I was in for another argument.

"No, Mother," I reiterated. "He writes that he is strongly opposed to any kind of a dowry. Besides, you have spent as much money on us, your daughters, for our education as you have on your sons. I do not think you should spend any more money on a dowry."

Personally, I was very sensitive about the subject of dowries given to girls. The hardships some families went through to get their daughters wedded because of the dowry demands of the groom's family flashed through my mind. During my posting in the burns unit, I had treated many young women for presumed accidental burns due to the spillage of kerosene on their trailing saris. They had cried bitterly, not because of the painful burns but because of the immense hurt in their hearts. I, of course, knew that those burns were rarely accidental. Either the young bride had been humiliated by the size of her dowry and had attempted suicide as her escape or the in-laws were so angered that they were trying to kill her. If the families were affluent and had connections, the matter was hushed up, and no one heard about it anymore. In other situations, a police report was filed only to be stashed away in some rusty, overstuffed file cabinet. The case would be reopened only if a fat bribe was offered from either party. As a young intern, I treated the physical burns and loathed the *system*.

Now, when Mother brought up the subject, I spoke up. I reminded her about the Dowry Prohibition Act that had passed recently. In May 1961, Pandit Jawaharlal Nehru had passed a law against the giving of dowries. It was considered a crime punishable by law.

Hearing our conversation, my father came and stood at the doorway of the small bedroom. "What humbug! You argue in such childish ways," he said. "You don't understand the depths of our culture. The giving of a dowry has been documented in our Vedas going as far back as three thousand years. It has a deep and sacred connotation, and now bloody Jawaharlal Nehru wants to abolish the age-old custom."

He flailed the newspaper that he was holding in his hand toward me.

"Don't I read the newspaper?" he said. "I know what you are getting at. Am I not aware of Nehru's ban on the giving of a dowry? He is imposing fines on those who unload their daughters with a bundle of cash. Then the husband's family uses that money to get their own daughters married or to pay off other long-standing debts. We are not doing any of that. What we are giving you is not in response to any demands from your in-laws. It is out of sheer love. It is just a small trousseau. The British give their daughters a trousseau, don't they?"

Not giving me a chance to respond, he continued, "We are not breaking the law in any way. I agree with Nehru's principles and feel such people should definitely be punished heavily. But you know what? They are never caught. Everything is still being done under the table, and corruption has increased seven-fold since the law was passed."

It was Mother's turn to take over. "Beta, you don't understand these things," she said in a persuasive voice. "When you immerse yourself into a new family, you must enter it with dignity. That's the only way you gain instant respect from them. The first year of marriage is very crucial for a proper footing. God forbid, but ... *anything* can happen." She paused and looked me in the eye. Pronouncing words such as ill health or death or even the loss of a job was a bad omen. She stressed on the word *anything*. She reiterated Pita-ji's views. "Anything can happen, you see, and then if you become an added burden to the family, it can make your marriage very rocky. You should be able to provide some support to your husband in time of need. That is our only intent. We are not giving money to his father to pay off any debts. What we are giving you is just an assurance against any kind of possible mishap."

Maybe there was some point in what Mother was saying, given the fact that I did not know the family that I was about to embrace. I did not know how my new family would really receive me or how they would react if indeed there were hardships. I realized that the difference between the giving of a dowry versus a trousseau lay in a gray zone and depended on the motives of the two families. I gave up my arguments. My entire endeavor at this time was to make my parents happy and give them the pleasure of arranging my marriage the way they had dreamed. I wanted to fly out of the country with pleasant thoughts about them. I was the daughter through whom they were living their dreams. I let it all happen.

"Do as you please," I conceded.

We did not discuss the subject anymore, and I saw glee and joy return to Mother's countenance. She was in high spirits again. She worked on my trousseau meticulously. She made an itemized list of everything a young bride might need to set up her home. I did not realize how much she had already collected over the years. There were pots and pans, stainless-steel *thalis* and *katoris*, a dozen each. She included a silver tea set, serving dishes and flatware for those more formal occasions. Then she added linen and other household effects. She insisted on buying me a sewing machine, because that was something she had cherished in her own trousseau. I reminded her that I was flying overseas and would be allowed limited baggage.

"All right, then, let me put in this sewing kit. It will be symbolic," she said.

If her will prevailed, she would have provided a houseful of furniture, as well.

Pita-ji had the desire of giving each of his daughters a Fiat car as a part of our dowry. He had placed the order for the purchase of the two cars several years earlier. In those days, the wait time for the delivery of a new Fiat from the time of its down payment was six to eight years. As luck would have it, my car arrived during the eight weeks of my busy and perplexed life, adding to the commotion.

"Mother, I am going to the land of cars. America does not need another car from India," I said.

"But this was in our plans. The car is already here, and it is registered in your name." Mother was upset and flustered. "Maybe we can store it until you return."

Whereas I wanted to please my parents in as many ways as I could, I also wanted to respect the views of my husband-to-be. I felt a strong shift of loyalty deep inside my chest. My husband would not want a car in my trousseau.

"Rats and mice will chew up the upholstery. And what about thieves? The engine will be stolen, leaving behind nothing but a rusty shell," I said with as much diplomacy as I could muster. Arguments went back and forth. Finally, to Mother's disappointment, the car was disposed of.

The list of personal effects to go in my trousseau was detailed and lengthy. I received fifty-one silk saris, several sets of heavy and expensive jewelry, and a hand mirror framed in silver. I can also remember Mother including an entire case filled with cosmetics. In keeping with other professional women, I hardly used cosmetics, but her imaginations ran wild, and her desires had to be fulfilled.

"In America, you will go to so many parties amid the *angrezi-log*, where you will be expected to dress up," she said. She was reliving her own life when, at the age of fifteen, she had stepped out of her village and entered the life of the British Raj, requiring her to attend ballroom parties and late-night dinners. She was not equipped for it and had to learn the hard way. She wanted to make it easy for me.

No arguments, I reminded myself.

One day, as Mother handed me some envelopes to be dropped off at the post office, she commented, "It is so impersonal to invite a family for such an auspicious occasion by sending them a letter."

"How else would you invite them?" I asked.

"Oh, the proper way is to go to each one's home with a basket of fruits and sweets and deliver a personal invitation. But I guess times have changed." She sighed. "In my days, the invitation was never to the family alone. It always included their extended families and their friends. Everyone came for such auspicious occasions. It was our way of staying together as a close-knit family."

Chapter 9

Parents conferred with each other and announced that the wedding would have to take place in New Delhi. Bhilai was a small, upcoming factory town built around the needs of the steel plant workers and would be ill suited for a big Punjabi wedding. New Delhi, on the other hand, was a large city with an equally large Punjabi community. The amenities for performing the elaborate rituals would obviously be more readily available there. Pita-ji made some inquiries to see if he could find accommodations in Delhi large enough to house the bridal party. He found a bungalow, 10 Windsor Place. It was at a perfect location, and that clinched his decision. It was situated in the better part of the city, just a mile or so from the Parliament House and the Presidential Palace. Connaught Circle, the popular shopping center for the elite, was just around the corner. It would be Mother's haven to shop for any last-minute forgotten items.

Pramilla's horoscope had indicated that her wedding would be four days after mine. Hence, my parents were preparing themselves for a double wedding using the same venue. Pita-ji rented the place for the entire month of October. Who would run this large establishment for a whole month? Mother had queried. She tried to track down her old preretirement servants to go along with us. She located Chandulal, who had acted as the main chef for my brother's wedding three years earlier. She felt very relieved that she had at least one person she could rely on to coordinate the domestic help, the need for which would mushroom as more and more relatives arrived.

♦♦♦♦♦♦

All angles covered, my parents, sister, Chandulal, and I finally embarked on the long journey to New Delhi.

Since there was no railway station in Bhilai, we had to first go to Durg. Just a five-mile run, this was quite a trek by cycle rickshaws. At Durg, we waited for the westbound Howrah Express. It finally pulled into the platform some thirty minutes late. By now, it was past ten at night, and the train was crowded. Hence, we made our way into different carriages and occupied whatever seats were available. Most occupants had stretched out their holdalls and were in deep slumber. Respecting Mother's age, someone scooted in tighter and gave her a seat. I curled up on my sturdy steel trunk and cushioned my head on my holdall. It was an uncomfortable six-hour journey. We got off at Nagpur so that we could transfer to the northbound Grand Trunk that would take us to New Delhi.

A multitude of official railway porters in red shorts and shirts swarmed around us, pleading to get our business. Lean and small in stature, they all looked alike, their resilience reminding me of red-faced monkeys. Competing against them were unofficial coolies, dressed in tatters and offering their services cheaper. When I looked over my shoulder, I realized for the first time how much Mother was carrying with her: two large trunks filled with my trousseau, crates of pots and pans, bedding, spices, flour, sugar. She wanted to have a little of everything so she would not feel stranded as soon as she arrived at 10 Windsor Place.

"What will you charge for your services?" Pita-ji asked as we all stood in a vague circle guarding our luggage.

Each porter offered a price, trying to outdo the other. There was a quick response from one of the uniformed porters with a round face and a healthy mustache. "I official porter, sir," he said in broken English as he tapped on the brass badge pinned on his sleeve. "I take charge. Nothing stolen. Nothing lost. I take care of you until departure. You pay me only if you satisfied. Otherwise, no pay."

He was the one Pita-ji hired. He would be reliable and would stay with us faithfully until we boarded. Pita-ji counted the number of items in our luggage, muttering aloud, "Eleven, twelve, thirteen," as he checked them off his diary and assigned the responsibility to our porter. The porter's comrade, a look-alike minus the mustache, joined him as his assistant. Heavy and bulky items were loaded on a trolley, the suitcases and holdalls evenly balanced on the men's turbaned heads. We all gave a helping hand, carrying what we could. We moved to an isolated area at one end of the platform and prepared ourselves for a long wait. The northbound train was not due to arrive for several hours.

I strolled around the platform, browsed through magazines at the magazine stall, and bought the latest copy of *The Femina*, a popular women's magazine. While we were waiting, Mr. Mustache suddenly took off. "Where did he disappear?" Mother said, bewildered.

"He must have just gone to smoke his *bidi* with his friends," Pita-ji said. When he returned an hour later, he brought us the news that a bogie somewhere in the back was being opened up for boarding.

"It is for through passengers, destination Dilli," he said, pointing his finger north toward New Delhi. "However, it is a *janana*-carriage, only women. Sahib-ji, and this other gentleman," pointing to Chandulal, "will have to find their seats in the Express when it arrives. Not to worry. I help. I get you comfortable seats."

It was good that we had met up with this well-informed porter. We exchanged three of our tickets for the janana. Without delay, the porter and his associate took us to the back of the railway yard where the janana bogie was being set up. It was not quite ready for boarding. The sweeper was sweeping the floor, and the *jamadarini,* the untouchable help, was cleaning the latrine. The compartment smelled fresh, heavy on phenol. Mother, Pramilla, and I walked in and took possession of the best seats before the other passengers arrived. The porters helped us with our holdalls. They set up Mother's bedding on a bench and the other two on berths above. Then they stashed our belongings safely under our seats and in convenient areas that were in direct view of Mother's seat. Pilfering and thieving were not unheard of even in the janana carriages.

♦♦♦♦♦♦

Mother never traveled without food and water. She opened the knot of an off-white cloth bundle, and the aroma of coriander and curry wafted across, overpowering the smell of phenol, coal, and dust. We all had a hearty breakfast of *poories* and stir-fried vegetables along with mango pickle. Chandulal refilled our *surai*, the large clay pitcher typical for storage of drinking water. Evaporation of moisture from a wet towel wrapped around it provided satisfactory refrigeration.

While I was walking about in the railway yard, someone announced that the northbound Grand Trunk was making headway and was minutes away from the station. Our bogie would have to be moved to the tracks where the express train was to arrive. I quickly settled in my seat. A steam engine connected with our carriage with a thud, and we were finally moving. Slowly maneuvering its way, the engine brought us to the tracks on Platform 1 and deposited us in the rear of the Grand Trunk. Linemen dressed in blue overalls jumped under the train, hammers and spanners in hand. They clinked and clanked as they linked us to the incoming train.

The platform, which had been quiet and lifeless all morning, was suddenly a colorful mob of passengers getting on and off the train. Pita-ji and Chandulal battled their way, and with the help of our faithful porter, they got into a compartment a couple of carriages ahead. Later that afternoon, their carriage disconnected and veered off to the northwest. Pita-ji and Chandulal had to shift to another carriage. We, the women, were spared that hassle, thanks to the ingenuity of our porter.

In minutes, our janana also got filled to capacity, leaving only standing room. A Bengali lady in her midforties walked in and found a seat across from us. Accompanying her was an elderly woman, presumably her mother-in-law. Mother stared at them awhile. Then she broke the silence. "Where you come from?" she asked in her broken English.

"Calcutta," the lady replied. "I came by Howrah Express, reached here this morning, and waited at the platform for full six hours. Very hot and very tiring." She sighed.

We had come by the same train, picking it up at Durg. Mr. Mustache had spared us the agony of waiting at the congested platform. We had settled in the janana carriage while it was still parked at the railway yard. Our Bengali comrade was not as lucky. Mother tried to ease her suffering by offering her snacks and cold water from our surai. They were friends for the rest of the journey.

Finally, the conductor blew his whistle and waved his green flag. It had been fourteen hours since we had left Bhilai. We had twenty-four more to go.

♦♦♦♦♦♦

As the train picked up speed, a monotone chatter built around us. If the women were not disciplining their children, they were telling their woes to each other. What could be a better way to spend time in the train than to unload your troubles? You could get free advice from a sympathetic listener who would soon disappear into the oblivion. Besides the failed crops and the increasing prices of everything, they talked about their wayward husbands who cared little about them or their family. I spent my time eavesdropping and lazily looking out the window. The telephone wires whizzed past like scalloped strings strung between shiny aluminum poles, giving a dizzying illusion of movement in the opposite direction.

The day went by quickly. As night fell, the drone and chatter in the train quieted down. Women gathered their children and stretched out wherever there was space. Mother settled under her sheets and snored.

It was a beautiful night, and I was too excited to fall asleep. I walked across and stood at the open door of my carriage, gazing at the roundness of the moon. The fresh October air tainted with puffs of white smoke from the engine felt invigorating. I clutched the handrails on either side of the door and allowed myself to sway in and out of the carriage, filling my lungs with the cool air. Periodically, the engine fired charcoal particles that tickled the hairs in my nostrils, causing me to sneeze. Bathed in the milky light, the landscape was tranquil and peaceful. We passed by acres and acres of farmland separated by dark clusters of trees. Flickers of dim lights in the distance indicated that we were going by a village.

The monotonous rhythm of the train put me in a trance. Journeys of my past came alive. Every journey I had taken as a student, I had stood at a door similar to this one, dreamily living my past and planning my future. Someday, I would be done with the long and protracted years of my studies and would start a new and exciting phase, that of ghar-grahasthi. That day seemed so far away at the time.

An ember of live coal hit my cheek. The sting awakened me from my reverie, stopping my thoughts midstream. I returned to the here and now. The future is here. Soon I will be married. I will embark upon ghar-grahasthi.

I thought about Kris. I thought about my life in America.

I bundled all these thoughts and stored them away. Mother must not find me standing at the door. She must not worry about me. I looked around. The carriage was asleep. Every space—the floor, the benches, and the bunkers above—was taken. I tiptoed across the sleeping bodies, making sure that I would not stumble over a mother's arm or step on a baby's foot. I found my way to the berth where I had my holdall set up for the night. I climbed up and slid under the sheets.

The side-to-side rocking with a simultaneous forward pull of the train was a soporific. I fell into deep sleep. When the train lost speed, came to a grinding halt, and picked up momentum minutes later, I registered the passing of a station. It must have been a small station, for there was not much of a row on the platform. Occasionally, I vaguely deciphered the voice of the conductor announcing the name of a village. I changed sides on the narrow bunk, readjusted my pillow, and fell asleep again.

♦♦♦♦♦♦

Suddenly, there was a shrill, shrieking toot from the engine, and the train came to a grinding stop. It was five in the morning, and we had arrived at Agra Cantt. I got up, rubbed sleep from my eyes, and moved to a window seat. Predawn gray mingled with the dim lighting of the platform gave the station a nostalgic appeal.

The sleeping bodies stirred. Vendors came streaming in, selling hot tea in disposable earthen tumblers. "*Chai garma-garam,*" they chanted. "Hot tea at your service, just two *annas,*" they chimed in English.

There was commotion everywhere.

Passengers poured out of their cells to make the best of the long, forty-minute halt. They headed to the row of taps with running water at the far end of the platform. They scuttled around, brushing their teeth and washing their feet and their faces. Some stood steadfast in their dhotis and bare chests, facing the rising sun, pouring tumblers of water to give oblation to the gods and reciting their morning prayers. Passengers who had reached their destination or had to catch another train got off carrying their bundles, wife and children in tow. Newcomers elbowed their way in to occupy the vacated seats. There seemed to be no chaos in the midst of chaos. No one seemed to be in a bad mood or in a hurry. Everyone seemed to know what they needed to accomplish in the limited time on hand.

Chandulal brought us tumblers of wash water followed by a breakfast of *Cholle-baturae,* a satisfying dish made from chickpeas and served with fried naan.

The forty minutes came to a close. The conductor blew his whistle, and the mobs on the platform began to find their way back to their compartments. The noise ebbed into a low drone. The stragglers, those who had wandered off farther to urinate facing a wall or defecate in the fields beyond, came running back. Vendors made their last appeal for their sales, the aroma of fried *samosas* and *bhajiyas* lingering in the air. The conductor walked along the side of the train, disengaging the clutching toes and fingers of the young vendors as they clung to the doors and windows collecting their change. He made a quick check of the emptying platform, waved his lantern, and blew the third and final whistle. We were on the move again, the last leg of our long and colorful journey.

In about three hours, we finally reached our destination, New Delhi. Our rented bungalow that we had started referring to as home was just a couple of miles from the railway station.

Chapter 10

When we arrived at 10 Windsor Place, our temporary home in New Delhi, the *khansama* received us at the gate. He showed us around and helped us settle in. The bungalow, a government-owned guesthouse, was impressive with wraparound verandas and manicured lawns. Flower beds, hedged neatly with miniature English boxwood, were filled with clusters of freckled cannas and yellow and maroon snapdragons. Bougainvillea, with its ever-dependable blossoms, draped the front porch. Designed in the British style, the bungalow had high ceilings and large, airy windows. The interior was tastefully furnished with overstuffed sofas and comfortable armchairs. This spacious, five-bedroom bungalow would do well for the innumerable guests who would be staying with us. Pita-ji was decidedly pleased with his choice.

Soon our families started descending upon us from all directions. And I did indeed have a large family: besides my immediate family, I had my dad's three brothers, *chacha-jis*; their wives, *chachi-jis;* my mother's brother, *mama-ji;* his wife, *mami-ji;* and my *masi,* my mom's sister. Masi is considered to be the closest relation to a girl after her mother. The word *masi* translates as *ma*, mother, *si,* just like. My masi's love for me was just like that of my mother, and I was delighted that she and her husband, *maasar-ji,* could come. Added to this crowd were cousins, family priest, and Grandma. We were easily thirty and counting. Living arrangements fell in place effortlessly. As guests arrived, they settled in the bedrooms, sharing the space available.

The khansama, besides being an excellent cook, was also the keeper-cum-caretaker of the place. Having been in that position for as long as he could remember, he became a resourceful partner to my parents, who needed all the help they could get for organizing and hosting the two weddings. He introduced Mother to some men and women who were happy to work on a short-term basis. Mother hired a sweeper, whose job was to come in daily and mop the terrazzo floors of the bungalow and sweep the sunbaked earthen floor of the courtyard. At times, she came twice a day. The jamadarini came around ten every morning and cleaned the toilets. One maid stayed at mother's heel all day and pitched in wherever she was needed. She washed our daily laundry, made our beds, and helped Chandulal in the kitchen. A young *dhobi*-boy stopped in every afternoon, bringing with him all his paraphernalia on a hand-pushed cart. He set up his shop under the shade of the trees and starched and ironed our cotton saris with meticulous perfection using his old fashioned coal-fired iron. How he controlled the temperature of his iron to suit so many different fabrics was an art he must have learned from his ancestors, for he never ruined or burned a garment.

The courtyard was the hub for all activities. Large and spacious, it served as a kitchen and a socializing and dining area by day and as sleeping quarters by night. Chandulal set up his kitchen on a raised platform at one end of the courtyard, next to the *tandoor.* He and the khansama prepared *cholle-allo, palak-paneer, Punjabi-dal,* and various versions of vegetable *pullao* on kerosene stoves and coal braziers. Mother cranked out *roties* by the dozen, baking them in the outdoor tandoor. We ate in shifts of eight or ten. At night, the place turned into a dormitory, and the men slept on *khatias,* portable hemp woven cots set up in rows. October nights were pleasant and balmy.

Life started at dawn and never stopped until midnight at 10 Windsor Place. If the khansama was not assisting in the arrangements, he kept my father entertained with the history of the guesthouse, its ever-changing occupants, and the mistakes made in the past. Pita-ji learned from those mistakes. In order to stay organized, he made small, independent committees, placing different relatives as the heads. *Phooffer-ji* (that is how

I addressed my dad's sister's husband) was put in charge of purchasing grains and food items. Another uncle, Chacha-ji, offered to overlook the arrangements for the *shamiana,* the tent for the banquet, and the mandapam, the wedding canopy. He was also responsible for flower decorations and catering. Mother held her purse strings, paying all the expenses.

Pramilla and I made frequent visits to Connaught Circle. We bought saris to give as gifts to each of the female relatives in Kris's family. Mother wanted me to walk into my new home with dignity and respect, and this was the only way she knew—give generously. My trousseau was revamped and missing items purchased. She laid the jewelry, all made in 22-karat gold, on the dining table. She looked at it. "I see nothing that sparkles," she said as she sought advice from one of my aunties. "The trousseau will appear so drab when we show it to the in-laws. We need some dazzle that will catch their eye." My auntie agreed. I had gone through the argument about dowries and heavy gifting to daughters earlier and had lost the battle. Now, when my auntie was also in agreement with Mother, I decided to accept these gifts graciously. Generation gaps can never be bridged. My sister and I went to Connaught Circle again and bought a beautiful necklace studded with rubies and pearls and a pair of long dangling earrings to match. I selected it with interest and looked forward to wearing it.

♦♦♦♦♦♦

I did not see how anything could ever go wrong now. My parents had done everything they possibly could to ease me into my new life. Kris's frequent letters were reassuring, and I was feeling well prepared. Yet there was something missing.

One day, my grandmother expressed her personal desire. She announced that a marriage had a far better success rate if the bride had purified her soul with a dip in the Ganges prior to her wedding. Grandma's voice was frail but firm. Since my sister's wedding was to take place four days after mine, she insisted, "Both of you must go to the Ganges and take the *ganga-snaan*." I had submitted to so many things to make my family happy, why not this? It couldn't hurt. Then, if her beliefs held credence, all the suffering my sister and I had caused my parents in recent years would be washed away in the Ganges, and we would start afresh. Such an excellent concept. Pramilla and I accepted the idea.

Accompanied by our grandmother, we took the trip to Haridwar. Located on the banks of the Ganges, Haridwar is one of the most popular holy cities of India, and by the same token, one of the most crowded and polluted. After a three-hour train journey, we arrived at the sacred city. We hired a *tonga*, a small two-wheeled horse buggy. The tonga-wala knew exactly where to drop us. He had done this many times for brides like us. We arrived at the banks of the river about noon.

The place was mobbed with people of all ages. Everyone was washing away sins of one sort or another or simply collecting points toward their future births. Besides being crowded by pilgrims on a mission, there were beggars clothed in extreme poverty and lepers with missing fingers and toes. Fakirs walked around asking for alms. *Sadhus* sat cross-legged meditating, undisturbed by the humdrum of the world around them. Some laid on live charcoal or a bed of nails to prove the power of mind over body. Amid this throng was also a group of youngsters standing about, their hair sleeked with coconut oil, cigarettes dangling from their lips, and suspicious smiles at the corners of their slanted eyes. My sister and I stood out in the crowd. We were two young girls too well dressed to belong there. The cigarette danglers stared at us. Grandmother turned to them and snapped, "Why do you look like that? Have you not seen girls before? Don't you have sisters?" They turned their backs to us and left, and we never saw them again.

Pramilla and I stayed focused on our task. Just like the rest of the pilgrims, we had a mission to accomplish. We had to bathe in the Ganges. We elbowed our way through the crowds and reached the banks. We looked at each other as we looked around. No one was wearing bathing suits. They were just going into the water fully clothed in their dhotis or saris and coming out as wet soggy silhouettes. How on earth would we do this? How would we change? Where would we change? There were no bathrooms in sight. We observed how the women around us were managing. We came up with our own strategy.

We walked gingerly to the edge of the river. The muddy water was ebbing onto the cement steps. Holding hands, we walked down the steps. As the water got knee-high and then waist deep, we stopped and steadied our footing on the slippery slab of cement. This would be the last time we, the two sisters, the Siamese twins, would stand together, holding hands and giggling. In a few days, we must go our own separate ways, follow our own karmas. We looked at the expanse of the river. We looked at each other. We took a dip, simultaneously dunking our heads underwater. One dip is all that was required. We walked out of the river with our arms crossed in front of us, feeling giddy with laughter. Water was dripping from our hair, our elbows, and the hems of our saris.

It was a challenge to get dressed in fresh clothing in the midst of the crowd. We kept our eyes on a small group of four women. They were sitting on their haunches with their heels planted flat on the ground and chitchatting, engrossed in telling their stories. Simultaneously, they were changing their clothes. They appeared to be modest and yet did not seem to be self-conscious about their modesty. It came so naturally to them. They undressed and dressed in segments. First one *choli*-sleeve was undone. This arm was immediately covered with the sleeve of a fresh clean choli. Then they did the same with the other arm. They pulled and stretched the choli-blouse over their breasts and secured the buttons across the front cleavage in an orderly fashion. Next, they slipped a dry petticoat over their heads and slid off the wet sari and petticoat. Finally, they stood up and draped their brightly colored saris to perfection. Their storytelling never stopped.

We imitated our colorful friends following their strategy step-by-step. Six yards of sari fabric could be improvised ingeniously to create modesty barriers. Grandma helped us with that, shielding us from the crowd. She watched us change and smiled with contentment. As we were leaving, she folded her hands in front of her in prayer, closed her eyes, and chanted softly, speaking directly to the sacred river. The tranquility of her countenance was contagious. By the time we returned home, I also felt an idyllic calm.

♦♦♦♦♦♦

There was a countdown of seven days to the wedding, and the celebrations began. All the relatives who were able to make it had arrived, and the guesthouse was filled to capacity. Some workmen came and, under Chacha-ji's supervision, installed the mandapam, the wedding canopy, and the shamiana, the multicolored tent shelter for the banquet, in an open area on one side of the bungalow. Others sat on the porch and worked with fresh flowers—marigolds, roses, jasmines, and chrysanthemums—and put up multiple scalloped strands on the archway and a densely woven curtain at the entry door. They all worked furiously to clean up the already clean premises. Anytime was teatime, and Chandulal had his kettle constantly on the boil. Aunties parked themselves on hemp khatias in the courtyard, shelling peas and chopping vegetables. Merriment was in the air. *Chote chachi-ji,* my youngest paternal aunt, set up her *dholak,* the drum, and they all sang wedding tunes in Punjabi and in Hindi.

I looked forward to the upcoming events. The fear of marrying someone I did not know had dissolved.

A day prior to the wedding, the maidservant gave me a ceremonial bath, rubbing my body with a paste of chickpea flour and turmeric and then washing it off with sandalwood soap. After my bath, I came to the courtyard. Friends and relatives applied henna on my palms and feet, ingeniously creating convoluted carroty-red patterns.

On the eve of the wedding, I wore a silver brocade sari in readiness for the ceremony of *jai-mala*, the exchange of garlands, the first of a long chain of upcoming ceremonies. Kris was to arrive shortly, accompanied by his friends, relatives, and well-wishers. I had not seen him since our short encounter in Dehradun. I longed to see him again. I walked up to the bay window in the drawing room and waited. Finally, the *barat,* the wedding procession, made its way through the gates of the bungalow and came into view. The sound of drums and *bhangra*-dancers echoed through the compound. In the far distance, I saw Kris above the heads of the dancing crowd. He was riding a white horse with someone walking alongside and extending a large silver umbrella above his head. The procession stopped and started several times as if to give us, the bridal party, a fair warning that they would be arriving at our door anytime now.

Then the music stopped. The barat had arrived. There was utter commotion in the front rooms of the bungalow.

"Are we ready? They are already here and waiting, and we are not ready!" someone was shouting.

"Where is the bride?" someone else queried. "Is *she* ready?"

"You have to lead," a commanding voice said, and Mother was nudged toward the entrance door.

"Oh no! What nonsense! It is Pita-ji who has to be in the front," Mother said.

My father, uncles, and other male relatives and friends all hurried to the porch to receive the honored guests who waited patiently in the driveway for a formal welcome. Finally, the greetings began. The guests walked through the archway that had been decorated with flowers, and the two families met on the porch. They exchanged garlands with relatives of equal rank, starting with my father exchanging a garland with Kris's father. All the other male members of the two families followed suit. Since Kris had three brothers in attendance and I had just two, my male cousin was quickly sought out from the crowd. He was a substitute, a surrogate brother.

Kris alighted from the horse, wearing a token silver sword on his belt. He paid his respects to my father by touching his feet with the tips of his fingers. He walked a few steps and stood at the threshold of the open doorway in readiness for the *jai-mala* ceremony. Led by my bridesmaid, I stood in the hallway on the other side of the threshold. Kris and I were separated by the screen made of interlaced marigolds and chrysanthemums. Mother arrived with her thali. She parted the flower curtain and received Kris, blessing him with prayers, *tilak*, and *arti*. I stood in front of Kris, he on the outside and I on the inside of the threshold. I looked at the arbitrary strip of flooring that separated us and suddenly felt numb and devoid of all emotions. Soon we would overcome this barrier and become united.

My bridesmaid handed me the jai-mala, a special garland of red roses braided heavily with scented jasmines. I put it over Kris's neck. With that gesture, for the first time I publicly acknowledged Kris's proposal and made my promise to marry him. As I bowed to pay my respects to him, he put a similar *mala*, a flower garland, across my neck. It was such a short ceremony, but it has lingered in my memory forever.

Following the jai-mala ceremony, I returned to my room while Kris and the guests were led to the banquet shamiana. I was not allowed to join the feast that followed. I was not to be seen in public with Kris until I was wedded. I retired to the quiet of my room and ate a small supper brought to me by my bridesmaid. The noise of the banquet and the blasting music kept me distracted until midnight. When things quieted down, I tried to rest. As I closed my eyes, another commotion just outside my room aroused me.

"What is all this new commotion?" I asked my bridesmaid. She went out to inquire.

"They are setting up a cot for Kris on the veranda," she said. "Since the wedding ceremony must start at four in the morning, Pita-ji does not want Kris to go to his hotel. He does not want to rely on public transportation or a taxi at that early hour. You know Pita-ji."

Of course I do, I thought.

"And Kris has agreed?" I asked quizzically.

"Yes, they are scrounging around finding him some night pajamas and a toothbrush."

Kris's cot was set up on the veranda outside my bedroom.

Lying in my bed, I envisioned Kris sleeping just a wall away from me. I tried to think of how it would feel sleeping next to him. I would have so many stories to tell and to ask. Where would we start? And how would we start? There were a myriad of unknowns, and the more questions I raised, the more my mind went blank.

I returned to the present. In a few hours, I would wear the red silk sari, get bejeweled in gold and diamond ornaments, and be seated beside Kris and in front of the sacred fire. At some point in the ceremony, Pita-ji would rise and place my hand in Kris's, ceremoniously giving me away to him, *kanya-dan*. Teary-eyed, I would accept my future. I would begin to look at Kris as my husband. I would be his wife. Married to him, I would have to discover my own ways to love him, to serve him, and belong to him. I had yearned for this moment for so long, and now it was fast approaching. My heart began to pound. It was pounding not with fear—for that was all gone—but with a certain excitement, the excitement of the unknown, the change.

I tossed and turned in bed.

Tomorrow, I would change my name. I would scribe a *Mrs.* to my name. I practiced writing my new name over and over in my imagination, giving it different slants and squiggles.

Since sleep would not come, I diverted my thoughts to the mundane. I wondered whether Kris had liked me for my hair. My hair was long, black, and straight down to my waist. When I was in third year of my medical school, I had had a sudden urge to give myself a new look. I had wanted to be a sophisticated Western girl. I showed Mother the poster of Audrey Hepburn and Gregory Peck and asked if I could wear my hair Audrey Hepburn-style. She clucked her tongue and said, "Chhi-chhi, you are not doing any such thing. When you are married, you can do whatever you and your husband desire. Until then, you leave that hair of yours alone."

I could hardly keep up with the speed at which my thoughts were weaving in and out, going in multiple directions. At one moment, I saw Kris as a very demanding and unreasonable husband. How would I handle that? Then, at the speed of lightning, came the most charming thoughts of my being his princess. Since I knew practically nothing about him, I tried to rely on my karma. Isn't that what my grandmother had always taught me? "Fear not, beta, for fear gets you nowhere. When fear grips, bank on your karma." So I did. I trusted my karma. He would love me for who I am, what I am, I assured myself. That is what he had written in his letters.

Thinking these thoughts, time passed. At some point, I must have fallen asleep.

♦♦♦♦♦♦

I was awakened by a knock on the door. It was my cousin. It was 3:00 a.m. She helped me put on my wedding sari, an electric red with a green-and-gold brocade border. She draped the palloo of the sari over my head to partially cover my face and eyes. With her arm around my waist, she led me to the mandapam, where the ceremony was taking shape. It was a serene night, the darkest night of October. Stars appeared bright in the expanse of the celestial blue sky. Barefoot, I walked slowly across the cool, moist lawn, my steps being drawn toward the subdued lighting of the mandapam. The fragrance of burning incense felt sharp and intense in the crisp predawn air.

When I arrived at the mandapam, Kris was already seated on his *peedhi*, the low decorated wedding stool. As I came closer, I lifted my gaze to look at him. Not much of his face was visible. He wore a silver crown studded with flowers, and his shoulders were loaded with a multitude of garlands. From whatever I could see, he looked radiantly happy, confidence shining through his eyes. That lifted my spirits and gave me tremendous joy.

My father and Kris's father were sitting cross-legged under the same small canopy. All the other relatives, Kris's and mine, were in attendance. Some had taken the trouble to freshen up while others were still sleepy eyed. Mother, dressed in a casual sari, took a seat next to my father.

The priest had already started his chanting in Sanskrit and was busy with the preparations for the wedding ceremony. With a quick glance at me, he pointed to another small peedhi next to Kris and indicated that I should take that seat. His fingers moved deftly as he took pinch after pinch of colored powder and drew intricate geometric designs on a small sanctified area in the center of the mandapam. The design, a *mandala* in yellow, white and magenta, was enclosed in a circle, the Universe. He placed a *homa,* a metal grill, in the center of the Universe and started the consecrated fire using ghee and incense. As the fire developed into a steady flame, he began the ceremony. He invoked the gods *Ganesha, Shiv-Parvati,* and *Laxmi* to make their spiritual appearance into the canopy and guide us through the sacred event.

"This ceremony is being performed by the gods and goddesses who are now present in this sanctified place, not by me," he explained, looking at Kris and me. "The gods are just using me as their instrument. The words I will be chanting are merely words of wisdom, His wisdom. At the end of each *shloka*, you will drop small amounts of puffed rice or ghee into the fire to indicate that you have understood and acknowledged the Knowledge. I want you to appreciate that the promises you will make will not be made to me, to your parents, or to each other. You will make them to yourself and to the Omniscient, the Ultimate Reality."

I was in no mood to think through all these philosophical thoughts at the time. All I wanted was to be married. I had not studied the Sanskrit language, anyway, so what difference would it make? I agreed to abide by the rules of marriage as prompted by the priest, respectfully offering clarified butter or rice to the fire at the end of each chant. I did not need to understand the meanings implicated therein. After all, my parents and their parents before them had done the same. I went through the rituals with confidence.

Just about halfway through the ceremony, the priest conducted one of the key rituals of our wedding—kanya-dan, giving the bride to the groom. Kris put his right hand forward, palm up in readiness to receive mine. Pita-ji rose and placed my henna-speckled hand on his, again, palm facing up. Then Pita-ji placed his own hand on mine and the priest dropped a red rose in Pita-ji's palm. Time stood still with the monotone of the priest's chants as the backdrop. I saw Mother wiping her eyes. I willed myself to hold back my tears. I had been given away to Kris in marriage. Life was moving forward.

As the sun's first rays flooded the mandapam, we were approaching the end of the rituals. Kris and I were walking the seven circles around the fire. With each walk, the priest recited specific shlokas, asking for God's blessings that we may have a long and prosperous life together and that we may lead our lives according to His wisdom. In the first four walks, Kris was leading, and in the final three, our positions were reversed, indicating equal partnership in marriage. At the completion of the sacred walk, I had exchanged seats with Kris. I was now sitting to his left.

As the final ritual, my sister opened a small silver box of *kum-kum*, the vermilion powder. Kris performed the sindoor ceremony by taking a pinch of that powder and filling the parting of my hair with it. Then he dipped his ring finger into the same powder and placed a *bindi,* a red dot on my forehead. Our eyes met, and once again, I saw that spark of love in his eyes. We rose from our seats and walked side by side as husband and wife, bowing low to touch the feet of all our elders and receive blessings from them.

After the completion of the wedding ceremony, I went to my room. I was now asked to change to yet another sari, something given to me by Kris's family. I chose a shimmering, watery-pink silk with tiny silver tinsels embroidered into the fabric. I removed all the heavy brocades and jewelry and felt a bit more like myself, though still in a cloud. I was adjusting to the change. I had acquired a whole new family.

Breakfast was being served in the shamiana. Kris had removed the silver crown, his turban, and all the garlands around his neck. He looked handsome in his suit and tie, jubilant and very youthful, I decided. I joined him at his table, sitting next to him, our arms touching, our eyes catching quick, short glimpses of each other. It felt strange that now no one was objecting to our being together.

"Want a piece of toast?" Kris broke the silence.

"No, thank you. I am not hungry this early in the morning," I said.

"Have some, anyway, and drink your orange juice," he insisted. He buttered a piece of toast and put it on my plate.

I drank a few sips of the juice. I nibbled on the toast.

He ate well.

♦♦♦♦♦♦

After breakfast, we gathered in front of the bungalow for the final ceremony, bidai, the bride's send-off. A chauffeur-driven, flower-decorated car awaited us in the driveway. I stood beside Kris, mentally acknowledging my loyalty to him and his family. The tinsel on my soft pink sari sparkled in the sun's rays like bits of silver on rose petals. There was tension in the air, the tension of the final good-byes.

Suddenly, I recalled that I did not have my pocketbook with me. Just as I was about to turn around and go to my room to fetch it, my grandmother's outstretched arm stopped me. "It is a bad omen to turn your back at this juncture. You must only look forward. Let someone else get your purse for you," she said.

Yes, of course, I thought. Rituals and superstitions do have significance at times and must be respected.

My sister, cousins, aunts, and women servants all stood in a cluster on one side of the porch, the men on the other. The older women began to sing songs of separation, the separation of a daughter from her mother. The lyrics were very sad, and the slow, dragging tunes more so. Mother began to cry. The night gone by had changed her life too. She no longer had her little girl to pamper. I was leaving her, moving forward. She gave me a hug and whispered in my ear, "Go, beti, dear daughter, go. Go wherever your husband takes you. Always trust him and respect him. God will be watching over you."

"I will do my best," I whispered back. "Don't worry, and stop crying, Ma. Trust your instincts. The son-in-law you have selected will take good care of me," I comforted her.

My sister gave me a hug and wished me the best.

I moved on to say good-bye to my grandmother. Throughout the ceremony, she was stoic and tearless, as most women her age generally are. I looked at her. Her tiny shriveled eyes spoke of confidence. "It is all written in your karma, dearest," she whispered as I hugged her.

All the women in my family, including the maidservants, were now sobbing. They were singing the parting songs with intermittent sobs, setting the mood. Much as I had built my courage and had not shed a tear throughout the wedding ceremony, I could not control myself now. I walked up to Mother and gave her a tight embrace. I cried and sobbed and cried some more. Finally, Kris's sister intervened. She separated me from my mother's embrace, walked me to the car, and helped me into the backseat next to Kris. He searched for my hand and squeezed it gently. I put my head on his shoulder and sobbed.

Chapter 11

We left 10 Windsor Place and came to the hotel where my new family, Kris's family, had their accommodations for the wedding. I accompanied Kris to his room. Overtaken by days of emotional and physical fatigue, all I wanted was to collapse into the inviting big bed and take a nap. However, I was suddenly stricken by an awkward feeling about sharing a room and a bed with a stranger. So I just took a seat on the sofa by the window. Kris sat at the edge of the bed, his eyes glued on me. Even when I was not looking at him, I could tell he was staring at me, that indescribable stare of a new husband. Our awkwardness did not last long. There was a knock on the door, and Kris's sister walked in to ask about my comfort or need for food or drink. This was followed by a stream of other relatives. They made themselves comfortable, sitting beside me or sprawling on the bed. They talked among each other—mostly about how pleased they were with the wedding arrangements made by Pita-ji—or congratulated Kris on his choice. I listened. I had been instructed by Mother that I must ease my way into my new family and not be too quick in interjecting opinions.

Unlike my sister, who had planned her honeymoon with her fiancé, I was not going to have a conventional honeymoon. Having accepted an arranged marriage meant that I had also accepted the unwritten rules that go with it. I had not simply married Kris but had been married into his family. I was a bride, a daughter-in-law, a sister-in-law, as well as an aunt to many excited nieces and nephews. "Our daughter is marrying into a well-established family in Amritsar," Mother had been proudly announcing to everyone after my engagement.

♦♦♦♦♦♦

That night, we boarded the train to Amritsar, my husband's hometown, where I would spend the first few days of my marriage. We were in a private suite, and that gave us our first moments of privacy. Still awkward in each other's presence, we fidgeted around with our luggage, helping each other secure the suitcases under our seats. Kris flipped the switch on the wall, and the incandescent bulb went out, filling the room with a soft blue glow from the night-light. We settled in for the night.

"I have waited a long, long time for this day," Kris said, his arms encircling my waist as I undid my sari. "The only woman I have loved in my life was my mother, and she died when I was nine." Rims of his pupils glistened in the dim light. "Now that I have found you, I will never let you go."

"I hope I will be able to live up to your dreams," I said, my own eyes filling with tears.

We sat side by side on the berth, his hand cupping mine, and I wondered why I had carried such grim thoughts about arranged marriages.

"We'll have a great time when we get to America," Kris said, drawing me closer and changing the subject. Confidence and hope radiated in our private little world.

I wanted to continue talking and ask many questions about his mother and about America, but he said, "We have a lifetime ahead of us. Come now, we must get some sleep." It was late into the night, and we went to bed, only to be awakened in the wee hours of the morning when the whistle blew and the train came to a halt at Amritsar station.

♦♦♦♦♦♦

When we got off the train, the fragrance of fresh flowers brought me back to the here and now—my obligations to my new family. We were greeted by Kris's relatives and friends, who stood at the platform with marigold, rose, and jasmine garlands. Kris and I were showered with heavy, double-stranded garlands one more time. I brought my henna-decorated palms together in front of me in a gesture of a namaste to all the male members who looked about my age, hugged the women and children, and stooped down to touch the feet of those who looked older. There must have been thirty or forty who had come to greet us at that early hour.

I did not know anyone in this new family, so I grabbed onto the symbolic ceremony in our wedding where the priest had tied my sari-palloo to my husband's scarf, indicating that we were now inseparable. I stayed by Kris's side and depended on his cues to steer me through the maze of his large family and their expectations. Though they were also Punjabis, their culture was obviously different from mine. Seeing me overwhelmed, Kris whispered to me, "Bear with it; I do have a large family. I know they can be overbearing at times."

"Not to worry," I said.

Many rickshaws and auto-scooters had been lined up outside the railway station to take us home. Kris helped me into one of the two-seater bicycle-rickshaws. The rickshaw-wala peddled his way through traffic on some busy roads, crossing over the Bhandari Bridge and into one of the oldest sections of Amritsar. In a few minutes, he turned into a narrow cobbled street. "This whole block once belonged to us," Kris said, pointing to the row of homes on the right as we turned the corner. "With four hundred years of property divisions and subdivisions over generations, my family is now left with just a small strip." The rickshaw stopped in front of his house, a four-story, slim, up-and-down stucco structure sandwiched between several similar to this one. The community well, with its disintegrating parapet of mortared stone and brick, occupied half the width of the street in front of his house. Now dry and covered over with chicken wire, it served as a landmark, giving the street its name, *kuan-wali-gulli*, the street with a well.

I got off the rickshaw and walked over an open drain crusted with scum and algae, lifting the skirt of my sari to prevent the gold brocade border from soiling. My oldest sister-in-law, who had not made it to the railway station, received me at the doorstep with yet another flower garland. I entered my new home, ceremoniously stepping over a mound of rice placed at the entrance for good luck. As I was being shown around, I learned that this small house that Kris was referring to as his home was also home to three of his married brothers, each family occupying a bedroom. They all shared a common sitting area, which turned into a bedroom for the children at night. There was one common kitchen. I was led to the room assigned to us for our stay. "Watch your step," Kris said as he held my arm to prevent a fall. The windowless room was eight by eight and was sunken eight to ten inches below ground. As my eyes adjusted to the dim lighting, I found my way to the *charpoy*, a cot with a wood frame strung with cotton tape, the only furniture in the room besides a small table. "This was my room growing up," Kris said, his eyes circling the small room. "I used to share it with my nephew. I did not like it, because he always stole my pencils and paper."

Kris's home was a stark contrast to the bungalows with their large compounds that I grew up in. Reading my mind, he said, "It's not going to be long before we'll leave. It will be different in America." His tone was apologetic.

"Oh, you don't have to apologize," I said, smiling. "I have lived in all sorts of places in my life." I thought of my internship when I had a three-month posting in a small village in Madhya-Pradesh and was housed in very primitive dwellings. Actually, I was remembering my mother's words. "You should stretch your feet only as much as the coverlet you have been provided," she used to say every time I complained about my bedding being inadequate. Then contemplating the same thought, she would conclude, "You never know what future has in store. Learn to live with what you have been given."

♦♦♦♦♦♦

Wedding rituals that were important to Kris's family started soon after our arrival. The first of many was *muh-dikhai,* showing the bride. After my bath, I was told by Kris's relatives (now mine as well) to wear a sari of their selection, a gorgeous off-white brocade this time, and sit on a peedhi in the middle of their sparsely furnished drawing room, my head and face partially covered with the palloo of the sari. Women, neighbors, and friends came from all over, pulled my veil up, looked at my face, told me that I was beautiful, and left unknown amounts of rupee notes or a piece of gold jewelry in my lap. Most of them were people whom I would never meet again. As was expected of me, I said nothing, appreciating their generous gifts with an occasional smile. My new relatives hovered around me, whispering to each other their confidence that I was going to fit in with them because, in spite of my college education, I was accepting their rituals with a smile.

Next, my sister-in-law led me to the kitchen and asked me to sit cross-legged on a mat next to Kris. In the warmth of the hearth, we were supposed to bond with each other by sharing a meal from a common plate, a stainless-steel thali, piled with the delicacies of Amritsar. I tore a piece of the buttery bread, a *paratha,* and dipped it into the sauces of *matar-paneer* and spinach-saag. As I was about to partake of this, my sister-in-law drew my hand away from me and toward Kris. "Always feed your husband first," she said. I placed the morsel in Kris's mouth, apologizing for my ignorance. After this symbolic ritual, we enjoyed a casual meal, breaking the barriers of formality.

Later in the evening, we went to the Golden Temple and sat before the temple priest, who performed a ceremony welcoming me into Kris's family.

All these rituals were the cement that was gluing the two families together.

The following day, Kris's oldest brother, a homeopathic doctor, took me to his clinic and asked me if I could examine one of his patients. This was going to be a bit more challenging than merely submitting myself to all those rituals. First of all, I was a pediatrician, not an internist. Besides, I had quit my job several weeks earlier and was immersed in dreams of love, marriage, and ghar-grahasthi. I was not prepared for a medical quiz. "Respect everyone in your new family," Mother had advised. Thus, I obeyed. Dressed in silks and jingling bangles that my sister-in-law had insisted I wear that day, I accompanied my brother-in-law to his clinic. I stood by the patient's bed, a bit nervous. The man looked like he might be in his late fifties. Homeopathic treatment had not helped him. He had not been feeling well for months. Silently, I recapitulated my medical routine and started with details of the patient's history: evening low-grade fevers, night sweats, cough, weight loss, and loss of appetite. Then there were telltale signs of crackles in his left lung. "I think your patient has tuberculosis. We may want to get an X-ray," I said meekly to my brother-in-law. The patient's gaunt eyes lit up. Finally, there might be an answer to his long suffering. An X-ray confirmed the diagnosis, and the patient was transferred to a local TB sanatorium. I learned later that he recovered with the treatment he'd received.

"You have made a good choice, Kris," his brother said when we returned from his clinic. Besides being accepted by the women in Kris's family, I was being appreciated by his brothers, as well.

The next morning when Kris came out from his bath, I saw a rash on his back and chest. My diagnostic mind was churning again.

"Are you aware of this rash?" I said, walking him to a brighter light to examine the rash.

"Oh, I have had it for years," he said. "It is liver patches. My brother says my liver was damaged from the frequent use of quinine that I had to take for malaria in my childhood."

I looked at the rash again and offered an alternate diagnosis.

"It is *pityreasis rosea,* a simple fungal rash," I said. "Shall we try an antifungal salve and see what happens?"

The ointment did work. The rash began to clear after a few applications.

"Isn't it nice to have a doctor in the family," Kris said as I rubbed the salve into every fold and hard-to-reach area of his back. "Now you know why I picked you. I did not listen to my brothers and marry one of those local Amritsar girls."

After three days of rituals, festive meals, and overwhelming affection poured over me by Kris's relatives, we returned to 10 Windsor Place, New Delhi.

Chapter 12

In Delhi, we were like two college kids with just one ambition: get our papers in order so that we could leave India together. We spent the week going from one office to another, sorting out the necessary documents. Since we had been married at home by a family priest, the American consulate asked for an official marriage certificate from the court. I asked Pita-ji for assistance. He replied, "Marriages are personal affairs between two families. They are sacred, and I don't see any reason for the courts to interfere. No one in my family will go to the court to register a marriage."

"But Pita-ji, they are asking for an official documentation," I said.

He prepared a notarized affidavit and handed it to me. "Take this, and see if it will satisfy them. If not, I will go and talk to them personally." To my surprise, the American consulate did not question the notarized affidavit, and a spousal visa was issued to me without unnecessary delays.

The following Monday, Kris and I took off for the United States, and I felt a new mix of emotions. Ten days after my marriage, I was leaving the known and the familiar for a faraway land where I knew no one. When I was a little girl, I was always curious to see what was beyond that next bend in the road, what was hidden beyond the confines of the compounds where I grew up. The venture of discovering those unknown treasures overshadowed all other thoughts. Like most girls, I had also fantasized about being married. Mother often spoke of it as ghar-grahasthi, the life of a householder. I was ready to experience it all.

Excited? Yes, very!

Scared? A little bit.

Sad? No.

PART 2

Storrs, Connecticut, United States of America

Chapter 13

My oldest brother, Jagdish, and his wife, Raksha, were posted in Germany and had not attended my wedding.

"Do break journey on your way to America and visit us in Berlin," Jagdish had written to me. "It will be a great pleasure to meet your husband, and we will show you around a city that has made history in recent years."

I was thrilled at the thought that my longing to see the world would begin even before I set foot in my dream country, America. Kris was equally excited, not merely because he would be visiting a country that he had not been to but also because it would give him a chance to meet my brother and his wife.

We accepted the offer.

In West Berlin, we met up with Jagdish and Raksha and settled in a cozy little inn in the heart of the city. We took a self-guided walking tour in the nippy weather with my brother giving us a running commentary on the history and Kris stopping us from time to time to take our photo. In one photo, I am standing near the Berlin Wall. In the next, I am staring at the hideous barbed-wire fence. In yet another, my sister-in-law and I are standing at Checkpoint Charlie.

In the evening, we changed and came down for dinner. We walked around a few narrow streets and then into an alley where we located a small but elegant-looking restaurant. The dim lighting in the restaurant felt particularly romantic to my newlywed eyes. It had been a fantastic day, and I was jubilant.

"Let us celebrate your wedding with some champagne, shall we?" Jagdish said as we settled in the warm upholstered chairs in the restaurant. He was looking at me fondly.

I did not know the importance of champagne in Western celebrations, and I did not know the difference between champagne and wine—or gin or rum or whiskey, for that matter. My only experience of alcohol was the bitter taste of brandy that I had to swallow in a gulp to soothe an earache that was not responding to warm onion juice poured into my ear canal or to a poultice of cracked wheat, ghee, and turmeric. To make it more palatable, Mother often gave me my medicinal brandy on a spoonful of sugar.

"Sure, why not?" I said.

The bartender displayed his bottles in anticipation.

"Your choice," my brother said.

I did not want to appear ignorant before my new husband, who had lived in America for several years, so I said casually, "Make it his choice," looking at Kris with mischievous innocence.

"I don't drink," Kris said in a gruff undertone. "I am a teetotaler."

I had heard my father use that word, *teetotaler*, frequently during his groom-hunting days. Boys who came from good and well-bred families were teetotalers. I had just discovered that Kris was one of those.

The bartender moved his ice-filled bucket with an array of bottles toward me. I gulped the air that was building up in my throat and quickly made the choice.

"This one," I said, touching the bottle closest to me.

"This one it shall be," my brother said to the bartender. "You've made a good choice," he said to me.

I felt flattered.

My husband, who had been so enthused and energetic all day, suddenly became morose, his cheeks drained of color. He stopped talking. When the dinner came, he nibbled and poked at his plate.

"What's the matter, Kris? You don't like our German food?" my brother said.

"I'm not hungry," Kris said.

"Yes, plane journeys can be tiring," my brother said. "They feed you at all odd hours, don't they?"

International travel does indeed kill one's appetite. I, however, compensated for my husband's stubbornness and inflexibility and politely ate the liverwurst, sauerkraut, and potatoes that were on my plate.

"It is very good," I said, not knowing much about what I had tasted.

By the time Kris and I came to our room, we were not talking. I knew something had gone wrong, but not that wrong. What had I done? Or what had I said? I had been my usual self, frivolously happy, chitchatting with my brother. I had toasted with my champagne glass and delicately taken tiny sips just as I had seen in the movies. I thought I handled it all quite well. What, then, went wrong? Maybe Kris and my brother exchanged some private words that did not go well.

It was a cold night, and the rooms at the inn were not heated. The beds were provided with fluffy down comforters. I quickly got under the covers and tried to get warm by rubbing my palms together and massaging my calves and thighs. I waited for Kris to come next to me so I could share his warmth. He changed in slow motion and finally came and lay beside me, cold, very cold.

"I am sorry I married you without inquiring into your habits," he said, talking in riddles to the air above him.

Silence.

"I should not be surprised. After all, you are the daughter of a high-ranking official. You must be accustomed to a drink or two before dinner."

Silence.

"We will have to make some adjustments, I guess."

"What adjustments are you talking about?" I finally managed to say, raising myself on my elbow and facing him. I was three thousand miles away from home, ten days into a honeymoon, and my husband firmly believed he had married a woman with a problem. My heart was sinking, fears multiplying.

"It is a bad omen to turn your back [to life] at this juncture. You must only look forward. Let someone else get your purse for you." My grandmother's words at the bidai ceremony rang in my ears.

And then, *"Go, beti, dear daughter, go. Go wherever your husband takes you. Always trust him and respect him. God will be watching over you,"* Mother was whispering to me.

I took courage. I spoke. I tried to convince my husband that it was all a pretense, an act, an appearance of sophistication that I thought was appropriate and would certainly be required of me in the future. I was practicing to be a good wife with good Western etiquette.

"I don't believe you," Kris said, dampening my morale further. "The ease with which you twirled the glass, the way you toasted, the way you took those small sips—you were certainly not pretending."

I repeated myself over and over, but my words were unconvincing. I felt trapped. I felt helpless. I withdrew into my shell. Is it going to be like this day after day for the rest of my life? I looked at him and then at the dark ceiling above. We lay side by side, silent for endless moments.

"Life runs on mutual trust, so I guess I must have faith," Kris said at last, turning toward me and drawing me close to him.

I snuggled up next to him and let my tears soak his undershirt. Soon we both fell asleep in the softness of the down comforter.

The next morning, I woke up at the sound of chimes somewhere in the distance. I thought it might have been six or seven, but the clock struck eleven times. I awakened Kris, and we got dressed in a hurry. We said good-bye to Jagdish and Raksha and rushed to the airport. From Berlin, we flew to Frankfort, Heathrow, New York, and finally to Hartford, Connecticut. At Heathrow, we heard our names being announced repeatedly on the overhead PA system. I held on to Kris's hand as tightly as I could, giggling as we ran looking for our gate. When we finally found it, the flight attendant was holding the door open for us. We rushed in and took our seats.

What I remember most from that flight is gazing out the oval window of the 747 while Kris sat beside me, running his fingers through the tangles in my long hair, lost in thought. I was looking at the expanse of fluffy white cotton, above which the plane was cruising in a monotonous drone. I had never seen clouds from above. This was my first travel by air. I looked for the kingdom of Ram and Sita, for Krishna playing his flute for his consort Radha. I made imaginary homes for them in the distant horizon. I turned to Kris, interrupting his solitude. "Mother always prayed to gods living in the heavens above the clouds. Where are they?" I asked.

"They are in your head," he said, smiling. "Don't look so far away. Just look inside of you." I believed him but did not want to give up looking for them.

After a thirty-hour journey, we arrived at our destination, our home for the coming year. Three months earlier, Father was shuffling through newspaper ads finding the right mate for me. Standing at the baggage claims of the airport in Hartford, I kept staring at my mate as he unloaded our suitcases from the carousel. He was not a mate or a stranger. He was my husband, and I felt like I had known him a long time. The agony of finding my mate through an arranged marriage seemed a world away.

"I am glad we took that break in Germany," Kris said. "I enjoyed meeting your brother and his wife."

"That was good," I said, surprised that he made no mention about my brother's social drinking.

Chapter 14

From Hartford, we drove directly to the home of Kris's boss, Dr. Bobbitt, in Storrs, Connecticut. I inhaled deeply, taking in my first breaths of the United States. The air felt pure and thin. I felt exhilarated.

"Welcome back," Dr. Bobbitt said, greeting Kris with a hearty handshake and a pat on his back. He and Kris walked to the living room, and I followed a step behind. "Hope you had a good holiday in India, Kris," Dr. Bobbitt said. Then looking at me, he said, "And here she is, your new bride." Kris smiled broadly. My hands went halfway up in a gesture of namaste when I caught myself and sheepishly extended my hand for a handshake. Mrs. Bobbitt joined us, and there were introductions again. She looked at me, at my draping sari, my bridal jewelry, and the bindi, a red dot on my forehead. "So this is your bride, an arranged marriage. She is beautiful," she said. Kris smiled generously again. Not knowing how to respond, I stood quietly, looking at my toes.

We had a short formal visit. While Kris and Dr. Bobbitt exchanged news about the status of their research and upcoming publications, Mrs. Bobbitt and I made perfunctory conversation. It surprised Mrs. Bobbitt that I could express myself in English quite well. "I had my schooling in a convent," I said timidly.

"And she is a pediatrician," Kris interjected, inflated with pride as if I were a prize he had won in a lottery. I blushed.

It was a Friday afternoon, and the key to our apartment was not available until the following Monday. Dr. Bobbitt and his wife had made arrangements for us to stay in their home for the weekend. They were going to be away, and we would have the house to ourselves.

Mrs. Bobbitt showed us around. Her house was pristine, decorated in muted shades of white accented by splashes of brighter colors. The soft white wall-to-wall carpet extended right up to the tub in the bathroom. Our bedroom felt like an elegant honeymoon suite with an Irish bedspread and white sheers on the windows. Mrs. Bobbitt had placed a bouquet of white roses in a white-on-white embossed vase on our nightstand.

After the Bobbitts left, I surveyed the house again, tiptoeing in my bare feet and comparing every space to our homes in India. I admired the American home. "Imagine dedicating a whole room to laundry," I said aloud, peeking at the room with the washer and dryer. "It is the size of my dhobi's entire living quarters where he and his family have to set aside half that space for washing and ironing our clothes." The kitchen was particularly impressive. I ran my fingers over the expanse of the white Formica countertops and opened and closed the refrigerator door, astonished by its size, a burned-orange enameled mass. I turned the knobs of the gas burners repeatedly and admired the ease with which one could cook in America.

As I sat next to Kris on the cozy velour sofa that evening, I found myself whispering, as though walls might retain my conversations and relay them to Mrs. Bobbitt. "She has trusted her entire house to us. My mother would never do that. She would put locks on every door." And then, "Did you see how well she has stocked the refrigerator? I feel I am in a honeymoon haven." Kris smiled, got up to stoke the fire in the fireplace, and said, "I promised you a honeymoon in America, didn't I? This is just the beginning."

America was beautiful. Driving from Hartford, the expanse of the landscape had been quiet and peaceful, the changing colors of fall, vibrant. The highways and byways were so clean, as if someone had just run a mop over them. The weather was balmy—Indian summer, as I learned later.

Wherever I went in the following weeks and months, my youthful eyes absorbed nothing but beauty. Everyone I met was kind and considerate, always helpful. Shopping was easy, goods plentiful. I saw no corruption. There was no price haggling with vendors. I had finally set my eyes on the country of my dreams—America.

♦♦♦♦♦♦

We moved into a two-bedroom apartment in the university housing on the following Monday. Within a week or two, the unfurnished apartment was livable with all its creature comforts. The bed came as a spare from one of Kris's friends, the living room furniture from a thrift store, the dinette from the Sears catalog. I was amazed at how easily things got done in America.

Kris resumed his responsibilities at the school of pharmacy as a postdoctoral fellow. I, a stay-at-home spouse, took to domestic pursuits. Although our apartment bore no comparison to Mrs. Bobbitt's beautiful home, I stretched my imagination and worked hard at decorating it. It was, after all, my first home. As soon as Kris left for work, I got busy. The rusty headboard was sanded down and painted a patina sage. A batik print hung on the wall to give our home its Indian elegance. Using one of my saris, I stitched a ruffled skirt to cover a cardboard box and set it up as our dresser.

In a few days, I was ready to undertake bigger projects. Our neighbors, Nina and her husband, Bob, had ingeniously put three wood planks into a box frame and slid the whole unit into their living room window. My apartment was a mirror image of theirs. I could do the same, I decided. Not only would the open shelving be good for storing books, they would also provide space for me to display the few Indian knickknacks that I had brought with me: the pair of sandalwood elephants, the colorful clay doll whose head bobbed back and forth like a *bharat-natiyam* dancer, the brass peacocks. Nina drove me to Barker's, a nearby hardware store, and we returned with several boards of finished pine. "You can use Bob's pattern and tools," she said.

I got to work immediately. Using Bob's pattern, I measured and marked. However, when I tried to cut, the saw would not budge. I eagerly awaited Kris's return. When he walked in and saw me sitting on the living room floor in the midst of all the mess, he threw up his arms and said, "What on earth are you up to?"

I stopped struggling with the saw, looked at him, and explained my project with bubbling enthusiasm. "We can have a bookcase like Nina's in no time. Just help me cut these boards."

"Me? Cut boards? Who do you think I am—a carpenter? You married a scientist, not a carpenter."

"I am the daughter of an engineer. I can cut them myself. I can figure it out," is what I did *not* say. Instead, I said, "No matter. We don't have to have a bookshelf like Nina's."

I felt my spirits deflate. American couples had harmony. They called each other honey. They did projects together, not us Indians. But I had married an Americanized husband. He should be different. He should be like Nina's husband. He was not.

"We don't have to have a bookshelf," I repeated and set the boards aside.

That weekend, Kris was up before I was. He was sitting on the living room floor in his pajamas, making a racket, cutting boards and pounding nails.

"Come hold this for me," he said as soon as I woke up. We finished building the bookshelf, and Kris took to this newfound hobby with a passion that followed him for the rest of his life. The same day, he went out and bought more wood and built us a free-standing room divider, consulting with Bob for details and borrowing his design.

As days went by, I realized that with almost every decision we made, we seemed to be having an argument.

I wanted to learn to drive. Kris thought it was too dangerous for an Indian woman to drive on the fast roads of America.

I wanted to take evening classes in oil painting. "Women of our culture should not be out alone at night," he said.

I was persistent, and he was adamant. However, in the end, I always acquiesced, remembering my mother's advice about being subservient to my husband. I became sensitized to these frictions. I wanted them to end. Every argument made my heart race and my head hurt. It made me sad. To top it all, we received a letter from Kris's dad, the first after we had left India. He filled us in on family news, asked how cold it was in America, and ended his note with a brief message. "There is always give and take in life. You must adjust and adapt to each other's likes and dislikes and never quarrel. And if you do, never let those foreigners scent it," he wrote. The letter was addressed to me, adding further guilt to my turbulent mind. *Kris is the one who disputes me every time when I know I am right,* I thought. There was no one around that I could talk to. All my neighbors were good neighbors, very kind to me, but they were all Americans, foreigners, not friends. They would not understand. I had to depend on my instincts, always asking myself what Mother would have done in that situation.

After mulling it over for a few days, I said to Kris, "Why do we have to argue so much? When marriages are made in heaven, the couple lives in perfect harmony. Wasn't our marriage made in heaven?"

I expected another argument, another philosophical sermon. Instead, he said, "Remember your physics? Opposite poles of a magnet attract each other."

We were indeed those opposite poles of a magnet. My husband was giving his approval that we live our lives charging and discharging our positive and negative ions. *That is how my parents must have lived,* I thought. They were always arguing. On a deeper level, they were in perfect harmony.

Chapter 15

It was the one-month anniversary of our wedding. I decided that I would cook a small surprise dinner for Kris but just could not get around to it. All day long, my mind was flitting from one thought to another. My menstrual cycle had been absolutely regular in the past, and now I was two weeks overdue. As each day had passed and I had seen no signs of bleeding, I had considered it to be from all the excitement in my life—the wedding, the packing, the giant leap to America. Pregnancy was not on my mind. Kris had talked about a yearlong honeymoon. At some point, I would begin to feel intimate enough with him to talk about such things and make plans about our future. And yet, this morning, I had felt a bit queasy in my stomach with a hint of what might be morning sickness. I tried to convince myself to the contrary. Indian folklore has it that no one gets pregnant in the first months after marriage. It takes about six cycles for the body to adjust to the new hormones. Only then is the womb ready to do its big job, accept an embryo. Deep inside me, however, I knew better. I knew that I was pregnant. I spent my day sorting out my emotions. At times, I was ecstatic and then suddenly apprehensive, almost afraid.

"It can't be. I really wanted to wait," I kept hearing Kris's words coming at me from the silent walls of our apartment. "We are just starting out. We have no idea where we will be a year from now. Maybe I won't have a job."

I spent my day preparing my defense. "It's all because of you. You could have waited until I had a chance to go on the pill."

It was five o'clock, and Kris walked in.

"Hello, my *chammak-challo.*" These were Kris's personal words of endearment for me. "How was your day?"

With my heart pounding, and my voice feeble, I said, "I don't know why I feel this way, but I think I may be pregnant."

Having blurted out my fears, I waited for a storm. Instead, he gave me a hug, lifting me off the floor and twirling me round and around in the center of our sparsely furnished living room. "That's the best news in the world. I am going to be the proud father of a son."

My mood changed immediately. "Son?" I said, sitting down on the divan to let my vertigo pass.

"Of course! My precious, million-dollar son," he said, landing next to me with mischief in his eyes. "You are carrying my million-dollar son."

"How do you know it's going to be a son? I want a daughter … *our* daughter," I said between his kisses.

"Oh, I know it," he said, giving me another hug. "I know it's going to be a boy."

"It's going to be *our baby*," I said, melting into a pool of tears. Legitimate or not, my tears poured easily. I found myself laughing and crying at the same time.

My pregnancy had yet to be confirmed. But today, we were celebrating parenthood.

♦♦♦♦♦♦

In the solitude of our apartment, my thoughts were constantly on my pregnancy and my baby … no, *our* baby. We had no radio, no TV. It was Friday, November 22, 1963. Standing in front of the refrigerator and deciding what I could put together for supper, I was humming the tune of a love song from a popular Indian movie: "*my heart is restless, the weather so beautiful, I wait impatiently for you, who is so much in love with me.*"

I was startled by the sound of the key turning at the front door. Kris walked in. Next, he was standing behind me, his hands around my waist. Embarrassed, I bit my lip and stopped singing. Turning to look at him, I said, "What's the matter? You are home early."

He muttered that he had a terrible headache and that he could not concentrate on his work. He headed toward the bedroom.

"Are you not well? Shall I get you an aspirin?" I asked, along with a myriad of questions, as I followed him. "Do you have a sore throat? Do you have an upset stomach? Did you go to the bathroom this morning? Do you think you have a fever?" This was the first time I had heard a physical complaint from Kris, and it worried me. "You don't seem warm," I said touching his forehead with the back of my hand.

"Just come and lie down next to me," he said, lifting the bed covers and making room for me.

"What's the matter?" I asked again.

"The president has been shot, and he is dead," he said.

I did not make the connection between President Kennedy's assassination and my husband's headache. I had been in America only three weeks, and the assassination of the president meant little or nothing to me. In fact, I had not seen the president's photo or heard his voice. *It happens all the time to politicians,* I thought. *We all survive it. Wasn't Gandhi assassinated?*

I lay beside Kris, massaging his forehead, and we fell asleep. When we woke up, I said, "Why don't we go to the movies? Maybe it will be a good diversion for your headache."

In the evening, we went to the one and only theater in Storrs, paid ninety-eight cents a ticket, and watched two shows back to back. We saw the frivolous movie *Three Fables of Love* followed by a second feature, *The*

World by Night. That evening, as we sat through the two films, Kris did not let go of my hand. We returned well past midnight.

Next morning, we had a quiet breakfast. Kris said that he felt better and suggested that we go over to Sally's.

Sally lived next door and had given us her key, urging us to make use of the facilities in her apartment on the weekends when she and her family were away. Her apartment was far better equipped than ours. She had an Osterizer, which came in handy when I wanted to make mint chutney. She had a washing machine that spared me many a trip to the Laundromat. She also had a TV.

We went over, and Kris turned on the television. Through the crackling background noise, I listened to Walter Cronkite's commentary, and through the fuzzy snow on the black-and-white screen, I saw how the assassination had affected the entire nation. President Kennedy, judged by some to be the most popular man in the world, was dead. He was only forty-six and had left behind a wife who was not much older than I. As the media focused its camera on the young and beautiful widow and her two children, tears filled my eyes. I could not imagine that happening to me or to anybody else.

The assassination of the young president must have made an impact on Kris, as well. For many weeks, he was reluctant to let me out of his sight, and when he was away, he checked up on me with frequent phone calls. At times, he surprised me by showing up for lunch.

That weekend, he started updating his résumé and sending job applications to various universities in the States and to the Punjab University in Chandigarh, India.

"What's the hurry?" I said when I saw him sorting his papers at the kitchen table. "We have a whole year ahead of us."

It was that sense of vulnerability that was making him anxious. Looking for his next job would give him a sense of stability.

"Oh, I think I should start looking around," he said.

Chapter 16

Although my visit to the doctor was not until twelve weeks from my last menstrual period, I knew that I was pregnant. I had begun to feel all kinds of new sensations in my body. My ravenous appetite gave me an urge for this food and that, and my energy level was high. I often woke up with a tingling in my breasts—all the telltale signs of pregnancy.

Given this new dimension to my life, I resigned myself to the status of being a contented housewife. Any dreams of taking an exam for my medical degree to be recognized in America had to be put on hold. This is what I had signed up for when I had decided to join the institution of marriage and motherhood and embark on the venture of ghar-grahasthi. Although the thoughts of who I really wanted to be kept creeping into my head now and then, for now, I just practiced the art of a *pati-vrata-patni,* a wife who devoted her attention to nothing but her home and husband. I kept myself busy, learning to type on our newly acquired Remington, writing letters to our families in India, and knitting for the baby to come. My letters to my sister were frequent, long, and descriptive.

As the only Indian couple on campus, we were often asked to represent our country at university functions. Initially, I felt awkward being the center of such attention. As I got used to it, I proudly wore my national outfit, a pretty silk sari along with ample handcrafted gold jewelry. When not much was going on at the university, Kris and I took long walks or went to the movies or visited department stores or simply cooked together.

Kris was a member of a hiking group and a fossil club. He also participated in the Masonic brotherhood. These activities brought many visitors to my home, and I enjoyed meeting Kris's friends.

Cooking, about which Kris and I knew very little, became the center of our lives. We created Indian meals from the meager ingredients on hand. I remember making *paneer*, our popular homemade cheese. Kris tried to split the milk with vinegar, calculating the amount needed with the precision of a pharmacist, and I insisted that buttermilk would do a better job. Neither he nor I won this battle. The pasteurized American milk turned out to be different from the fresh buffalo milk that Mother used, and it refused to curdle. Whatever we had produced tasted awful, but our American friends thought it was great. We made chapattis, the Indian flatbread with whole-wheat flour that we had to procure from Canada. And we made a lot of chicken curry.

Since we were living on Kris's small income as a fellow, we had to stretch every dollar that we spent. The kitchen was our priority. One evening, we were at the section of kitchen accessories at Barker's. I was admiring all the items on display and checking their price tags. I picked up a napkin holder. "Do you think we should get this?" I asked. It cost a dollar. The value of anything we purchased had to be first converted to rupees. The napkin holder was almost five rupees. We enumerated all the items we could buy for that much in India—a good pair of leather shoes, a nice cotton shirt. "With all the company we get, it will be a good investment," I said. I held the shiny metal dispenser in my hand while Kris examined a plastic one, which was almost half the price. We compared the two and debated the pros and cons of our purchase. "This one will last much longer," I said.

"Then get it," Kris said.

To this day, I hang onto that napkin holder in memory of our initiation into ghar-grahasthi—a reminder of a foreign graduate student's value of money.

♦♦♦♦♦♦

We were invited for a dinner party by the Bobbitts. It was my first Christmas in America, and I wondered how everyone else would dress for the occasion. Laying out several choices, I asked Kris if I should wear the red silk sari with its gold-and-green border and palloo, the one I had worn for my wedding. "Will it be too loud and flashy?"

"Other women will be wearing red for sure. It's the season, after all," Kris said as he changed into a dark suit and his favorite maroon silk tie.

I wore the red. I slid plenty of gold bangles on my wrists. I wore my necklace studded with rubies and pearls, along with its matching long earrings. "Look okay?" I asked Kris as I took a pinch of kum-kum, the vermilion powder, from its little silver container and carefully placed a bindi on my forehead. Watching me struggle in front of the small mirror in the bathroom, Kris walked up to me and helped me put a streak of the same red pigment in the parting of my hair.

The Bobbitts met us in the foyer. I handed my coat and scarf to Dr. Bobbitt and patted down the pleats of my sari, dusting off flecks of snow.

"I love that red," Mrs. Bobbitt complimented me. "That color is so becoming on you."

"Thank you," I said, my cheeks flushing.

We walked into the living room. I was introduced to the other guests, three or four members of the faculty and their wives. All the women in the group were dressed in knee-length skirts in basic colors of navy, black, beige, red, or combinations thereof. I had worn my colorful sari along with the heavy matching jewelry. I made myself believe that I was not overdressed. I was their guest from India, after all.

While there was animated chatter around me, I stood quietly, looking at the transformation that had taken place in the Bobbitts' home. Pretty to begin with, it was even prettier for the party. A perfectly shaped Christmas tree exuding its fragrance of pine, studded with twinkling lights and dainty ornaments, all in perfect symmetry. Potted poinsettias were strategically placed everywhere. There was a steady orange-blue flame in the fireplace, its cinders making crackling sounds now and then.

After a while, we moved to the dining room. I was seated next to Mrs. Bobbitt. New to their culture, I was shy about asking many questions or participating in their conversation. When they talked, I had to strain my ear to understand their accent. Their words ran into each other with a musicality that was so different from my Indian-British inflections. I was accustomed to pronouncing each word separately and with emphasis. From time to time, I was unable to follow along and allowed my thoughts to wander.

This was a formal sit-down dinner. I compared it to the ones Mother used to arrange when she invited her British friends. It felt strange that there were no servants in attendance here. Mrs. Bobbitt, the wife of a department chief, had to excuse herself and take away the soup dishes while Dr. Bobbitt himself sliced the ham and passed the plates around.

As we ate, Mrs. Bobbitt made an effort to keep up a conversation with me, just casual sort of talk. "How do you like it here in America? Are you adjusting well to the cold weather? Where in India do you come from? Did it snow there?"

I grew up in Madhya Pradesh, a province not too far from the equator. The only seasons I had known were summer, monsoons, and a hint of cool weather in between. I explained this to Mrs. Bobbitt.

"I had never seen snow in my life," I said. "I woke up the other morning and was in awe; I had not seen anything so beautiful. I ran out in my bare feet to catch those flakes in the palloo of my sari."

We both laughed.

There was a break in our conversation, and I saw that Mrs. Bobbitt was looking at my face, at my bindi. "I have always wondered why you wear that red dot on your forehead. I mean, is it a caste symbol or a religious thing?" she asked.

Do I have to do this again? I thought. *Does she not know that everyone in India wears a bindi? It's so basic. It's a ritual. It makes us look pretty.*

"It's just the way we dress. I mean, it's just a part of our makeup," I said.

"Oh, I thought it was a symbol of your caste," Mrs. Bobbitt said apologetically.

"No, no, it has nothing to do with castes," I replied quickly.

"Then what is it?"

Brief explanations that had satisfied the cashier at the grocery store and the teller at the bank did not satisfy Mrs. Bobbitt's curiosity. I had to tell her more. I could not decide what and how much I could explain at this formal party. I glanced at Kris and hoped that he would take over and answer this complex question. He was sitting at the opposite end of the table, and I was left to my own devices.

I recollected the sindoor ceremony, one of so many that were performed at our wedding. Directed by the priest, and under the watchful eye of parents, relatives, and spectators, Kris had colored the parting of my hair with kum-kum. Then, clumsily locating his ring finger, he had dipped the tip of that finger into the red powder, and placed a bindi on my forehead. With that, we were declared a married couple, with mutual promises of love, faith, and sincerity toward each other. These words were not verbalized by the priest, merely understood by the act of this ceremony called sindoor.

"It is just a symbol of happiness, a symbol of my being married," I said, and I told her about the sindoor ceremony performed at our wedding.

But that was not the answer, either. I had been wearing a bindi ever since I was a little girl. So I continued to explain. "In our culture, a girl can wear a bindi through her childhood and into her marriage, but not if she is widowed."

"Oh, I didn't know that," Mrs. Bobbitt said, briefly interrupting our discussion and offering me another helping of mashed potatoes and green beans.

"It's not a strict requirement that unmarried girls always wear a bindi," I tried to clarify.

"Why is that?" Mrs. Bobbitt asked.

"Well …" I fumbled for answers. Mother's explanations came to mind. As a child and into my teens, I was not allowed to wear lipstick or cheek color, but Mother always approved of my wearing a bindi. When I questioned her, she said, "It is a symbol of hope. You wear it in the expectation of finding a good husband and living a long and happy wedded life." I was barely ten at the time and had given Mother a quizzical look. "Yes, trust me. That day will come for you too." According to Mother, there was a potential husband for every girl in India, and I was to wear a bindi in anticipation of finding a good one.

I recapitulated these thoughts and expressed them to Mrs. Bobbitt. It satisfied her, but I needed to delve into the subject further to satisfy my own curiosity. The symbolism of a bindi is far more complex.

Typically, Muslims, Jews, and Christians in India do not wear a bindi. On the other hand, in the Hindu culture, the custom has existed from prehistoric times. The Ramayana has it that Ram had placed a vermillion dot on Sita's forehead and colored the parting of her hair with the same red powder when he took her as his wife.

Priests give their own explanations. They believe that the spot between the eyebrows, *bhrumadhya,* is the area of the frontal cortex wherein lies the center for concentration. They refer to it as the third eye, the eye that can see the unseen. It looks beyond our visual fields. By touching that spot with a clean finger after bathing, we invoke concentration and clear thinking. Thus men, particularly those with a religious orientation, often place a colored dot, a bindu, on their forehead, as well.

All this was too complex to discuss at the party, so I kept it to myself.

"Does it always have to be red?" Mrs. Bobbitt raised another question.

"Well, red denotes power, lust, and love, so I prefer a red bindi," I said. "Some wear it in colors to match their clothing."

After dinner, we moved to the living room, savoring Mrs. Bobbitt's homemade apple pie. One by one, the guests departed. Kris and I stayed on, enjoying our conversations with our hosts, talking about the vast differences in culture, climate, and socioeconomic situations between our two nations. By the time we left, I felt I had established a closer friendship with Mrs. Bobbitt. In the following months, she visited me often and became familiar with many of our customs and food habits and even ventured to wear a sari at one of my parties.

Chapter 17

It was a cold day in January. As usual, after breakfast, Kris got ready to leave for the university. I handed him his overcoat and gave him a hug as he was stepping out the door. He said he would be back soon.

"How soon?" I asked. There were times when he left in the dark and did not return until it was dark again.

"As soon as I can finish my experiments," he said, giving me another hug.

Our apartment was a boxlike unit identical to the one next to it and to the one after that, the entire row with black doors, all doors shut all winter long. It snowed all the time. At least that is how it felt to me that winter.

I stood at the half-open door and watched Kris as he walked up to his car, snow crunching beneath his boots. Looking at the dense, ominous clouds on the horizon made me dizzy. *Another bleak, snowy day,* I thought as I shut the door. I took a shower and got dressed in a sari, the only apparel I wore. I made the bed and collected the laundry. When I looked out the bedroom window, the sun was struggling to break through the dense clouds. Clumps of evergreens stood silently in the far distance. There was not a soul in sight—no hawkers selling their wares, no comings and goings of rickshaws, no honking of cars and scooters.

I walked across to the kitchen and opened the back door, pushing aside the snow that had blown against it. There were stretches of clotheslines in the quad, and one of my neighbors was taking diapers and baby clothes off the lines. She was dressed in dark gray leotards, a plaid skirt, a black heavy sweater, and knee-high boots. She did not seem to mind the cold. I watched her walking back and forth, touching the clothes on the lines, clutching some in her fist—checking for dryness, I supposed. I touched my tummy, caressing the baby that was growing inside of me. I talked gibberish to my baby. The woman continued with her chores.

I shut the door and moved to the living room. I put a couple of rows on my knitting and then set it aside. The hands on the clock had barely moved. Kris had left a long time ago, so I thought. But the clock betrayed me. I was hoping it was lunchtime. Kris had said that he might come home for lunch. I sat on the couch and waited. I thumbed through the small collection of books piled up on the corner table. There were texts on pharmacology and organic chemistry, nothing that interested me.

I located a small book sandwiched between the rest—*Marriage: East and West*, by Dr. David and Vera Mace. The authors were describing the favorable outcomes of arranged marriages of the East and were comparing them to Western traditions. Kris had earmarked some pages and underlined pertinent paragraphs that described the reasons for their success. I flipped through the pages back and forth, wondering what Kris was thinking when he had made his choice to marry me. Was he overlooking the fact that I was neither eighteen nor an uneducated village bride, as were the samples used in this book?

When it was past one o'clock, I knew that I would be eating lunch alone. I put the book aside and made myself a sandwich and a cup of coffee. Sitting at the kitchen table, I wrote a letter to my sister. The textured parchment paper made rustling sounds as I scribbled pages after pages. I complained about the weather. I told her that I was wearing my rosy-pink silk sari with the maroon and green batik, the one she and I had bought at the little bazaar. No one in America wore colorful clothes like I did, I wrote. Everyone, women and men, wore black, gray, or brown. I also complained about Kris. I said he did not care about me. I said he was gone all day and that I was eating lunch alone and that life was dull and dreary and cold in America.

As my pen moved faster and faster, the contrast with India became unbearable. I began to miss the very things I used to despise in India. I wanted to see a stray dog on the street, hear Mother's screams after the menace a feral cat had caused in her kitchen. I wanted the pounding monsoon rains.

I read and reread my letter. Then I shredded it. It wasn't true. It wasn't fair. Kris did care. In fact, he cared too much, in his own way. He did not understand why I was unhappy. How could he? He had fulfilled all my dreams. I was in America. I was living in comfort. I was making new friends. I was going to have a baby. There was no reason for me to be unhappy.

"What's the matter? You don't look too happy," Kris said when he came home that evening and I did not rush to the door to greet him.

"I don't like it here," I said.

"How can you not like it here?"

"Because … I'm lonely."

"How can you be lonely?"

"Because …" I looked at the still and lifeless expanse of snow through the fogged-up window.

"Don't I count?" he said.

"I want to see someone who looks like me, someone who wears a sari," I blurted out and began to cry.

It had been three months since I had seen another person in a sari. Three months since I had touched, tasted, or smelled the familiar. Three long months since I had stood in a hospital corridor, my stethoscope and doctor's bag in hand.

That night, Kris made us an Indian dinner, boiling yellow split peas—which resembled our Indian legume, *toor-dal,* in its outward appearance.

He flavored it heavily with onions, stewed tomatoes, and curry powder to camouflage its taste. Having a simple meal of rice and *dal* comforted me.

After dinner, he picked up the phone book and located an Indian name in the directory, one Mrs. Bawa in Deep River, Connecticut. He called her up, introduced himself, and learned that she also came from Amritsar, his hometown. She was in America on an exchange teacher program. After chatting with her about their common friends and acquaintances in Amritsar, he planned a visit with her for the following weekend.

I looked forward to meeting Mrs. Bawa. I would finally meet someone who dressed like me, spoke like me. She would give me tips on making Indian meals without turmeric, coriander, cumin, or garam masala. The Spice Islands brand of curry powder that I had bought from Universal and used for all my cooking had cumin, coriander, fenugreek, turmeric, cardamom, and more. It had all the commonly used Indian spices, and yet the taste of the dishes I prepared with it was so un-Indian. I did not need all of them in the same recipe. The proportion in which they are used is also different from one recipe to another. I needed those spices in individual jars. Fresh ginger root, an essential ingredient in our cooking, was not available. "What's that?" the grocer had said when I had asked for it and directed me to the spice racks. I brought home a bottle of ground ginger and found that adding it to any of my recipes ruined the taste further. Mrs. Bawa would answer all my questions. She would comfort me.

♦♦♦♦♦♦

When Mrs. Bawa opened the door to greet us, I felt an immediate sense of camaraderie, quickly overlooking the fact that she was wearing jeans and sweater and not a sari. A smell of curry wafted from her kitchen, and a familiar print of elephants and camels covered her sofa. We sat at the small kitchen table in her studio apartment and chatted for a long while as she brought out ham sandwiches and chips. When she spoke in English, she threw in many Hindi words, her accent matching mine. I did not have to strain my ears to understand her lingo. She was pronouncing *bӑth* and *glӑss* and *clӑss* just the way I liked.

"You must stay for dinner," she said as she served us the afternoon tea with cardamom, milk, and sugar. "I have prepared some nice chicken curry."

Mrs. Bawa's invitation was persuasive. We stayed overnight in her cramped apartment, and I felt a small part of India in my bones.

"How do you cook curries without our spices?" I asked as we settled for dinner.

"Oh, just learn to improvise. You get used to it," she said. "I had tried to order some staples from New York. They were not of good quality, and some of the dals were wormy."

"Can't trust those Indian merchants even in America," Kris said.

I ate the rice and curry with my fingers like I used to in India and talked about the bounty in America. I told her how the supermarkets and department stores had fascinated me. I had never seen such brightly lit stores with so much of everything. "And it's all fixed price, no bargaining," I said. We both laughed as if we had made a pleasant discovery.

"In spite of it all, I'm lonely," I told Mrs. Bawa. "As soon as Kris leaves in the morning, I feel like I am a bird trapped in a golden cage."

"Only way to avoid loneliness in America is to have a job," she said. "Everyone is so busy here. No one has the time to sit and gossip. It is different in India. You have family, servants, vendors. Something is going on all the time. Not here. It is very quiet here."

I realized that it was not my sari that had made me pen such a letter to my sister. In fact, everyone I had met in America had adored my sari. It was not the food either. I enjoyed the challenge of creating Indian meals with the meager ingredients on hand. I was simply missing my career.

I returned from Mrs. Bawa's with a resolve.

Chapter 18

The following morning, our breakfast started with a feud.

"I am going to look for a job," I said to Kris as he came to the table.

"But you are pregnant," he said. "You need a lot of rest."

"I'm pregnant, not sick," I said as I slid half the onion and cheese omelet on his plate and sat down next to him with the other half. "I went sledding last week, didn't I?"

"And left me worried, of course."

"Pregnancy and delivery are nature's norms, you know. Have you not seen women working from dawn to dusk, carrying heavy loads on their heads and at times delivering right in the fields?"

No women in Kris's family had worked outside of their home, pregnant or otherwise. It was hard for him to understand that besides being a pati-vrata-patni, I had another self that desperately needed to emerge. Our mutual warfare continued.

"Where will you find a job? You don't have the credentials," he said, optimistic that he had a chance to win.

"I can look for something at the university," I said.

"What can you do at the university? You are a doctor."

"I can always find something."

"I don't want our son to be hurt in any way," was his last plea.

"Don't worry. I will take good care of your million-dollar son," I teased.

We finished breakfast, and I picked up the plates, my dilemma unresolved.

A week later, we were invited to another dinner at the Bobbitts. There, I was seated next to Dr. Dolyak, the chief of the department of poultry sciences. I happened to say something about my credentials and the obstacles I was facing at working in the medical field. "Oh, I have the perfect job for you. I have a research grant and am looking for someone to run the experiments," he said. He told me that he needed a technician to set up the equipment, calibrate it, and analyze human and chicken blood samples for similarities and differences in their protein contents.

In spite of Kris's reservations, I accepted that job. I learned the lab techniques with ease, and—being a pediatrician—had no trouble drawing blood from tiny chick veins.

♦♦♦♦♦♦

The temporary job at the university put me in a good routine and helped me break many cultural barriers. I mingled with my coworkers, and my friendship with my neighbors grew. Sally had introduced me to her friends, a group of women connected with the auxiliary services. I had met Ruth and Nancy and Connie and Shirley and Joan and Jackie and Mabel and Aula and Sara. These names had sounded so foreign, so different from Sarojini, Revathi, and Vasanti, my friends in India. Now, as I memorized the names of my new friends, I thought less and less about those that I had left behind. I began to look forward to our bimonthly meetings where we worked at a new craft or experimented with a recipe.

Wherever I went, I was called upon to demonstrate something that was typical of India. I showed our group the art of henna decorations and gave them cooking demonstrations. One day, when I had them over for dinner, I made chapattis, the Indian flatbread. "It looks like a flying saucer," Ruth said as the chapatti puffed up on my griddle. I also showed them several different ways of wearing a sari. "It feels like a lot of fabric, but you carry it so well," Mabel said. "And look how it works so nicely as a maternity outfit. I bet you don't have to invest in maternity clothes." Questions regarding my bindi or the Indian caste system never escaped me.

As my friends learned about the diversities of the Indian culture, they enlightened me about America. I took in bits of the American history, learning about the pilgrims and the initial disputes with the Native Americans—they called them Indians. Then, realizing that I was also an Indian, they amended, "I mean, the *American* Indians." I wondered what these American Indians looked like and whether they had anything in common with me. I also heard stories of the riots that were occurring in the southern states over issues of desegregation.

One night, we sat in a circle with our embroideries and knitting in Jackie's apartment. Everyone had questions regarding my arranged marriage. I explained our customs. "We slowly fall in love after we are married," I said. This was a concept difficult for them to grasp. It opened up the subject of love and marriage. "In America, we choose our own partners," one of them said. "When a girl turns eighteen, she does not have to get her parents' consent for anything," another woman explained.

How strange, I thought.

The women began to talk about their personal lives. One of them told us about her four-year-old daughter being a flower girl at her wedding. "She looked so cute," she said. I considered that for a moment. I was naive, and it never occurred to me that a woman from a university setting could have a child without being married and then talk so openly about it. It also shocked me to hear about the frequent breakups and divorces among my American friends. It surprised me that they did not consult with their parents or grandparents on these matters.

"Maybe we should introduce the concept of arranged marriages in America," I said.

We all laughed.

Chapter 19

Prenatal checks were the highlight of our lives. Each month, on the day of my appointment, Kris took the day off and drove me to Dr. Sandler's office in Willimantic. He waited patiently for that smile on my face as I came out of the exam room. I gave him a detailed report of the progress our million-dollar son had made. Following our visit, we went to lunch and talked about baby names—only those for baby boys, of course. I tried to throw in some of my girl favorites, Radhika or Monika or Digiti-Minimi—a name I used to fantasize about when I studied human anatomy—but we always ended up with the name Rajiv. Relaxing in the little deli next to the doctor's office, I described to Kris the ticklish somersault going on inside my tummy. "Next time, I am going to take on that task of carrying the baby," Kris said.

"Jealous? I will never give you that privilege," I teased.

Our visit to the doctor in June stopped us in our tracks, putting a damper on our carefree lives. We learned that the baby was in breech position. The doctor performed retroversion, a procedure to manipulate the abdomen and gently turn the baby around. When I returned for my weekly follow-up visit, however, the baby had found its comfort back in breech. After three such attempts, we had to talk about alternatives. Dr. Sandler took X-rays of my pelvis and measured the opening against the size of the baby. He discussed the results with us. "You have an adequate pelvis. There is a good chance that you could deliver vaginally," he said. That enlivened my spirits. Throughout my pregnancy, I had looked forward to a normal, vaginal delivery. "However, if you want to feel more secure about the baby's health, you should consider a C-section." Cesarean was considered to be a major surgery and not without considerable risk to the mother in those days. I looked at Kris and tried to read his thoughts. His face was grim, his brow furrowed. He squeezed my hand when Dr. Sandler used the words "not without considerable risk to the mother."

When we did not give an answer, Dr. Sandler said, "We don't have to make a decision today. Think about it, and we can make a definitive plan when you return next week."

"What do you think?" I asked Kris as I cried all the way home.

Kris was silent. On reaching home, he placed a call to his brother Shadi-lal in India. He wanted to talk with someone from his family, someone with experience as a father. After six hours, when he could not get a connection, he gave up and turned to me. "You are a doctor; you should know," he said. It was one of the hardest decisions I had ever been called upon to make. The doctors in America were well trained, and Dr. Sandler had come highly recommended. I trusted his judgment. I tried to be optimistic. I opted for a vaginal delivery.

"That's a reasonable choice," Dr. Sandler said. "We will keep the operating room staff on alert. We can take you in for a C-section if you don't make the desired progress."

The availability of this alternative was comforting.

"Could I still go for a natural, drug-free delivery?"

"Of course," Dr. Sandler said.

♦♦♦♦♦♦

I went into labor on the expected date of confinement. We drove to Willimantic and checked into the hospital.

Kris was allowed to stay in the delivery room with me, a new trend in those days. Not having a single friend or experienced female family member by my side, I was pleased that at least Kris would be there. From the time I had known him, he had projected himself as a confident, self-assured man. I expected him to hold my hand through this ordeal. However, each time I had a contraction, his face turned the color of my drape sheet. I squeezed his clammy hand. "I am all right. I will survive this," I found myself comforting him. After a couple of hours, when my contractions became strong and the pain excruciating, he left the room. I could see him in the lobby coughing and retching. Then the nurse shut the door.

I felt very alone. There was no one to hold my hand, no one to support me. I missed my mother. I clutched the cold metal railings of the delivery table and pushed. As I labored, Dr. Sandler disregarded my request for a drug-free delivery. The medications relieved the pain, but they also slowed down the contractions. Finally, Rajiv, Kris's million-dollar son, was born vaginally after almost twelve hours of hard labor. He came into this world with a brilliant Apgar score. I, on the other hand, sustained a large tear in spite of an episiotomy and had a miserable, slow postpartum recovery.

The customary five-day hospital stay gave me the much-needed rest. Although I missed my home, I was pleased to be in the hospital. I spent most of my afternoons in an open grassy area, an extension of the obstetric ward, convalescing and nursing Rajiv. Kris was allowed unlimited visiting hours.

I was the only brown-skinned woman in the Windham Community Hospital at that time. Nurses, staff from different departments, and even patients on the floor visited me to see the special baby with long dark eyelashes and a head full of silky black hair. The million-dollar son was worth all the trouble and anxiety I had gone through.

My stay in the hospital was also an introduction to mainstream America. One morning, I had a new nurse assigned to me. As she wheeled baby Rajiv's crib to my bedside, I heard her say to the aide beside her, "Such a cute baby, and such a beautiful mother; it is a shame she is not married. I understand that there is a guy who comes regularly to visit her."

The aide looked at her quizzically. So did I. She had assumed that I did not understand English.

"Did you not see her hand?" she said. "She wears no wedding band."

"Oh my!" the aide said.

These women, living in the little town of Willimantic, were so far removed from the rest of the world. India, its culture and its customs, was nowhere on their radar.

♦♦♦♦♦♦

Rajiv blinked and grimaced in the bright sun as the nurse wheeled us to the waiting car outside the hospital. Kris opened the passenger door of the small two-door Saab and helped me get settled. I held Rajiv securely in my lap, and Kris drove the fifteen or so miles from Willimantic to Storrs slowly and carefully, avoiding the bumps and potholes on the road.

When we came home, I lay Rajiv in the center of our bed. Kris and I stared at the baby as he slept peacefully. It felt as if all my medical knowledge had drained out of me, totally erased from my memory. I stood in awe, admiring the miracles of nature. I had gone to the hospital with a big tummy and had returned with this fully carved little baby. We stroked his feet, his cheeks, and his belly until we made him squirm. "He's smiling, he's smiling," we said as we looked at each other with pride.

As days went by, we realized how inexperienced we were at parenting. Is he hungry? Is he fussy because he needs to pass gas? No, he just wants to be picked up and cuddled. I found that we were not arguing as much anymore. We were always consulting, experimenting, guessing, and most of all concurring with each other. We were learning to understand the language of a baby—our baby.

Chapter 20

Kris returned to work, and I settled into a new routine, that of motherhood. Rajiv was a contented baby, easy to care for. Each day was full of excitement. Life was perfect, and I wanted those days to last forever. However, Kris's year of fellowship was nearing its end, and a change was inevitable. We had to make decisions about our move. In response to the innumerable applications that Kris had sent, he had received offers from a few universities in America. None of them were permanent positions, just another year of fellowship. He had also applied for a position at the University of Punjab in Chandigarh, India.

I was not ready to return to India. I had not had a chance to enhance my career.

"Don't you want to consider these offers from American universities?" I asked. "Maybe we can stay on for a few more years. I would also like to study and get some training in my field. That will help me get a better job in India, don't you think?"

"I will if I have to. But if I get the job that I have been vying for, it will be best that we go back. It will be good to return and get settled in our home country," he said, ignoring my question.

In a few weeks, Kris received the much-awaited letter.

"My colleague in Chandigarh has offered me the job I was seeking," he said. "It is a reader's position with the prospect of moving to a full professorship in a few years. I will be working in the university of my choice, and we will be living in a city I love. How much better could it get?"

I had never seen Kris so happy and excited. I could not share his joy. I looked at him, my face expressionless.

"Don't look so sad," he said. "Once you get to Chandigarh, you will also love it. It is the most desirable place to live—the cleanest city in India, the least congested. I have always dreamed of making it my home. And now everything is falling in place."

"And you are sure you want to go back?" I asked again.

"Yes, of course," he said with confidence. "My opportunity is now. The job is not going to wait for me forever."

I was not convinced, and he could read my mind.

"When we come to America to study, we should not think we have become Americans. I am an Indian, and it is that great Indian soil that has made me who I am today. I must return and give back to that country that has given me so much."

Kris described his visions of working at the Punjab University and giving it his all. He envisioned modernizing their lab, teaching undergraduates, and having graduate students of his own.

"I will be able to produce and publish quality work once I get the lab set up to American standards," he said.

He was not thinking of the bureaucracy in India—the hardships of getting anything done. Or maybe he was a bit too ambitious. We continued to argue.

"You feel confident that you, a single individual, will make a difference?" I asked, reminding him of the corruption and the general inertia of the land.

"Oh yes. If each one of us will do our bit, the whole country is bound to improve."

At this point, I knew our fate was sealed, and I did not want to dampen Kris's enthusiasm. I was a new bride, weaving my life into his and trying to know him better. He was stubborn and strong in his convictions. I conceded. I started wrapping up my life in America with the determination of making a permanent home in Kris's dream city.

♦♦♦♦♦♦

Since I knew so little about the place, I started asking a lot of questions. Kris explained to me how the new city of Chandigarh, the capital of Punjab, was born. During the 1947 partition of British India into two separate countries, India and Pakistan, the state of Punjab had to be split. Lahore, the original capital of Punjab, lay within the boundaries of Pakistan and remained the capital of Punjab, Pakistan. The Indian state of Punjab needed its own capital. Pandit Jawaharlal Nehru, the first prime minister of independent India, wanted to portray his progressive outlook to his people. He wanted to create a city like none other in India or Pakistan. He commissioned several foreign architects to design the city of Chandigarh, Le Corbusier, the famous French architect, being one of them.

"It is a beautifully planned city—methodically laid out in neat squares and quads, and all sewage runs underground. Just like America, there are large parcels of land set aside for lakes, gardens, and parks," Kris explained.

I had never been to Chandigarh, and I tried to take it all in.

"It will be no different from living in America," Kris said. "You will be living in a clean, hygienic city with the added advantage of raising our children with Indian values and culture."

I planned to return to India with the same optimism and passion that my husband felt. Maybe Chandigarh was a dream of a place. I willed to make it my home. I sealed my memories of the year in Connecticut and prepared for our move back.

PART 3

Chandigarh, Punjab, India

Chapter 21

Kris and I arrived at Chandigarh on a Sunday afternoon in early November 1964. After returning from America, we had spent a couple of weeks with my parents in the sweltering heat of Madhya Pradesh. As I got off the train, the weather in Chandigarh took me by surprise. It was cold, windy, and overcast. I covered our three-month-old baby, Rajiv, with the palloo of my sari as we walked across to the taxi stand. There were taxis, auto-rickshaws, and cycle-rickshaws for hire. We hailed a cycle-rickshaw, the cheapest mode of transportation.

As the rickshaw-wala peddled along Madhya Marg, the main artery of Chandigarh, I was impressed by the canopy of flowering *gul-mohar* trees planted along the city's divided parkway. Next to them were rows of rosebushes. The fragrance of the flowers mixed with the smell of diesel emissions sputtering from the passing auto-rickshaws made me feel quite at home. I was in India, no doubt. True to Kris's descriptions, Chandigarh was an open city neatly laid out in sectors. Our rented duplex in Sector 15 was four or five miles from the railway station. We wove in and out of many sectors and inner roads to get to our destination.

The roads in our development were also paved, litter-free, and wide enough for two-way traffic. Except for the *tring-ring-ring* of a cycle-rickshaw or the chant of an established hawker or the bark of a stray dog, our street was quiet. What a contrast this was from the congested, overcrowded, bustling city of Amritsar, Kris's hometown. I was going to like Chandigarh, I decided, and I said something to that effect to Kris.

"I told you that you would love it," he said, beaming with excitement.

♦♦♦♦♦♦

Our landlord was waiting for us at the rental unit. He opened the door to let us in. A pungent smell of the fresh coat of lime wash wafted through the air. We walked in and looked around. The apartment was a decent size: a central hallway that led to a covered porch in the back; living room and dining room on the left of the hallway; a bedroom on the right. The kitchen was off the back porch next to the dining room, a small bath on the opposite side. Kris and the landlord stood in the hallway and discussed the business aspects of our rental agreement. Their voices echoed in the empty shell. I walked through the rooms, mentally arranging the furniture that we would buy. With the permanency of our stay in mind, I imagined that we would buy the best. Heavy drapes and area rugs would help absorb the echo and some of the damp chill.

As the landlord was showing us around, he commented, "You have come from America. There, I understand people take care of their property, even a rental home. Don't they?" Without waiting for an answer, he continued, "I have no qualms in renting this brand-new house to you all. To a local, absolutely not. They are such rascals. They have no value for other people's property. Once you let them in, you cannot get them out. You take the matter to the court, and the case goes on and on through your lifetime. Eventually, you surrender, or if you die, the case gets transferred to the next generation. The dispute continues."

Kris and I listened and took his comment as a compliment to us as well as to our American friends who had opened their homes to us with such implicit trust when we were in America.

Standing in the walled-off courtyard, I looked at our duplex from the rear. The covered porch and the cemented courtyard were appealing. That's where we would be spending most of our time. The ubiquitous house gecko appeared on the wall near the kitchen. She greeted me with an endless stare. Her three-inch tail, just about the length of her slender grayish-green body, was moving back and forth, back and forth, ever so gently. I stared back, hoping that she would go away. Instead, she just blinked. She was joined by her mate, his soft white belly pulsating in rhythm with hers. Almost simultaneously, as though they had formed a strategy, they attacked a mosquito caught in a cobweb in the corner. Their meal done, they disappeared into the dining room. The geckos had obviously settled in this house before humans had a chance to inhabit it. Having lived in the comforts of American homes for just one year, I was forgetting the conditions I was returning to. I had to remind myself that these geckos would be our companions from here on, sharing our home with us whether I liked it or not. They help us keep down the population of mosquitoes, flies, and other critters, I convinced myself.

After the landlord left, Kris walked over to the other half of the duplex to meet our neighbor, Dr. Bhatnagar. Kris had known him as a colleague over the years. They exchanged warm and friendly pleasantries, and Kris asked him for assistance with a few essentials that would help us tide over the first few days. Dr. Bhatnagar, a bachelor in his forties, was not much help. He lived with his elderly mother, *Amma-ji*, and being single, had very few items to spare. He offered us a quilt and a khatia, a hemp woven camp cot.

Later in the day, we cooked a small meal on a borrowed kerosene stove and then spent a romantic evening checking out our neighborhood. Rajiv slept comfortably in his stroller, making clucking sounds as he sucked his middle and ring fingers. The sun had broken through the clouds, glorifying the famed city with a transparent orange glow.

"See? What did I tell you? There are no *gandi naalis* running beside these homes," Kris pointed out. "All the homes look so clean, because the sewage is underground."

Again, he was comparing Chandigarh to his hometown of Amritsar, where water from kitchen washings, as well as from bath and laundry, drained into narrow channels built along the sides of the homes. Young ones squatted across these open drains to do their business. Pedestrians took advantage of the running water in the drains and dropped their banana peels into them. The words, *gandi naalis*—filthy channels—described it all.

"And see how pretty our street looks with its rows of lamps with no clumsy overhead wires," Kris said.

We continued to compare our new city to Kris's hometown. Just about a year ago, I had visited his family in Amritsar after we were married. During that stay, when we had taken a taxi to visit a relative, our driver had to leave us sitting in the car on the side street while he walked the narrow cobblestone *gulli*, flailing his hands in the air and clearing the passage of children, cows, and pedestrians. "*Hato, hato,* move aside, make way for Sahib-ji's car to come through," he was shouting in a commanding voice. When he returned and drove us through, the pedestrians stood glued to the walls of the tall buildings, holding back their children. The children, excited at the novelty of a car on their street, hailed at us with gleeful smiles. The cows, however, were back on the street and had to be steered out of the way once again.

Kris and I chuckled over those memories as we strolled around our streets in Chandigarh.

♦♦♦♦♦♦

When the sun went down, the chill returned. We had set up our khatia in the dining room, assuming that it would be shielded from the cold by the living room on one side and the kitchen on the other. One half of the borrowed quilt served as an underlay, a sort of a makeshift mattress, and the other half as the cover over us. Rajiv was tucked in the middle to benefit from our body heat. As the night progressed, the room turned into an icebox, and the stone walls felt as if they were blocks of stacked ice. We pulled the cot a foot or two away from the wall, and Kris lit the Primus stove to create some warmth. If any part of my body got exposed to the room air, I felt an icy sting, and if I tried to readjust the quilt to cover myself, the warm air escaped disturbing the balance inside our tentlike igloo and left me shivering.

When we woke up the next morning, we were greeted with bright sunshine. By afternoon, the temperature rose to the comfortable sixties. As days went by, I realized that this was the normal pattern of winters in Chandigarh: invigorating balmy days and chilly nights—except for the weeks when we got the northwestern rains that left us cold, damp, and frigid. I could deal with that, I thought, and I began to like the Chandigarh weather. I was going to like settling in India permanently.

Chapter 22

Kris left for the university at an early hour, leaving me to work on organizing our home. With a small baby in my care, I did what I could. Mother shipped the two trunks of my trousseau that she had kept in storage while I was abroad. When they arrived, I opened them and peered through their contents. I unpacked the gleaming stainless-steel pots and pans, utensils, and thalis. I had frowned when Mother was putting my trousseau together with such meticulous attention to detail. I had argued that she was spending too much money on my wedding unnecessarily. Now I valued her thoughtfulness.

The kitchen in our duplex was a bare room with four recessed shelves on one wall and a small cement platform at the far end. This was certainly an upgrade from the Amritsar kitchen, where the cooking was done squatting on the floor beside a charcoal grill. However, I could not help comparing it to the one I'd had in America, and I knew I would have to adapt. I arranged the utensils neatly on the upper two shelves, leaving the lower two for rations and spices.

The doorbell rang.

"So you must be the family moving in from America," the lively voice said as I opened the door. She introduced herself as Harnam, a neighbor. Her oval face, hazel eyes, and rosy cheeks were all smiles. "I live off that street." She pointed to the street perpendicular to mine. "Not far, just about five houses down. And this is my son, Subhash." She pinched the toddler's cheek in affection, and he recoiled shyly.

"Won't you come in?" I asked.

We moved to the sunny courtyard where I had set up the khatia for day use. We chatted for a while and got acquainted. I learned that Harnam's husband also worked at the university and that she and her husband had grown up in Amritsar and knew Kris's family.

Later that day, Harnam took me to the market, and we bought some basic necessities. We came home with packages of rice, flour, yellow, green and black lentils, tea, sugar, salt, and essential spices—turmeric, cumin, coriander, and red chili powder. My kitchen was up and running.

"You will need beds and bedding," Harnam said as she was leaving. "When Kris comes home, send him over, and we will help you get settled. I'll send you our guest bedding."

"That's so very nice of you," I said.

In the evening, Kris and Harnam's husband transported two beds and ample warm bedding.

♦♦♦♦♦♦

The next morning, I went over to visit Amma-ji, Dr. Bhatnagar's mother. I gently knocked at the open door and then walked in. "It's me, your neighbor," I said. Amma-ji walked toward the door and greeted me. She looked quite like my own grandmother, a peaceful, wrinkled face with a dimple on her chin, her gray hair braided and tied into a knot at the nape of her neck. The simple white sari she wore suggested that she must be a widow. I introduced myself. "I know who you are, beti," she said with endearment. "I already met your husband when you arrived. A delightful young man you have for a husband."

Whether it was due to or in spite of my husband's charms, I felt pleased that I was being so well received by Amma-ji. She took Rajiv from my arms and sat down on a *chatai*, a mat made of natural fibers spread on the cement floor of her courtyard. She had been working on a cup of lentils, placing them on a thali, a large steel plate, and fingering through them to remove stones and other extraneous material. A basket containing a paring knife, a few potatoes, an onion, and a green chili lay next to the thali. I made myself comfortable beside her. Keen to spend time with me, she offered me tea. As I shared a cup of tea with her, she poured out her woes in a tone of despair. Intermittently she cooed and cajoled Rajiv, losing herself in her thoughts and in the baby's innocent splendor.

"Look at my son," she said. "He is forty and is not married. Krishan married at a good age, and see how happy he is? I wish my son would marry and I would have company. Anyway, now I am glad you have moved next door to me. You are like my daughter-in-law."

This was the first time a woman had addressed me as her daughter-in-law. Kris had lost his mother to an attack of cholera when he was nine. Amma-ji's words felt soothing to my ears.

"Don't hesitate to ask for any help you may need," Amma-ji said. "You can leave the baby with me whenever you wish. I am always home."

I began to leave Rajiv with Amma-ji when I needed to run errands. It was amazing to see how she could continue working on her daily chores with an infant in her care. As she sat cross-legged on the floor beside the blazing charcoal brazier and made chapattis, she bundled Rajiv in his blanket and tucked him between layers of her soft muslin sari. He slept peacefully in her lap. If he whimpered, she rocked him back to sleep by gentle rhythmic movements of her thigh and a few reassuring words. The rolling and roasting of the *rotis* continued without a break. I, a young mother and a pediatrician, worried that my baby would suffocate under the layers of her clothing or roll off and get a burn from the hot coals. She was never concerned. These were time-tested methods, and I was not to worry, she assured me.

Chapter 23

When Kris had decided to return to India, he was determined that he would make a difference in the uplift of our country. He had envisioned how he would utilize the knowledge he had gained in America to expand his laboratory, introduce new techniques, and improve the standard of graduate education. I had returned with my own convictions. I would carry over what I had learned in America and take the life of an Indian housewife to a new level. I would do away with servants. As a child, I had had mixed feelings about the status of our servants. They were treated well by my parents and lived far better than their counterparts in the villages. However, the thought that they were captives of the rich always bothered me. *I will try a different path when it's my turn to run a home,* I had concluded. Now that I was living in my own home in the most modern city of India, I had my chance.

My determination, however, crumbled rapidly. It started with the latrine. This was a small room with a squat toilet and an overhead tank with a pull chain. Surely I could clean this rather easily, I thought. I bought a special broom made of bamboo bristles and a jug of phenol. I mimicked the procedure I had seen so often through my childhood. Wearing flip-flops set aside just for this purpose, I entered the room, sprinkled a cup of the phenol everywhere, and scrubbed. I got into the nooks and crannies of the grout on the raised, foot-shaped platforms on either side of the lavatory and pulled the chain. As a final touch, I poured a bucket of water. The water hit the back corners of the room and drained into the toilet with a gurgling *whoosh*. When I was done, I looked at Rajiv, my only companion at that hour. He was attempting to scoot around on the floor in the courtyard. I cooed at him and told him my success story. He smiled back, and I was sure he had appreciated my good work.

By the next morning, however, the room had developed a strong odor of ammonia all over again. Cobwebs with entrapped mosquitoes appeared in the corners, and rat droppings lay at the edges of the floor. I broke down. *This is not what I envision doing every day for the rest of my life*, I thought. The young girl Shakuntala, whom I had observed entering Amma-ji's house via her back entrance, was passing by. She was the jamadarini, the latrine cleaner, who served several families in my neighborhood. She was from an untouchable family and so, as was the custom, entered the homes via the rear entrances. I hailed for her, interviewed her, and hired her to clean my latrine. That settled, I felt a weight lift off my shoulders.

I started on the next essential task, that of sweeping the terrazzo floors. Where was so much dust coming from? It was not quite a week since we had moved into this brand-new house. India was a dusty country. Crucial for cross ventilation, the windows had to be open all the time. That explained why Mother had her maids sweep her house twice a day.

As I went dusting from room to room, I also collected the laundry. I looked at the mound that was building up in the back porch. There was a shirt, an undershirt, underwear, pajamas—all this from what Kris had shed after his bath in the morning. I added to it my own garments and those of the baby. It was a humongous pile. All this would have to be soaked in Surf powder for a couple of hours, taken to the wash-stone in the courtyard, beaten with a paddle, rinsed and wrung, and then hung on the line. I sighed at the thought of the lengthy process as I continued to work. I put the clothes in a bucket, sprinkled a cup of the soap powder, and poured a kettle of hot water over them. I was stooped over the bucket, stirring the load with my paddle when Harnam walked in. I straightened my back, the paddle in my hand. She greeted me with her usual pleasantries, looked at me, and then looked at the clothes in the bucket.

"Servant help is such a rare commodity in Chandigarh," she said.

"Is it?" I asked out of curiosity. Growing up, I had seen plenty of servants around our house. Why would it be any different now?

"Oh yes," she said.

"Has India changed so much in just the year I was in United States?" I asked.

"It is a problem innate to Chandigarh at the moment, although it is spreading all over the country," she explained. "Here, thanks to that famous architect Le Corbusier, or whatever his name is, there are no *jhopar-patties*, hutment colonies, anywhere. He demolished them all. The labor force has to come from the surrounding villages. Those that make it in get absorbed immediately with the government or in industry. You cannot woo them to work in your home. You cannot afford their price."

I made a pot of tea, and we made ourselves comfortable on the khatia.

"There is a way out, *didi*," Harnam said reflectively. "Shakuntala tells me that you have hired her as your jamadarini. As long as you keep it hush-hush, she will do other house chores as well for you. Many of us in the neighborhood use her, but we don't talk about it openly."

"She belongs to the caste of untouchables and is crossing her boundaries. If that's what you mean, that does not bother me," I said. "She is such a sweet thing. I did not know she was taking on other household tasks, as well."

"Oh yes! And she does a good job."

Next day, I asked Shakuntala to take on more responsibilities. The coarse-featured, dark-skinned young girl who visibly belonged to the untouchable caste began to show up at my house daily around nine. She wore clean homespun cotton saris that she tucked up to midcalves while working. She swept the floors, washed the daily laundry, and cleaned the bathroom and latrine, finishing all her assigned work in a couple of hours. When she was done, she often spent time with me, narrating the neighborhood gossip. I loved seeing her animated, smiling face as she told her stories. When I offered her tea, she received it in her own chipped china mug and sat on the floor several feet away from me in accordance with her upbringing. Although I had asked her to take care of all the house chores, I too held the prejudice that I grew up with. I did not hug her or allow her to work in my kitchen.

Bit by bit, I succumbed to the traditional life in India. I ended up hiring a dhobi for taking care of the heavier laundry and a gardener for the upkeep of our small garden.

♦♦♦♦♦♦

Harnam and I saw each other frequently and spent a lot of time together—our bond two stay-at-home moms with young children. She walked me through several aspects of ghar-grahasthi as it applied to the running of a home in India. It should have come naturally to me since I grew up in India, but my shielded childhood put me at a disadvantage. As a young child, I had been raised in the privileged society of the British Raj, surrounded by servants. Then, in the post-British era, I was in medical school and spent most of my time living in dorms. When I did come home for holidays, I was always studying and was exempted from any kind of housework. If Mother asked me to help her in the kitchen in order to learn the trade, Father snapped at her for taking my attention away from books. Now in Chandigarh, I had to learn new skills.

One thing I had to learn was the art of bargaining with vendors. The cart selling fresh fruits and vegetables came by our neighborhood around nine or ten. The hawker's high-pitched yodeling could be heard a block away. I dropped whatever I might be doing and joined Harnam to buy my vegetables for the day.

"You must start with a very low offer," she said to me in a whisper as we approached the vendor. "And don't ever mention how things are done in America. If he hears the word *America*, we'll lose all bargaining power."

We stood by the roadside and browsed through the produce in the cart, touching this and that and checking for freshness. Harnam kept up a friendly conversation as I silently picked four baby eggplants and a dozen okra pods. She piled up some peas and a head of cauliflower for herself. She did the bargaining, haggling about the price, complaining about the quality, and watching the vendor's fingers closely as he weighed our purchase on a handheld scale.

"Narayan," that was the vendor's name, "could cheat us with the weights?" I asked Harnam as we walked away with our produce.

"Oh yes. These people are so clever. All he has to do is use his little finger and tip the bar of the scale ever so slightly. You will never know," she explained.

I realized that there was much to learn.

After our purchase, we often sat together at Harnam's and peeled peas and chopped vegetables, letting our children, Rajiv and her toddler son, entertain each other. To save time and effort, we cooked together, dividing the finished products. Harnam's hands worked deftly as she added scoops of spices to the wok. I watched her intently as the aroma of fried onions and garlic mixed with the warm sunshine in her courtyard. I was learning Punjabi cooking from Harnam. She, on the other hand, was reflecting on how things are done in America. One day, she abruptly stopped the stirring and focused on the subject. "Tell me, didi, is life really, really good in America? Is it true that when you pluck an apple from an apple tree, it turns into gold?"

I looked at her bewildered.

"That's what everyone in India believes," she said.

"Oh, that! Yes, I have heard that too. America is indeed a country of opportunities. With honest hard work and some good luck, one can certainly get rich there," I replied.

"I would love to go to America," she mused.

♦♦♦♦♦♦

Mother had included two quilt casings in my trousseau. These soft, midnight-blue silks with inlay of silver roses could be made into beautiful comforters. I showed them to Harnam, and we set out with our project. We first headed to the cotton market. Every vendor on both sides of the street in this market had stacks of cotton on display in front of their stalls: a snow-white pile from the recent harvest, another from the previous year, and yet another of the lumpy, yellow, recycled variety. Harnam pointed out the differences between the various piles. Then she walked up to a vendor who had done some work for her in the past and presented our project to him. Whatever prices the vendor quoted, Harnam rebutted. "I bring you all these customers, and this is the price you are giving me? You have to do better than that," she argued. The vendor lamented that it had been a terribly bad year for cotton. The rains had come at the wrong time and had ruined the crops. Harnam and he continued to higgle-haggle until they arrived at an agreeable price. The vendor weighed two kilos of clean new cotton and passed it to a young boy, his assistant, who was working a ginning machine in the back room. Harnam and I stood by the door while our cotton was being fluffed. My eyes took some adjusting to the dim lighting in the workroom where the air was dense with floating particles of dust. Soon the assistant appeared at the door, his face, hair, and clothing covered with white strands of cotton. He handed us our casings, each filled with the measured amount of fluffed cotton.

"You have to watch these people carefully," Harnam said as we waited by the roadside for a rickshaw, each one carrying a sack of the fluffy, freshly ginned cotton. "Even after we have paid the price for the better cotton, these people can bungle you up. As that *mundoo* was ginning your cotton, he could have easily pilfered, thrown in some of the old stuff in place of the good one. You would never know the difference. I was watching him like a hawk."

"Hmm," I said.

We hailed a rickshaw and took our silk sacks and fluffy cotton to our next stop, a bazaar around the corner from the cotton market, where women were sitting on the sidewalks on either side of the street, quilting.

The more complex the design, the higher the price I would pay. "Let us stay with a simple design," I suggested to Harnam. She assigned the work to a group of four women who worked simultaneously on our project. In a few hours, we brought home two finished quilts.

♦♦♦♦♦♦

On weekends, Kris and I ran errands together. I needed his input for the purchase of bigger items for our home. We went to the sector that specialized in furniture and met the manager in one of the showrooms. We got immediate attention when we mentioned that his company had come recommended to us by Kris's boss. Things always moved faster if you started your dealings with a general praise of the proprietor and the mention of your own connections. It worked better if the connection was someone with money or a high rank or both. Choosing the proper reference for a particular job in itself was an art I was learning.

We sat at a table, and our assigned salesman showed us various wood samples. We looked at teak, walnut, and rosewood. I selected rosewood with a patina finish. Though it was the most expensive, it was also the perfect hardwood that would last us our lifetime. The salesman opened his file and began to show us line sketches of the designs he had built in the past. "Hold on a minute," I said. "May I show you what I had in mind?" I took out a Sears catalog from my bag, wherein I had flagged my selections. His eyes widened as he saw the catalog. His interest in us doubled. "So you have come from America," he said. We did not need any further credit check to place our order. Cups of tea appeared from nowhere. We placed an order for a five-piece bedroom set and the entire dining room furniture. The bedroom furniture would be delivered piece by piece over the next six months and the rest slowly thereafter. As we were ready to close the deal, the salesman said to me, "If you don't mind, may I keep the furniture section of your Sears book? We can offer all the unusual designs to our future customers."

I looked at him in total surprise.

"Oh yes, madam," he continued. "You can actually sell the Sears catalog in sections—furniture section for its furniture, ladies' section for women's designs, and children's for children's clothing. Even the toy section has value. Toy makers see the photos and recreate the toy for our children. The Sears catalog has a large market. Did you bring just one book from America?"

I nodded to say yes and declined his request for purchasing my catalog.

Chapter 24

Whereas I was enjoying the novelty of the experiences of ghar-grahasthi in India, the energy required to get through each day was beginning to get to me. Keep an eye on the vendor's weigh scale. Make sure the cotton you are getting is what you paid for. Never leave loose change on your dresser. That could be a temptation for Shakuntala. Never hire a rickshaw at his asking price. By the end of the day, I felt exhausted.

To top it all, I discovered that I was pregnant again. I was not ready for this, certainly not until I was well established in Chandigarh and had found full-time help to assist me. Rajiv was not walking yet. He was eight months old. The optimistic orange glow that I had seen on the day of my arrival began to fade.

"I can't take this," I said to Kris as I sat picking at my food at the dinner table. "I think I am pregnant, and I don't feel well at all." Seconds later, I felt queasy, rushed to the sink at the far end of the porch, and threw up.

"What's the matter? We wanted two children, didn't we? You should be happy," Kris said when I returned to the dining room. I had tears rolling down my wet, weary cheeks. I stood clutching the edge of the table, still nauseous.

"Pregnancies are hard, I know. The sooner you get them over, the better," Kris said, continuing to eat the rice and dal on his plate.

I tightened my grip and raised my voice. "What do you know about pregnancies? You have never been pregnant. How can you understand?" Then in a more somber voice, I said, "I sure want another child, but I just wanted to thaw out from the winter and get accustomed to living in India before I undertook another pregnancy."

"You have already thawed out; summer is around the corner," he said. "I know life seems a bit hard now, but just look at the brighter side. Once you get through these early years, you will have all the time in the world to pursue your career."

He got up from his chair and, putting his arm around my waist, led me to the bedroom. "You need to lie down for a bit," he said.

So he does appreciate that I desire a life outside of pregnancies and ghar-grahasthi? I thought and slowly dozed off. I woke up the next morning rejuvenated. Kris's words resonated in my mind. Someday I will return to my career.

I soon realized that this pregnancy was in sharp contrast to my first. With Rajiv, I had yearned to experience the novelty of morning sickness. It never happened. Except for a day or two of a mild nausea, I had felt strong and energetic, almost euphoric. With this one, I was sick all the time. The so-called morning sickness lasted all day, bringing with it extreme fatigue that carried on through the night and into the following morning. I was unable to manage much housework. The thought of entering the kitchen made me nauseous. The last thing I wanted to do was to cook.

During these difficult times, Amma-ji always surprised me. At about noon, there was a knock on the wall that separated her courtyard from mine. Then I heard her feeble voice. "I have some food for you." I could see a hand stretch over and across the six-foot wall. I would stand on a stool on my side of the wall and graciously receive the *tiffin* she had prepared for me. The aroma of fresh spinach simmered with cinnamon, cloves, and ginger dissipated my nausea. Thanking her with words would have been superfluous. Paying her for her services was out of the question. She did what she knew needed to be done. "You are pregnant, and you need to eat.

It is no trouble for me to just throw in a little extra vegetables or a cup of lentils as I cook for my son and me. You must rest, and you must smile. Don't let the weight of the pregnancy get to you. A smiling mother gives birth to a smiling baby," she would say, extracting a weak smile from me.

Encouraged by her counsel, I diverted my attention to other things. I started taking an interest in my baby and my home. I worked on the small garden space in the perimeter of our courtyard, planting green beans and *karela,* the Indian bitter gourd. As the weather warmed up, we moved our bed to the courtyard. Sleeping under the starry blue skies was pleasant and refreshing. In the morning, I brought our tea to the bedside on a small trolley and lounged around while Kris read the newspaper. As I lazily sipped my tea, I admired the bright yellow karela flowers strewn amid the creeper's lattice pattern on the far wall. I watched the dewy petals lose their moisture in the shimmering sunlight. Slowly they opened into full blossoms, dotting the creeper's green tapestry. Rajiv, sleeping on his belly in his crib beside our bed, squirmed and yawned as the slanted rays of the sun hit his face.

♦♦♦♦♦♦

It was mid-April when things happened to disrupt our peaceful life. I was sitting beside Kris with my cup of tea as he opened the *Hindustan Times* and read the headlines. There was breaking news. India had declared war against Pakistan. As Kris continued to read, horrid images of the aftermath of the India-Pakistan partition in 1947 flashed through my mind. I shuddered at the thought of the consequences of this war. Chandigarh was the capital of Punjab, the state bordering Pakistan, and it would certainly become a target city.

"You worry too much. This war is about the Kashmir dispute. It is not going to affect us," Kris comforted me. "Besides, we should not fear wars. Wars come and go. We always survive them. Amritsar being just eighteen miles from the border, we sure saw our share of the Hindu-Muslim riots in 1947. I was right in the midst of the big upheaval, and I survived, didn't I?"

He put the newspaper down and continued, "There was so much random killing in Amritsar. People get crazy when there are riots, you know. Because of my fair skin and facial features, I was often mistaken to be a Muslim, and the Muslims wanted me to be on their side during the riots. I would insist that I was a Hindu. 'Show us proof. Show us what you've got in there to prove that you are a Hindu. You sure look like one of us,' they would say and mockingly poke their sticks at my privates, calling me a coward. I would be forced to pull my pants down and show them that I was not circumcised—I was indeed a Hindu."

"That's embarrassing. How did you get out of it?"

He turned his right hand over and, making a fist, pointed to a tattoo in the middle of his hand. It was the symbol of *aum*. I had noticed that tattoo the day we had first met and he had extended his hand to accept a cup of tea from me. It had never occurred to me that there would be a story behind it. I always thought it was the result of one of his teenage whims.

Making his fist tighter to highlight the tattoo, he said, "I got this done, and it solved the problem. I just stuck my hand out. They saw the aum and left me alone. I was fourteen at the time."

I held his hand in mine and stared at the aum, speechless.

We read the paper every morning and kept abreast of the progress of the war. It was something happening far away in Kashmir. We were nowhere close to that region. However, in a few weeks, the effects began to trickle down to our areas. Military tankers were seen on our peaceful roads. Officers drove around in open jeeps, monitoring the city and announcing on loud speakers that we, Hindus and Muslims, were to continue with our routine work peacefully during the day. After dark, however, we were to observe a strict curfew. Anyone not observing these rules would be handcuffed and put in jail. If there was resistance, those resisting would be shot without questioning.

My friends and I walked to the store to buy black fabric to cover our windows. The cheerful markets and streets seemed dull and quiet. Fear and suspicion prevailed. At night, the streetlights were turned off, and the blackouts gave an eerie feeling to our town. Airplanes covered the dark skies. We were never sure whether these were Pakistani planes that might bomb our city or our own air force protecting us. We stayed huddled in our rooms until daybreak. We ate by candlelight and went to bed early. We could no longer enjoy long evenings in the courtyard or sleep under the stars.

The war lasted six months. Finally, in September 1965, the United Nations intervened and mandated a cease-fire in Kashmir.

♦♦♦♦♦♦

While we were dealing with the war, the baby within me was growing actively. The fatigue from carrying the weight of two babies, one within and the other outside my body, was overwhelming. With Kris's work schedule, he was not much help. The part-time assistance I got from Shakuntala was not enough either. I needed an ayah, someone who could take care of Rajiv and in due course help in the care of the second baby as well. I spread the word. A buxom woman of mature age came by for an interview. Before I had a chance to put forward my needs and requirements, she laid down her own.

"I will take care of your children during the day, but at nights, no. Once I retire to bed, you will not disturb me. I need my rest," she began. Without giving me a chance to put in a word, she continued, "You must provide me meat curry at least two days a week. Don't tell me later that you could not afford the price of meat. I speak from experience. Many people do that. A promise should be a promise. And don't serve me the bones, reserving the good meat for yourself. I see that also happening very often." She stated this among a long list of dos and don'ts.

Her tone intimidated me. Being young, inexperienced, and desperate, I yielded to all her demands and hired her. Harnam had already made me aware about the scarcity of help available in our area.

In a couple of weeks, I noted that Rajiv was becoming more and more subdued under her care. I began to suspect that the tobacco she chewed might be laced with opium. I discussed this with Kris, and we decided that rather than confronting her, we must let her go as soon as possible—a difficult task. She was just about twice my age and three times my size.

Next morning, I served her gobhi-paratha smothered with butter, her favorite breakfast, along with a tumbler of hot tea. She burped with satisfaction. She appeared content with the security of her job. As she was wrapping up her meal, I managed to say, "You have been very helpful, *Mai*. However, I don't think we can utilize your services at the present time." I had said it and was expecting a burst of obscenities.

She surprised me. She did not ask for explanations. Instead, she mumbled, "You Indian *mem-sahibs*, you don't know what a good ayah means. I have worked with British mem-sahibs for years. They never questioned my skills. They fed me well and paid me well. Ever since those *gore-log* have left the country, I have trouble finding steady employment."

With that, she rolled up her bedding, put the money I gave her for her services in her hanky, and tucked it in her bosom. She left just as peacefully as she had come.

I was back on an ayah hunt.

♦♦♦♦♦♦

One day when I was visiting Harnam, I noticed some tentlike structures that had come up in the vacant lot across from her house.

"That's new," I commented.

"Yes, it's a small *banjara* community that has just moved in. They travel from place to place and halt wherever there is prospect of work. They camp in any open space they find and stay until there is work. Then they move on. They are day laborers. This group is from Kashmir."

Sitting on Harnam's patio steps was a girl of about nine or ten. She was sewing a doll with scraps of fabric. "This is Dharma," Harnam said. "She resides in one of those tents in the gypsy camp. She trots over to my place after her parents leave for work. She spends most of her day here."

Dharma continued to work on her project uninterrupted, her lower jaw angling this way and that as she poked the sewing needle through the fabric.

There was something about this little girl that caught my attention. She was a typical urchin girl from an obviously deprived background. She was wearing a loose-fitting frock that was ripped at the waist and hem. Her features were ordinary, medium complexion, forehead lined with wrinkles. Her hair, down to her shoulders, was matted and uncombed. In spite of all this, I thought she was very attractive. I pondered over the absurdity of my logic. Could it be her name? It is her name. That's it, her name, Dharma: the law and principle that keep the universe in balance.

"She is very adept at housework," Harnam interrupted my reverie. "I asked her to wash my utensils and make dough for chapattis. Didi, you will be surprised—she makes better dough than me."

Dharma looked at me and smiled.

"Take her with you, didi, and show her where you live. She can do all sorts of odd jobs for you." Then, reverting to English and talking softly between her teeth, Harnam continued, "I give her twenty-five *paisa* for the day, and she is very happy with that."

I was pleased that Harnam had already set Dharma's rate, sparing me that hard task. She walked home with me, taking charge of the stroller and talking to Rajiv in baby talk.

When we reached home, I asked Dharma, "Will you watch my baby for a bit? I need to go for a bath."

She nodded with confidence.

I put Rajiv down on a mat in the shady part of the courtyard and asked her to play with him. I was still ambivalent about her maturity. She sat across from him, cooing and talking to him. He babbled, crawled nearer to her, and reached for her face and hair. The two of them giggled. I knew they had bonded. I proceeded for my bath.

Later in the day, Dharma chopped my vegetables and made dough for chapattis. I gave her a quarter of a rupee in coins and sent her home before dark.

"Will you come again tomorrow?" I asked as she was leaving.

She returned the following morning and the day after, and the day after that. She began to come daily. Eager to improve her skills, she was always ready to take on new responsibilities. In a few days, she was able to bathe Rajiv, change his nappies, and take care of his feedings. She played with him all day long as though he were a living doll, choosing his clothes, brushing his hair, encouraging him to crawl across the courtyard. With the extra time on hand, I took to some relaxing hobbies. I stitched two sets of Punjabi outfits for Dharma. She delighted in coming to work in her new clothes.

Chapter 25

As planned, Mother arrived in Chandigarh a couple of days before my date of delivery. She came on a weekend, which gave her and Kris the opportunity to get reacquainted. "Mummy," he commented as she was serving him breakfast, "I love the curry you make from lotus stems." Sure enough, we had lotus stem *koftas* for dinner that night.

Losing no time, Mother took over the responsibilities of running the house, giving me the status of her little girl of a long time ago. The rifts that had gone on between her and me during the years of finding my suitor were long forgotten. They were now a hazy past. In her eyes, I was her baby, all grown, and yet her baby, ready to give her another grandchild.

The following Monday, I felt something happening inside of me. It was like I was going to have my period, a mild cramping sensation. I recognized it as the start of my labor. Mother nodded as she put her hand on my belly. "That's what it is, beti," she said with confidence. Then she realized that Kris had already left for the university, and she was not fully prepared for this eventuality. She was new to the area, and her little girl had gone into labor.

"Go, go," she said to Dharma. "Run as fast as you can. Your uncle left just a short while ago; he may not have reached the university yet. Find him, and tell him to come home soon."

Dharma put on her sandals and took off.

"I don't know which hospital you are supposed to go to. I don't know anything about this town. I hope Kris will come back in time to take you," Mother said as she walked hither and thither, repeatedly opening and closing the front door.

Amma-ji came over to see what was going on. Shakuntala was in the courtyard in the midst of beating the wash clothes with her paddle. She set her work aside and asked if she could help. There was pandemonium.

My own calm and composed temperament gave way to impatience, tainted with some kind of a remote sense of worry. I sat at the living room window, restlessly tossing back and forth some of the unpleasant memories of my first pregnancy and delivery and wondering how this one would go.

Rajiv was born in America. Just like everything else, I knew that my obstetric care would also be better than what I had seen during my training in India. However, having studied about the vast armamentaria of drugs available to women in labor in America, I had made just one request—that of a natural, drug-free delivery. I wanted the experience of labor without the influence of drugs. "Oh yes, that is what we always do. However, if we feel the need, either for the baby's safety or for the mother's comfort, we may use some medications," I recalled Dr. Sandler's words of reassurance. When I was wheeled into labor and delivery (L&D) however, I was taken by surprise. I was hooked up to monitors, EKG machines, and IV lines as if I was a case of acute appendicitis. The doctors and nurses, dressed in their robotic garbs, were moving about in total silence giving me a feeling of being in an operating room. Although the place was decorated in warm, soothing colors, I felt desolate, isolated and cold. The silence in the room was chilling. The only way I expressed my pain was by looking at Kris and silently letting a tear roll down my cheek. After a while, he had also deserted me, and then I had felt really alone and silent. Pretending to be brave I gritted my teeth and muttered under my breath that my stomach hurt a lot. I was drugged, slowing down my contractions. When I timidly complained that it still hurt, I was drugged again, further slowing my progress. I was drugged every step of the way, first with medications in the IV drip, and then with a spinal injection, and at the final stage, a general anesthesia with a mask. I did not awaken from the anesthesia for several hours. When Rajiv was brought to my bedside, I had difficulty acknowledging him as my own. "Go away, that's not my baby. My baby is here," I had babbled, curling up on my side and rubbing my sore belly. "Don't you see? My baby is right here." The nurse rolled the crib back to the nursery, laughing. I, in my delirium, laughed with her. Some eight hours later, I finally held and nursed Rajiv for the first time.

Dr. Sandler was a competent obstetrician. However, I had learned later that his philosophy of readily using medications during labor and delivery was based on the popular demand that was cropping up among his patients. They wanted comfortable, pain-free deliveries. Drug companies were tooting the benefits of their medications and La Leche League philosophies about natural labor and delivery had not yet taken hold. I was Dr. Sandler's odd Indian patient asking for a drug-free delivery and willing to bear the pain.

Now, sitting in the living room in Chandigarh, anxiously awaiting Kris's arrival, I pondered over those events and wondered if this one will really be drug-free as my current obstetrician had assured me.

In a few minutes, I saw Kris's aqua Lambretta turn the corner. Following him was a rickshaw-wala, pedaling speedily to keep pace with him.

Dharma, having taken a ride back in the rickshaw, hopped off the carriage and quietly slid into the background. She stood with Rajiv in her arms and watched the commotion as though it was something totally unwarranted. In the past, when Dharma was living in Kashmir, she had accompanied her mother many times when she performed the duties of a midwife. There was no anxiety, no drama. Birthing was an ordinary procedure in an ordinary day. And so it was for Dharma today—an ordinary day.

♦♦♦♦♦♦

Kris and I headed to the hospital. The rickshaw-wala knew the shortest route. Ringing his bell and weaving in and out through the traffic, he cut across the inner streets and onto Vidyapath and in minutes came to a halt in front of the hospital entrance. I felt much calmer in Kris's company. My pains were certainly marching along, but my amniotic sac was still intact.

At the hospital, I was received in a wheelchair and taken to registration. While Kris was filling out the necessary forms, a nurse's aide dressed in a white cotton sari came in and took my vital signs. She affirmed that my pains were for real. Once the admission papers were completed, I was admitted to a private room. My pains kept coming with stronger force and at shorter intervals but were totally bearable. *Easy,* I thought to myself. This is going to be easy. In an hour or so, I was transferred to labor and delivery. This was off limits to males, and I said a hurried good-bye to Kris.

"Take care. I'll send Mummy as soon as I get home," he said.

When I arrived in L&D, there were four delivery tables arranged in a row about four feet apart. The green privacy curtains between the tables were pulled back, giving the room an airy, spacious feel. A large picture window brightened the room with natural light. Table 2, which was nearer to the window, was vacant and had been prepped to receive me. I was pushed, shoved, and lifted off the gurney and onto the delivery table. My legs were propped up in stirrups. I turned my head to the right and to the left and met my neighbors with faint smiles. We were four women in camaraderie, our feet up in stirrups. I did not feel alone.

Mother came barging in. "I am so glad I found you," she said. "This is such a big hospital. I could not find my way around." Then, directing the question to the nurse, she asked, "Sister, how is my baby? Is she all right? I am so worried for her."

Sister Julie, an Anglo-Indian nurse in her thirties dressed in a white, knee-length uniform, stopped at the foot of my bed. She pulled the disposable mask down from her nose, exposing her scarlet lips. "She looks fine to me," she said in a nonchalant manner and walked on to the next patient in the room. She was moving from one delivery table to the next, assessing each one's progress. Hearing her words, Mother felt a sense of relief. She took her position at the head end of my table, ready to help as necessary.

My neighbor on the left, whose fat belly seemed to fill the girth of the table, gave a loud scream. "God, God save me! My life is in your hands!" She did not have her mother or aunt or sister by her side. Mother walked over to her and squeezed her pudgy arm. Suddenly, the woman quieted down, dropping her head and chest in repose. She may have fallen asleep. Her drape sheet rolled off her bulging tummy. The aide came by and pulled the sheet back over her. Mother returned to attend to me.

"It's a good thing you are here," Sister Julie said to Mother. "Some of these poor women have nobody to pull them through their ordeal."

Mother's status was affirmed.

Finally, it was my turn. A monster wave came rolling in. I clutched the railings of my delivery table. "Mummy, I want to die! I just want to die! Can't you give me something so I could die?" I yelled, my voice overshadowing all the other screams and cries that were going on in the room.

Mother's face became scarlet with anxiety. She took a washcloth and wiped my brow. It was November, and yet I was sweating. She looked at me sympathetically and then at the others in the room. She spoke to us at large. "I feel for you women. This is our curse, and we have to bear with it. It never gets easier, I know. But you'll all get through it."

I took courage from Mother's words and relaxed.

Another contraction came. I screamed again. "Here comes the monster! Mummy, please, *please* save me from this one!"

Mother wiped my forehead again. With a furrowed brow, she said, "Have faith. This is all God's doing. He starts it. And if He starts it, He has to end it. It is not in your hands. Just have faith in Him." Then when my contraction receded, she looked around at her audience and continued,

"This has gone on for millennia. It is the fate of us women. We cannot live with it. We cannot live without it. What can we do?"

The women chuckled in the middle of their contractions. There was a momentary silence. The room felt like a sleeping dormitory. Then there was a sudden shriek from the bed at the far end. The nurse was checking my blood pressure. She removed the stethoscope from her ears and snapped, "Will you shut up? It's not so bad. Do I have to listen to this racket all day long?"

There was silence again.

There was never a question as to whether Sister Julie would administer to me—or the other women in labor—any relief medication. I screamed louder and louder with every contraction, hoping that would diminish my torment. It did not faze our nurse. She continued to walk back and forth, performing her duties and ignoring our screams as if it was background noise in a fish market. Two aides, self-trained midwives, floated through the room and were a great help. When my contraction mounted to a peak, an aide stood beside me, placed a firm hand on my belly and directed the contraction. Her gentle touch softened the monster.

"*Hoshiar, hoshiar*," she said. "You are very courageous. Just breathe easy and push down."

"I am trying, but this is a real monster," I said, shivering. "It won't let go."

"A couple of monster pushes, and you will be done," she said calmly.

And so it was. I finally dilated to Sister Julie's satisfaction. She pulled the green curtains on both sides of my table, converting the area into a private delivery room. She sent an aide to fetch the doctor. She rolled in an instrument trolley and uncovered it. She turned on the goose lamp and adjusted its light. Shortly thereafter, the gowned and gloved doctor walked in. She took her position on a revolving stool between my legs and inspected me under the drape sheets.

"Hold that contraction. Don't let it go," she said. "Keep holding," she repeated. I heard a soft crunching noise. It was that of a scissors cutting something. She was giving me an episiotomy. I gave one last push, and the baby was born. The doctor cut the cord, and I heard a loud, high-pitched cry. "You have a boy," she announced, smiling.

The nurse held him, slimy and wet. She covered him with a blanket and brought him to me. A minute after I had delivered, I was holding my son Ravi, counting his fingers and toes. I looked at him in awe. I ran my finger over his cheek.

All the noise and commotion in the room receded, and I felt an inner peace—a moment of inexplicable bliss. I smiled, dropped my head on my pillow, and dozed off. I slept peacefully for several hours. The memory of that blissful moment surfaces in my mind as I write.

When I awakened, I was back in my room, and Kris was by my side.

"How did it go?" he said to me as he looked at the little bundle in the crib beside me.

"Very well," I said.

"I must have been in deep sleep," he said. "I was awakened by something that must have been a dream. It was a voice—sounded like Mummy's voice—'Wake up, Kris; you have slept through the whole thing. You are the father of another son.' The voice was so clear. I jumped out of bed, changed, and came quickly to the hospital. Admissions told me you had delivered a boy and had been transferred to your room. I hurried and came up the elevator." He tapped the watch on his wrist marking the time he was awakened. "The dream was amazingly vivid. You were probably at your last push at that time."

With that, he held my face between his hands and planted a kiss on my forehead.

Mother, standing by, smiled. "See, you are starting it again. Cannot live with it and cannot live without it," she said.

♦♦♦♦♦♦

The doctor came in for her daily rounds in the early afternoon. In two more hours, Ravi would be two days old. I had been urinating well since my delivery. I had had a decent bowel movement. I did not have a fever.

"I feel very well, and my episiotomy does not hurt anywhere as much as the one with my first baby," I said to the doctor. "It just feels a little sore."

"Yes, you were very cooperative when I did your episiotomy," the doctor said. She was thumbing through the pages of my chart as she spoke. "As you know, that makes all the difference. If the doctor has the patient's cooperation to keep the tissue taut and stretched, she can make a quick, clean cut. As long as the incision is midline, it is virtually bloodless and pain-free. You are familiar with that, aren't you? You must have done a few of these during your training?"

"Yes, of course. It was a part of our curriculum," I said, remembering the painful, jagged tear when Rajiv was born.

"I did not need to give you a local when I made the cut. I infiltrated a cc or two of Novocain later when I put in the stitches. You were fast asleep by then. You merely winced," she said.

She put the chart down, pulled my hospital gown up, and examined me.

"The wound looks good and clean. I anticipate it will heal quickly and very well."

At this point, I requested an early discharge. I was missing Rajiv and the rest of the family. The conventional five-day hospital stay was cut down to two. I signed the necessary discharge papers and collected my belongings. I had enough change on me to take a rickshaw home.

When Mother saw me walk in with Ravi in my arms, she was all upset. "What are you doing here? You need to be in the hospital and resting. I was just preparing to visit you and bring you a hot meal," she said in her usual loud voice, wiping her hands on the palloo of her sari.

"I will rest at home," I said.

She took Ravi from my arms and, pulling up an easy chair, insisted that I sit down. With the help of Dharma and Shakuntala, she hurriedly set up a cot on the porch.

I spent the following month slumbering lazily in the winter sun. A village midwife recommended by Dharma's mother came in daily to attend to me. She manipulated my stomach as if she was kneading flour to make dough. She explained that that would expel all the dirty remains in my womb and align the womb back in place. This was followed by a total-body oil massage. After the massage, I sat on a stool in the courtyard, and she assisted me with a hot bath. Ravi and his brother were also included in the massage and bath sessions. With all the care around me, life was as it should be for a postpartum mother.

Chapter 26

At the end of four weeks, Mother left, and I began to face reality. With an additional infant at home, I had anticipated my domestic responsibilities to double, but for some reason, they seemed to have multiplied manifold. The frequent power outages, water supply cuts for several hours a day, and the milk turning sour due to lack of refrigeration were all common occurrences. I was used to such inconveniences and had developed my own ways of dealing with them. Now they began to test my patience. We had no phone that would allow me to pour my grievances to Kris while he was at work. Days were long and tedious. Sleep became a rare commodity.

The difference in the temperament of the two boys was quite a shock to me. Unlike his brother, when Ravi needed nourishment, he never gave a warning whimper. The very first signal was an ear-piercing, blood-curdling cry. In the early weeks, I catered to his demands. As he turned eight weeks old and then twelve, some of his daytime feedings did stretch out to six hours. However, his demand for the 1:00 a.m. feeding never changed. I tried to modify the day feedings, hoping that would change the pattern. He did not skip the 1:00 a.m. feed. I gave up breast-feeding and introduced a bottle, hoping that that might give him more calories than my breast milk and help him sleep through the night. It did not work. That hour of 1:00 a.m. was etched in his feeding cycle.

♦♦♦♦♦♦

In three months, I began to feel the strain. In order to improve my morale, I needed to do something different—something beyond taking care of Ravi's feedings. I announced to Kris that I would look for a part-time job.

"How do you think you are going to manage that? We've gone through the business of finding ayahs and servants without success. All we have is little Dharma. Who will take care of the children? She certainly can't," he said.

"Well, I have some leads. If it sounds good to you, I am going to pursue it some more," I said.

Mrs. Malhotra lived around the corner from us. I had bumped into her during my pregnancy. On occasions we had walked together, and as we pushed our toddlers in their strollers, I had learned a few things about her. "I don't tell this to everyone," she said to me one day. "When my husband was doing his graduate studies in America, I used to do babysitting. I don't mind telling you because you have lived in America. You will understand. If I tell our Indian people, they think I was working as a servant or an ayah in America. It's kind of stupid, isn't it?"

"Babysitting is a very noble and respectable job," I said. "You were helping other mothers go out and achieve their goals." With this, our philosophies had clicked, and we became friends.

I told Kris about my encounter with Mrs. Malhotra.

"Go ahead, follow your leads. See how it pans out. It will all depend on how you present your needs to her. So long as she does not see herself as an ayah," Kris said.

"I know," I said. "I will have to think about that."

I met with Mrs. Malhotra and proposed that Dharma would go to her house along with my two. She would bathe Ravi and feed him. She would also be in charge of changing the dirty nappies. While Rajiv played with her toddler, Mrs. Malhotra could supervise them all. Dharma could be an extra pair of hands to help wherever she was needed. Mrs. Malhotra found this arrangement satisfactory and agreed.

"You are persistent, aren't you?" Kris said with a smile when I gave him the news.

I began to look for a job. After a couple of interviews, I found a part-time job that was perfect for my needs. I was hired as a research assistant in the department of pharmacology at the Postgraduate Institute of Medical Education and Research in Chandigarh. It helped my spirits tremendously. I was in the company of intellectual adults and could temporarily dispel the grim thoughts of the never-ending domestic duties.

♦♦♦♦♦♦

Ravi's determination, however, was steadfast. No matter how good a day he had had at the sitter's, his alarm clock did not fail him. In fact, it was so precise that I could set my watch by it.

Giving up breast-feeding had been a mistake. Now when Ravi's alarm went off, I had to get out of bed and find my way through the cold patio into the equally cold kitchen and go through the long process of fixing his bottle. Putting on my warm socks and wrapping a shawl over my shoulders, I tiptoed to the small kitchen. I brought the Primus stove into the open space the patio provided and tried to light it in the dim illumination of a solitary bulb. The stove flooded with kerosene. I cussed and complained and hollered for help.

"I don't know what I am doing wrong," I said. "This dumb thing won't light."

Kris put the screaming baby back in the crib and joined me. Receding sounds of exhausted crickets coming from a distance in the blue night gave me hope that the wailing from the bedroom would also eventually cease.

"Let me light it for you," Kris said as he crouched next to me and arranged the woolen shawl over his head and shoulders.

"Check the fuel; maybe it is low on kerosene," I advised.

Kris lifted the stove and shook it. That was not the problem.

"You have to be patient with these guys," he said. "They have a mind of their own. Once they get flooded, they are much harder to light. We'll just have to wait."

"The way Ravi is screaming, he will awaken the entire neighborhood," I said bitterly.

"So?"

He started lighting the stove again. He filled the little receptacle at the top with denatured alcohol, struck a match, and lit the alcohol. It burned with a soothing blue flame. "This cold weather does not help," Kris lectured, as though I did not already know that. "You have to pump it at the precise time when the fuel pipe is warmed up and the flame in the receptacle is just tapering off." I knew that too. When the flame in the upper chamber became a flicker, Kris rubbed his hands briskly against each other and pumped the belly of the stove with a few gentle strokes. Kerosene vapors rose and ignited. The stove was finally lit.

Kris returned to the screaming baby.

The buffalo milk that had been delivered to us in the morning was kept in a cool spot in the kitchen so that it wouldn't turn sour. The stainless-steel saucepan in which it was stored was icy cold, and it took several minutes for the milk to warm up. When the milk came to a good boil, I poured it into the banana-shaped glass feeder. Corking one end and mounting the nipple at the other, I placed it in a bowl of tap water to bring it to the right temperature. To hasten the process, I poured handfuls of the cold water over it. Thirty minutes later, I rushed the bottle to the bedroom. As soon as Ravi got the nipple in his mouth, the screaming ceased, and the drama ended. Ravi was smiling again, and the household was at peace, only to be awakened again at six with a piercing scream.

Kris and I convinced ourselves that our son was born with the anomaly of an alarm clock in his stomach, and we were not able to find the switch to turn it off. We became obsessed with finding that switch. We tried several techniques. When one failed, we tried another, feeling confident that that would work.

We gave Ravi his last bottle at eleven o'clock, hoping that he would be content at least until three or four. This did not work. At one, Kris was again standing beside Ravi's crib. "Shut up, Ravi!" Kris shouted at a pitch louder than the cry. "This noise you are making is enough to disturb the sleeping gods. Don't you understand?" On hearing his name, Ravi stopped for a moment, stared at Kris, smiled, and started yelling again, now his pitch louder to match up to Kris's.

"Don't shout," I said to Kris. "You are the one who will awaken the gods."

The following night, I came up with a new theory. "The baby had been in my womb for nine months and misses me," I said to Kris. "Babies can smell their mothers. I think I will hold him and comfort him while you go and prepare the bottle." So I held and cajoled Ravi. Kris prepared the bottle. Same result.

We decided to try Dr. Spock's method. I located the book that was given to me in America during my first pregnancy and read the pertinent pages aloud, paraphrasing them in Hindi for emphasis. I stated, "Let the baby cry for twenty minutes. Ignore the cry. Do not lift him. Do not attend to him." We put all this into practice.

One night, as we were trying the twenty-minute guideline, Amma-ji dropped in. "Is he ill?" she asked. She held him in her arms, rubbing his cheek and gently pressing the area in front of his ear. He quieted down. "He must have an earache," she suggested.

Had I missed the diagnosis of an ear infection? Was he really sick? I was failing both as a mother and as a doctor. I felt embarrassed. I hurried and brought him his bottle. Once he got his fix, he was all smiles again.

So he was not ill, after all. He was simply responding to Amma-ji's time-tested ways of handling a baby. By rubbing around the ear and cheek, she was satisfying his rooting reflex. Why, then, had it not worked for me? The difference lay in Amma-ji's confident and experienced touch versus that of my young and nervous fingers.

I explained Dr. Spock's philosophy to Amma-ji. I do not think she bought into it. She shook her head and walked away. We, the two exhausted, powerless young parents stood beside our son and witnessed his victory.

Now that we had convinced Amma-ji that our child was neither ill nor being neglected, we decided that we would extend the twenty-minute theory further to a whole thirty minutes. "We have a smarter kid than the American babies from whom Dr. Spock drew his inference," Kris said. He was keeping up some humor in spite of our frustration. The following night, we left the bedroom and sat huddled in the cold living room. Covering ourselves with a wool blanket, we patiently listened to the tick-tock of the clock and to the screams coming from the bedroom. Thirty minutes later, we were lighting the stove again.

Winter gave way to spring and then to summer. Ravi was seven months old. He had trained us well. Whereas he ate all the table foods I had introduced him to, he diligently kept up his nightly routine. He was a happy baby—and I a miserable mother.

Chapter 27

I was sitting on the step that led to the courtyard, exhausted. My head was heavy with lack of sleep. I had managed to give the children their breakfast. I let them play awhile so that I could revive myself, after which I would have to get up and prepare their baths. Rajiv was content patting puddles of water at one end of the courtyard. Ravi, seated closer to me, was playing with the stainless-steel dishes and spoons strewn about. Opportunistic flies had descended upon us, looking for their own share of the breakfast.

I was enwrapped in self-pity.

This is what marriage is all about, I was musing. Mothers tend to babies. Lucky fathers go away to earn the daily bread. They have no clue as to what transpires at home between the hours of eight and five. That's what translates to a perfect married life, I am told. I have all the ingredients for this perfect life. I have a house, two healthy children, and a perfect husband. My life should be perfect.

In the midst of these thoughts, I found myself amused watching two of the flies taking turns landing on Ravi's sticky face and then on a piece of toast on the floor. It was the red guava jam that they were after. I did not have the energy to shoo them away. My two babies were dirty and unkempt, but they were content and safe. That would have to do for now.

This is life, I was repeating over and over as I was trying to enter into the lives of the two flies. Both were going after the same guava jam. They both wanted more. *They are striving too,* I mused. *But they are content. Or are they?* I was lost in my soliloquy.

I lost track of time. It was 11:00 a.m. The doorbell startled me. I wondered who it could be. Harnam was accustomed to just walking in. It may be Shakuntala. "Come in, I am just running a little late," I said. "I'll get your laundry ready in a minute."

"It's me, your sister," Pramilla's voice echoed. She walked in and stood beside me. She was dressed in a soft silk sari, her hair neatly pinned in a bun at the nape of her neck, a mild touch of color on her cheeks and lips. She held an elegant handbag, the type a professional woman would carry.

"Oh my gosh, what a pleasant surprise! You are supposed to be in Bhilai and working. What brings you here?" I said, brightening up.

Before I could rise, she sat down beside me and gave me an old-time hug. We had not seen each other since our weddings and my departure to the States soon thereafter, almost two years earlier. She had also given birth to two children. She explained how she had come to New Delhi for a meeting, and since I was just a few hours away, she'd decided to take the bus and come see me.

"That's so nice," I said as we hugged each other again and again.

"How are you?" she finally asked. It felt like a generic question.

"Very well," I gave a generic reply.

"You don't look it," she said. Her eyes studied my crumpled sari, my uncombed hair falling to my waist, the breakfast dishes strewn all over the courtyard.

She reflected on our life when we were living together in Bhilai, unencumbered with men, marriages, and babies.

"I have never seen you like this," she said. "You were always dolled up so prim and proper. What happened to your bangles?" She looked at my bare wrists. "You used to match your bangles to your saris. I remember how you painted designs on your bangles to match the prints on your sari. And now look at you. It looks like you've not attended to yourself for days."

Then she focused on the children. I suddenly felt exposed and naked.

"My goodness, look at them. They look like little refugees. Is this the way they are all the time?"

I tried to cover my guilt. "Oh no, it's just been a bad day." Then, looking at Ravi's mucus-covered face, I quickly added, "I was awake all night with Ravi. We all have a cold, you see."

A minute later, my head was on her shoulder, and my eyes were tearing up. "Life is hard, Pramilla. You will not believe this boy of mine has not slept through the night since I brought him home from the hospital," I said between intermittent sobs. I counted the number of months on my fingers. "It's almost seven months. I feel so wiped out."

The midsummer sun had moved over head, leaving just a sliver of shade in the courtyard. I pulled Ravi's mat closer toward us to keep him cool.

"Look at those darling little eyes," Pramilla said. She leaned forward and pulled Ravi into her lap. "I can't believe these innocent eyes could be any trouble whatsoever." She wiped his face with her handkerchief and kissed him.

"You want to bet on that?" I said.

That night, Ravi did me the favor of holding up to my truth. He woke up at 1:00 a.m., and Kris and I went through our full routine of preparing his bottle. Pramilla, sleeping in a bed next to ours, turned on her side and muttered something that I did not understand.

Next morning, after Kris had gone to work, she said, "I have made up my mind. I am taking Ravi home with me. You need a break, and I want no arguments."

"You will do that?" I asked.

"Oh yes. I mean it. It will be no trouble at all for me. I have a good setup in my home. I have an ayah for my older one, and my mother-in-law takes care of the baby. All I'll need is to find one more maidservant, and that will not be difficult in Bhilai. My mother-in-law loves children, and she will welcome Ravi. She can easily supervise his care as well."

"I am not sure I can do this. I will have to ask Kris. I wonder what he might have to say. He might have objections," I said.

Various thoughts ran through my mind. Kris might feel that he was failing as the head of the household in the eyes of his in-laws, or he might think of the separation and bonding issues and all the psychological effects thereof—something I, as a doctor, should have been concerned about. Or he might simply not want to burden Pramilla and her family.

When Pramilla broached the subject with Kris that evening, his response was brief.

"Sure, go ahead. Just don't send us a telegram in a week saying, 'I've had enough; you need to come and get him.'"

"Don't worry," Pramilla said. "That will not happen. I am comfortable with my decision. The two of you need a break, and Ravi will fit right in with my two. They will have a great time together. You can come for him whenever you want."

"I will not have any time off until the end of the year. You will have him for at least five months," Kris said.

"Not a problem," my sister said.

The following day, Kris and I took Pramilla and Ravi to the railway station. Pramilla took Ravi from my arms and found her seat in the train. As the train whistled its departure, she waved to us through the iron bars across her window. Mimicking his aunt, Ravi also raised his hand, smiling. I waved back.

Sending a child away to live with a relative was not an uncommon practice in India. In fact, my mother had sent Pramilla to my grandmother's for two years when I was born. Ravi would be gone for just five months. I did not have to engulf myself in feelings of guilt or regret. However, when I came home, I did begin to feel sad. The place felt vacant and somehow incomplete. Except for the nocturnal malady that required the preparation of a midnight feed, Ravi was a delightful baby, always babbling, scooting around on his hands and knees and chasing after his brother. Now the house was going to be a quieter place.

It took a few days for us to get adjusted to the new setup. After seven long months of sleep deprivation, I finally had the luxury of a full night's sleep. With just one child to care for, I felt that a new life had been bestowed upon me. I enjoyed my time with Rajiv. Feeding him, bathing him, and telling him fairy-tale stories was no longer a chore. He rarely woke up at night. When Kris came home, he had just one focus—time with his firstborn son who had been neglected for months due to the needs of the second baby. "There he is," he said as soon as he walked in the door. They tumbled together in the front lawn, tossing balls back and forth.

"You are glued to your son as though you have not seen him in ages," I would say.

"Seems like that, doesn't it?"

Chapter 28

Kris and I were adjusting well to our simplified life, that of parenting just one child, when we were faced with another hurdle—a political issue.

I had made a pot of tea and brought it to the courtyard where our bed was set up for the summer. Kris was still asleep. I woke him up and handed him his tea along with the *Hindustan Times* and then got busy with my day's chores. It was always helpful to finish the cooking early, while Rajiv was sleeping and the temperatures were still bearable. I set a saucepan of milk on the Primus stove to prepare some cream-of-wheat porridge for Rajiv. Sitting beside Kris, I was chopping the vegetables for the day when he read the headlines on the front page printed in large bold lettering. THE RUPEE TAKES A TUMBLE. Taking a couple of sips of his tea as if to shake off his sleep, he reread the headlines, this time a bit louder, and then he continued to read intermittent paragraphs from the lengthy article. His brow furrowed, and he threw the paper across the courtyard. "What a damned government we are dealing with. They just don't know what they seem to be doing," he muttered.

"What's the matter? Is it bad news? Is anything wrong?" I asked, wondering whether we were going to face a war again. It had not been a year since the last Indo-Pakistan war had ended.

"Wrong? Everything is wrong. Just last night, Prime Minister Indira Gandhi spoke on the radio that she would not succumb to foreign pressures.

The last thing she would do would be to devaluate our currency. And look what's in the paper today."

I stopped my chores midway and collected the flying sheets of the newspaper. What did this devaluation really mean? Why was it so upsetting to Kris? That June morning in 1966, the value of the rupee fell almost 50 percent. The dollar exchange of our currency went from just about four and a half rupees to seven and a half. Foreign aid from the United States and other allied countries was abruptly cut off.

"How will it affect us?" I asked.

"Well, to begin with, we will see a horrific inflation. We will have to make major adjustments in how we live," Kris explained. "Other effects will trickle in bit by bit. All imports from foreign countries will come to a halt."

"So we just won't buy foreign-made tins of cheese or biscuits," I said.

"It's not that simple," he said, thinking deeply. "After months of perseverance, I had finally convinced my boss that we should order a mass spectrophotometer from the States. I was looking forward to setting it up. It would have been such an asset to our research capabilities. I might as well forget about getting it now."

That would indeed be another major setback for Kris. Recently, one of his publications had been rejected by a British journal because his experimental mice were not housed in a temperature-and-humidity-controlled environment. When he expressed his frustration, his boss shrugged his shoulders and said with a mocking laugh, "What do these people expect? Do they want us to build five-star hotels for our mice when we ourselves do not have air-conditioning in our offices? Just publish your article in one of our own journals. Be practical." Kris had appreciated the sense of humor and yet had felt disheartened with the futility of his hard work.

"We are facing one setback after another," I said. "Do you think we should consider returning to the States?"

I did not get an answer. I left him to his newspaper and went about fixing breakfast and getting Rajiv up and changed.

"What do you think?" I asked Kris again at breakfast.

He considered for a moment and then said, "You don't give up just like that. You face challenges head-on, not run away from them."

I did not bring up the subject again.

♦♦♦♦♦♦

A few weeks later, we received a notice from the university that a new section of the faculty housing had been completed. We were allotted a lovely end-unit townhouse. This made me feel one step closer to Kris's job security and to the permanency of our life in India. I cherished the idea of the move and got engrossed with making new and more stable arrangements for the running of our home. I found a trustworthy milkman who milked his buffalo at my doorstep in order to provide me with fresh, unadulterated milk. I also had a woman delivering fresh-baked *tandoori-rotis* every evening in exchange for some flour. The furniture that I had ordered several months earlier was beginning to arrive a piece at a time, and the house was slowly getting filled up. I bought a refrigerator, an area rug for the living room, and a bicycle for myself. I modernized my kitchen. I graduated from the Primus stove to a countertop two-burner gas range that used propane from a portable tank. In short, I was beginning to feel well settled in India and the Indian way of life.

I continued to work as a research assistant in the department of pharmacology. I was productive with publications, and my boss gave me the leeway of fixing my own hours, a privilege he did not give to his staff easily. However, I could not develop a passion for the subject of pharmacology. I just worked diligently, following the protocols of the lab procedures and writing up papers. I missed pediatrics. My dreams of ever returning to it seemed remote. Conditions in India were not conducive. Getting into a salaried hospital job in Chandigarh was next to impossible; there was too much red tape. The thought of a private practice was depressing. I could see myself working up cases, making diagnoses, and then facing frustration. With so much poverty, there was no money for medication to treat the patient. Sometimes I dreamed about what my life might have been if I were in America. However, since that was not on the horizon, I settled for what I had. After all, I was publishing and learning something new every day.

Kris and I did not talk about the inflation, the country's political situation, or the devaluation. We did not discuss the logic of why we had returned to India. Inflation soared, and the prices in the market rose sharply. We learned to get by without imported cheese and biscuits and the like. I stopped buying eggs on a weekly basis. Instead of rationing one orange for Dharma and one for Rajiv, I asked Dharma to share one fruit between the two of them.

♦♦♦♦♦♦

In December, we took our planned trip to Bhilai. Spending two weeks with my sister and her family gave Ravi plenty of time to readjust to me. On the first day when I talked to him, he stared at my face with a blank expression. He could not quite differentiate me from my sister; we sounded so alike. However, children pick up quickly. In a day or two, his memories of me were refreshed, and he learned to call me Mummy. Pramilla was always *amma,* a Hindi word for mother.

After an endearing holiday, we returned to Chandigarh with Ravi. He was not only sleeping through the night but was also toilet trained. Pramilla had reinforced our Indian method of training babies, something I had failed in miserably. I had neither the energy nor the time. In Bhilai, Ravi had one maidservant all to himself. Every morning Sheila started a leisurely day with him, introducing him to the concept of toilet training. She sat down in the courtyard with her knees bent, soles facing each other. The inwardly turned feet served as a toilet seat, and a scrap newspaper served as a disposable potty. Ravi squatted across her feet, leaning forward, resting his chest against her shins, skin touching skin. Sheila whistled a soft hissing sound suggestive of running water, a universal sound used all across India for toilet training. She waited patiently, talking to him, sometimes cajoling, sometimes scolding, but always whistling the universal sound, until Ravi got the message. In a few weeks, he was trained. I had managed this in some haphazard way with Rajiv, and now having both children fully trained was a great blessing.

Chapter 29

When Rajiv turned two we began to look into preschools. We were told that the waiting period for enrollment in the local Montessori school, the one that took pride in being the best in the area, was long, and therefore we must start early. We gave ourselves a year. We visited the school and met the headmistress. She was pleasant, courteous, and friendly. She showed us around the classrooms, and we were pleased with what we saw. The children were polite, well behaved, and followed the teacher's instructions. We talked about different aspects of the school—its curriculum, the uniform, and the fee. Then she took out a register from her drawer and proudly pointed to the list of kids on her waiting list. She added Rajiv's name at the bottom of the page.

During our visit to the school, I did not pick up any cues that enrolling a child in a school required a bribe. I became suspicious about it when I discovered that our name never seemed to move up on the list. The initial sweet-sounding voice of the headmistress was becoming more and more abrupt and sour. Each time I called to inquire about our status, I got the same answer. "There is a great demand for our school, you see. You still have a long wait. We are doing our part. You must do yours." She was clearly pointing out to me that I was not doing my part; I was not offering a bribe. When I discussed this with Kris, he shrugged off my doubts. "Not in an institute of learning. Certainly there could be no corruption there," he said.

We continued to wait.

♦♦♦♦♦♦

One evening, Kris came home excited about the new ration system that was being implemented in Chandigarh. He handed me a passport-sized booklet, our ration card.

"By presenting this card at the local depot, you will be able to buy rice, flour, sugar, lentils, and Dalda [an Indian brand of Crisco], all at a fixed and fair price," he said.

I perused the card. The family was listed on the first page, with our birth dates, first and last names, and Kris's name as the cardholder. The following page listed the items available on ration along with the schedules for the pickup. The quotas were calculated according to our gender and age, and the items were staggered, so I would have to go in every two weeks.

"Finally, the government is doing something about corruption," Kris said. "Now we will not have to buy anything from the black market and feed into the greed of those scoundrels."

I looked at the quantities sanctioned on the card, and I knew we would have to live frugally.

"We can do that," I assured Kris.

With the card in hand, I began to go to our depot every two weeks and pick up whatever our allotment was for that day. My neighbor argued that I should claim Dharma as my daughter since she was now living with me and eating from the same rations. That would help with the quantities I received.

"I would rather let her parents claim her on their card," I said.

"They have moved to a different district. They can claim her there, and you can claim her here. Nobody will find out. And if they do, you have proof. After all, she lives with you," she said. I was being bombarded with lessons on how to beat the system in justifiable ways.

I did not accept her wisdom. Instead, I became strict about not wasting food. I began to cut back on the amount of sugar in our tea and in the children's milk. I stopped making desserts. I economized on fuel by using the pressure cooker and cooking two and three meals at one time.

♦♦♦♦♦♦

I remember one particular ration day. The day started out cold and cloudy. As usual, I had taken the day off from work so that I could get the rations. I walked to the depot and stood in line for my kilo of sugar and a tin of Dalda. As the wind picked up, I wrapped my shawl tightly over my head and shoulders. The queue was long. Servants stood smoking cigarettes and spitting betel juice, waiting to collect rations for their masters. Coolies and workmen were in line, surrendered to their fate of losing a day's wage. A few women dressed in crumpled homespun saris interspersed the line. Dressed in a crisp, well-ironed cotton sari, I realized that I was the only one of my kind. I felt as though I was being stared at. However, I looked ahead and concentrated on the line that was moving along smoothly. The vendor, a man in his late forties, dressed in a white dhoti and shirt and wearing a thick, oily mustache, sat cross-legged on a raised platform. He looked well nourished, multiple rolls of his belly resting comfortably against his thighs. As each client came to the head of the line, he perused the card, collected the cash, and ordered his assistant to bring out the goods. The depot was going to be open until noon, and I hoped that its doors would not close before I had my turn.

As the line got shorter, I became encouraged that I would have a successful day. When I moved to the top of the line, the vendor looked at me from head to foot, as though he was making some kind of an assessment. I was young and, to some extent, beautiful. I was too well dressed for this queue. I became self-conscious. I handed my card over to him and kept my distance, not looking directly into his face. He stared at the card for a very long time, saying nothing. I continued to look at his fumbling hands and waited. He finally said, "*Bibi-ji*, we are out of sugar and ghee. Maybe you can come back next week." He turned his head to look at the mounds of groceries in the hazy depths of the depot. My eyes followed his, and I saw a stash of the yellow tins of Dalda with their bold black lettering. He returned my card.

I had no courage to confront him. I could not come up with a tangible argument. Silently, I put the card in my pocketbook and started my journey home. The black clouds burst into a downpour, and I was soaked in the proverbial winter rains of Chandigarh. When I came home, I realized that I had left our bedroom window open. The rain did not spare the sheets and quilts on our bed. I clenched my teeth lest I begin to complain and spent the afternoon drying our bedding on strings stretched across the bedroom.

After awhile, I lay down on the couch in the living room and tried to take count of the events of the day. The replay of the cinematograph was revealing. The robust and happy vendor was giving me every hint and opportunity to offer him a bribe. I saw the sly look on his greasy face, the hesitancy with which he returned my card, and the affect with which he said, "Maybe you can come back next week." What he was telling me was to come better prepared the next week. Come with your bribe in hand. I was torn between following my husband's exacting ethical ways and my own inefficiency of not being able to provide the rations for my family.

"How was your day?" Kris asked when he came home that evening.

"Well, we will have to do without sugar and ghee until the next ration day," I said.

I told him what I had witnessed at the depot. I wanted him to say, *Why, then, did you not press a five-rupee note in his palm*? Instead, he just looked at me grim faced. There was no advice, no apology, no pity, no sympathy, just internal anger and the utterance of obscenities under his breath.

♦♦♦♦♦♦

The following weekend, Kris's older brother Shadi-lal and his wife dropped in for a casual visit. They lived in Ambala, a couple of hours from Chandigarh. Without the convenience of telephones, they usually dropped in unannounced. Shadi-lal was an income tax officer. Because of his position, he had easy access to cars and drivers from area merchants, a gesture on the part of these merchants for the favors they might need at a later date. He utilized these privileges to their fullest. He had a car and driver at his disposal that day. Usually, I enjoyed seeing him. In contrast to my husband's quiet temperament, he was a loud and lively man who could brighten anyone's day.

That day, however, when I saw the couple arrive, I felt like a clam that wanted to withdraw into its shell. I would have to serve them tea, and I had no sugar. Embarrassment began to grip me. Then I took control of the situation. After exchanging our usual *how are yous*, I slipped into the kitchen and sent Dharma by the back door to borrow some sugar from the neighbors. By the time she returned with the bowl of sugar, my sister-in-law had walked into the kitchen asking if she could help. The secret was out. I had no sugar in my house, and everyone knew it.

"I can't understand why you have to live like this, like beggars begging for sugar," Shadi-lal said to Kris in an authoritative tone, that of an older brother. "You know I can get you anything you need. All you have to do is ask. Merchants are only too eager to please me. They send me so much stuff. Sometimes I don't know what to do with the surplus."

My sister-in-law nodded both in agreement with her husband and in appreciation of her being so blessed in life. "I distribute the extras to my servants," she interjected.

"Ask, and your goods will be delivered to your door," Shadi-lal repeated.

Kris looked at his brother. "I don't need such favors. I can handle my own affairs quite well," he said. His voice was calm.

I served the tea with samosas that Dharma had fetched from a nearby stall. Conversations switched from one to another as I continued to refill our cups with fresh tea. Kris mentioned Rajiv's enrollment in the Montessori. "How long will we have to wait?" he asked his brother.

"You don't understand, Kris," Shadi-lal said. "The going price for school admission is around fifty thousand rupees. If you have not paid that under-the-table money, you might as well contemplate raising an illiterate street urchin. No good school will ever take your child unless you first pay their price. On the other hand, if you wish, I can call the principal. Once she knows you are related to me, your name will move up pretty damned fast."

Kris did not respond. He was known as the odd and stubborn one among his siblings. Arguing about principles and morals with his brother would have been futile. We continued to talk about this and that, and the evening ended on a good note. However, several concerns kept flooding my mind. I realized that in order to exist with any kind of respect and dignity in India, I had to be somebody, be related to somebody, or be able to bribe somebody. I was proving to be a failure at all three.

Chapter 30

After Shadi-lal's visit, finding a good school for our children began to weigh heavily on our minds, though neither Kris nor I spoke about it. Finally, one evening, I broke the silence on the subject. "So what do you think we should do about our children's schooling? Shadi-lal was not optimistic that we will be offered an admission at the Montessori, and I don't think the local government schools are an option for us."

"I have been thinking of an option," Kris said.

"And what is that option?" I asked.

"We will take them to America."

"What!" I said in amazement. "After almost three years of setting our roots here, we will return to America?"

"Yes. Our children deserve the same opportunity for education as Pandit Jawaharlal Nehru. He studied in Oxford, because he had family money, and he had connections. I don't have either. Paying black money for the education of our children is out of the question. There is no way I would instill that moral in their young minds. However, with our savings, we can certainly buy tickets to take them to America. There they will get the best education. Free."

Kris rambled off the costs for airline tickets and a few figures from our savings account.

"But what about all that you have vested in your work here? You have so much research in progress, papers to publish."

"I will take my knowledge back to America."

"Your publications will then be considered as American, not Indian." I was thinking about Kris's strong spirit of nationalism.

"Just like the wind, knowledge has no fences, no boundaries. It can be disseminated from anywhere and should be allowed to penetrate the world freely."

"Why, then, did we not stay on when you finished your doctorate and I joined you in marriage?" I argued.

"That was then. A lot has changed since. We have gained experience, and nothing can replace personal experience," he said.

I realized that Kris was serious about returning to America.

♦♦♦♦♦♦

Our dialogue about the possibility of returning to America began to flow like a river without end. Interspersed in the mayhem of the children's needs and getting through hurdles of the basics for sustenance, we snatched every opportunity we could get to talk about the reality of our taking this leap.

"In America, I will not have to worry about milk going sour," I laughed when I was unable to serve breakfast one morning until the *dudh-wala*, the milkman, arrived at my doorstep with his buffalo. His timings were quite erratic. "We won't have to deal with this musty odor in our bedding," I said another day when the monsoon rains had poured buckets for three straight days. What good was a refrigerator if the power went off for several hours every day? And what good was my gas stove if the propane delivery trucks were on strike for weeks on end? I could not recall a single day without a fiasco, be it from an act of nature or the result of our system. I exulted at the thought of leaving all these hurdles behind.

Kris was equally excited. He had silently tolerated the indolence of his fellow workmen and colleagues for three years. If he arrived at his desk at the scheduled time, he was considered to be a workaholic. "Give the orderly some time to unlock the doors, open the windows, and air the rooms," he was told. And if he worked over the lunch hour, "Are you trying to outrank the rest of us and make some kind of a sneaky impression on the boss? Go home. Be like the rest of us," they said.

"This lethargic, laid-back atmosphere is understandable and indeed very contagious," Kris explained to me. "All year round, the weather impregnates laziness and hampers productivity. In winter, the labs are so damned cold. Everyone huddles around the solitary room heater until the sun hits the windows and warms up the labs. In the summer months, it's too hot. Everyone disappears into the shelter of their cool and darkened homes. Even the boss goes home for two and three hours in the afternoon. It's a culture that penetrates the whole society and is difficult to change."

We found ourselves constantly enumerating the struggles each of us would be leaving behind.

"I will never have to walk away stone-faced from the masses of beggars in the bazaar. You shell out one quarter, and so many come running and tug at your sari-skirt as though you were a maharani," I said. "Amid them, there are so many professionally trained little urchins collecting coins for their masters. You never know who really deserves your quarter."

"In America, you pay your fair share of taxes and let the government worry about the rest," Kris said.

"And I won't have to deal with these unending ayah and servant issues," I said.

"I will never have to see you standing in a rations line," Kris said, his eyes glazing over.

♦♦♦♦♦♦

There were days, however, when another side of me, my dark side, emerged. We would be returning to America on a green card with the intent of becoming American citizens. The permanency of our move and the need to give up my nationality preyed upon me.

"We will lose our roots in India. Our children will become American," I said to Kris one day.

"Yes, indeed. And I will be the proud father of my two American children."

As we discussed the issue, the differences in the cultures of the two countries became exaggerated in my mind. I could not see myself raising our children in a foreign land with a foreign culture. Kris appeased my anxiety.

"You worry too much, and I cannot help you in that. I can assure you that the children will be fine. Nationality and culture are two separate entities. Culture starts at home, and their home in America will be no different from what it is here. It is you who will impart the values to them, no matter where you are raising them. Besides, every culture has something good to offer. Hopefully, they will pick up the best from the American culture, as well. In fact, they will be at an advantage. They will have the benefit of exposure to both cultures."

In due course, my doubts dissipated, and I felt elated at the thought of returning to America.

"Will I be able to study in America?" I asked Kris.

"I don't see why not," Kris said. "You will spend a fraction of the time you spend here in running the house. You can do whatever you wish with your spare time."

I could see the feasibility of realizing my dream: studying in America and being a board-certified pediatrician.

"We must do whatever it takes to go back," I said.

Chapter 31

When Kris perused the package of papers from the American embassy, he learned that there were various ways we could apply for a permanent resident visa. What stood out was the Immigration Act of 1965 that had been signed by President Lyndon B. Johnson. In this new law, the quota for immigration from several third-world countries had been significantly increased. Besides, the economy in America was strong at the time, and there was emphasis on advancing research in all the sciences. Popularly known as the "brain drain quota," this quota was luring trained scientists from different countries to come to the United States and fill the slots that could not be filled by the locally bred.

Kris fulfilled both criteria—he was an immigrant from the third world and a well-trained scientist. His application was accepted without delay. However, in order for a visa to be issued, Kris had to show proof that he would be able to support his family for at least a year, which meant that he had to procure a job in the United States. Not having access to job openings in America, he began to apply blindly. He sent his résumé to every university that was doing research in a field that was even remotely connected to his training. Some sent rejection letters; others simply ignored his application. However, after almost two hundred applications and the passage of ten months, he was offered a research assistant's position at the University of Michigan in Ann Arbor.

♦♦♦♦♦♦

While we were busy procuring a better life for ourselves, we began to announce our decision to our families. The responses were varied and interesting.

Pita-ji to Kris: "Immigration is a serious matter. What you are doing now will reflect on your children and their children. They will always be treated as second-class citizens by the white Americans. I know what the Japanese went through after WWII. You are young and therefore shortsighted." He was looking at our lives with a long-distance lens.

Kris: "I have thought it through, Pita-ji. The children's education is crucial to me right now. No one can predict the future. But I know one thing for sure: America will not make the same mistake twice."

Pramilla to me: "You have painstakingly done your studies here. And now when you have the opportunity for giving back, you are running away from your responsibilities. Look at the masses of sick babies here that you could help."

Me: "Babies are innocent creations, Pramilla, irrespective of where they are born. I can help a baby anywhere, and I would love to help the babies here if I could. I can't seem to fight the red tape. I feel certain that I'll have better prospects of utilizing my talent in America."

Shadi-lal to Kris: "Wives have no respect for their husbands in America. They demand equal rights. I can assure you, you are the one who will be cleaning the latrines. Why would you want to do that? Look at me. Look at all the help and servants I have. Why would you want to leave such comforts behind?"

Kris: Silence. Arguing with his older brother would have been disrespectful.

Mother to me: "Take my blessings. I know you will adjust. I did. I had felt like an immigrant when I came to Madhya Pradesh all the way from Punjab. I had to adjust a great deal—the language, the culture, the clothing, everything was different. I had to also learn English. Pita-ji expected me to write invitations and thank-you notes to his British friends and colleagues. I was a village girl, and it was hard. I did it, and so will you. You are educated."

I felt blessed to have a mother like her.

My father-in-law to me: "Take my blessings and go. America is a country of advancement and innovation. Write to me often, and tell me about all the discoveries you make there. I have read that people have something called the television in their homes. Send me a photo of your television when you get one."

When I came to America, I wrote to my father-in-law regularly. On July 20, 1969, I described the awe I felt when I turned on the TV and saw Neil Armstrong's hazy image taking the giant leap on the moon. When he received my letter, he replied with a phone call congratulating me for having taken my own giant leap.

♦♦♦♦♦♦

Irrespective of the advice and opinions of our friends and family, we continued our pursuit. The paperwork required for leaving the country was unending and kept us very busy. We had to make innumerable trips to New Delhi. Most of it was laborious paperwork. One incident stays alive in my memory.

We were to collect our signed papers that would give us the final clearance for emigration. We had submitted all the necessary documents: our income tax clearance, our health exam reports, birth and marriage certificates, and a myriad of other papers. We were so elated that this was to be our final stop, after which we would be set free from the Indian bureaucracy. We arrived at the Secretariat Building around ten o'clock, the time when the offices opened. We parked our Lambretta and hurriedly walked to the entrance of the large, four-story brick building. The Ministry of Overseas Indian Affairs was on the third floor. We climbed the wide, centrally located stairs, and a peon opened the ornate wood door to let us in. We entered an open area with something like a breezeway on either side. I was glad to see that the benches along the side walls of the breezeway were practically empty. The masses had not yet arrived, and our wait time would not be lengthy. The clerk who was the intercept between us and the officer we were to see was seated at his desk in the center of the open area. He greeted us by name. That was a good sign. He recognized who we were.

Kris responded to the clerk's greeting with a smile and a hearty Indian-style handshake, taking the clerk's hand in both of his own.

"So has the boss had a chance to look through our file and give us his autograph?" Kris asked.

There were innumerable files on the clerk's desk—files, I suppose, of hopeful and anxious people like us. The files were weighted down by irregularly shaped river rocks, their edges smoothed by age. I spotted our file beneath another hefty one, a big stone weighting them down. At least the file was visible to me and not in "Status—Lost." The clerk leaned back in his seat, his foot tapping the footstool rhythmically, his eyes staring at the air in front of him. There was no response to Kris's inquiry.

"I hope you found all our papers in order. Have they been signed?" Kris repeated.

The clerk continued rocking back and forth in his chair, his eyes focused on something far away.

"If we can pick up our papers now, we can go directly to the American embassy and file them there, avoiding another trip to Delhi. I have come all the way from Chandigarh," Kris said.

"Sir, do you feel the breeze?" the clerk spoke at last.

I looked to my right and to my left. Windows at both ends of the long breezeway were open, and there was indeed a soothing breeze. The clerk's desk was strategically located to catch the breeze. It was a hot day, and I appreciated the gentle wind wafting through the folds of my sari. The clerk continued, "Your papers will fly away in these currents, sir, unless you weight them down with something."

His statement drew our attention instantly. Simultaneously, Kris and I came to the realization that he was not referring to the breeze in the breezeway. I looked at Kris, wondering what he would do at this crucial juncture. If he followed his track record, he would just walk away. He smiled, put his hand in his pants pocket, and pulled out a ten-rupee note. The clerk gave him a warm, two-handed handshake, and the note disappeared.

"Come back later in the afternoon, sir. You will be able to see the boss and have your papers signed."

We left our clerk in good humor and stopped at a café for a quick lunch. When we returned, our file had moved up to the boss's desk. We were graciously shown in. After a short, casual, interview our documents were signed.

We headed to the American embassy directly. The contrast was noticeable. Our papers moved in an orderly fashion from one desk to the next, and we did not have to worry about bribes or about our files being lost or misplaced. In a few weeks, we received our green cards and permanent resident visas.

At a later date, I mentioned the incidence of the bribe to my brother Jagdish, a successful engineer who had studied and worked both in India and abroad. His answer to my dilemma was convincing. "You see, choti-baby, the poor clerk probably had five children under five whom he had to feed and clothe. Do you think his meager salary from the government could see him through the month? You probably helped a poor child get his first school uniform. It is not a bribe. It is just one human being helping another. We all have to help one another."

I gave some thought to my brother's explanation. He is right. This is what keeps India alive and flourishing. They refer to it as helping each other. They call it favor swapping, not a bribe. I realized that it is a system that has worked in India for centuries. I looked beyond my brother's household—at the mobs on the streets who have accepted this unique way of life. In spite of the poverty and corruption, and the calamities that they go through, their faces have a peaceful glow. They appear content and accepting of their fate and the country keeps churning.

I prepared myself to leave all this behind and strive for happiness in a new land and a new culture.

PART 4

Ann Arbor, Michigan, and Toledo, Ohio, United States of America

Chapter 32

We returned to America on January 29, 1968, this time on a permanent resident visa, our destination: University of Michigan in Ann Arbor. Rajiv was three, and Ravi had just crossed his second birthday.

Because of restrictions in foreign exchange, we were permitted to bring just eight dollars per person. I was glad that unlike the ration system where we collected rations based on our age and gender, the Indian government was generous enough to permit a full thirty-two dollars for the four of us. This sufficed for us to open a bank account and pay for the initial expenses. I had carefully packed small containers of rice and dal to tide us over the first night or two.

Having had some experience in Storrs, Connecticut, it did not take long for me to establish a workable home in Ann Arbor. The basic household needs came from the Pound House, a service provided by the women's auxiliary to help foreign students like us: a few dented pots and pans, mismatched crockery, and faded floral towels to function as window coverings. This was not the time to think of luxuries. Surrendering whatever wealth we had accumulated in India, we had come to America with an ambition to further our educations and to provide better opportunities for our children. We would have to make-do with whatever we were offered. When Kris got his first paycheck, after budgeting for the necessities, there was just enough money to pay for snowsuits, snow boots, and a bunk bed for the children. We managed and settled in, each paycheck allowing us to buy just a few more household needs.

Kris started his regular eight-to-four job and was gone all day. I was again a housewife and a homemaker. With two young children, facing a chilly winter and living in a tiny apartment, I began to feel the impact. The children loved the snow-covered slopes in the back of our apartment and spent a great deal of time sledding and making snow castles. It was too cold for me to be outdoors. I stood at the window, watched the children play, got bored, and felt lonely. I needed to find myself a job, something that would give me an opportunity for adult conversation and to see America beyond the view from my two-bedroom apartment. I felt starved for any kind of intellectual stimulation. With the vast expanse of the university, the air smelled of intellect. I, however, had no job and nowhere to go.

I asked Kris for advice. "Where will you find work?" he asked. "You know how difficult it was for me to land my job. I had made over two hundred inquiries before I was hired. Remember? Why don't you enjoy the luxury of staying home for a while? We can easily live on one salary," he suggested whenever I brought up the subject.

I received no encouragement from him. Once again, I felt stranded in a new country with a culture of its own and no friends. No one, not even Kris, understood my boredom and loneliness.

I made a plan. Every morning after Kris left for work, I got the children dressed, gave them breakfast, and sent them to the snow-covered quad to play. I now had a couple of hours, intermittently interrupted for cookies or hot chocolate, wherein I could look for a job. I picked up the university directory and started making phone calls. I started with the department of anatomy and went on to biology, cytology, endocrinology, and geology. I could cover only two or three letters of the alphabet each morning. All the phone interviews were monotonous, almost identical. I started by introducing myself and giving them my background. The secretary at the other end was always polite and took time to note down all the information. I spelled my name, told her the country of my origin, my education. After our lengthy conversation, the reply was always the same. "We do not have anything at the moment. However, we will keep your data on file. We will call you if something opens up."

I came to the letter *M*. Mathematics was not my favorite subject in college, but I had managed to graduate. I called. This could just be my lucky letter in the English alphabet. The secretary passed the phone to Dr. Jonathan, a postgraduate fellow. I was excited that I had gone past the secretary. I became hopeful. I went through my routine. "I cannot work in the medical field until I clear the ECFMG [Education Council for Foreign Medical Graduates] certification, and that will take at least a year. In the meantime, I would like to get a job and do something worthwhile."

"Like what?" he asked.

"Like … spend my time in an intellectual environment."

"With your background, what do you think you would do in the department of mathematics?" Dr Jonathan's voice was crisp.

"Well, I can do any kind of statistical work you may have. I have basic knowledge of math, and I can do almost anything you need me to. Ee-er … I can add, subtract, arrange data in columns." My words began to come out in a stutter, and the sound of my voice kept dropping. I wanted to tell him many other things I could do in the field of mathematics. He interrupted. "Why don't you send us your application with your curriculum vitae," he said.

This interview ended exactly like the others. He would keep my résumé on file and give me a call if an opening comes up. However, it was different in some ways, and I was somehow hopeful. I had actually spoken to a fellow, a person who had the authority to hire assistants. He had asked me to send in an application with my curriculum vitae.

I shared my hopes with Kris that evening. "You know what that means, don't you? Your application will be carefully placed in basket thirteen." I did not know exactly what that meant. I knew it was not good just from the way Kris said it. I was glad the interview was on the telephone and not in person. At least Dr. Jonathan would not recognize me if he and I were seated at the same table in the cafeteria.

I did not send my application to the department of mathematics.

Frustrated and humiliated, I stopped making phone calls. I had covered *A* through *M*, thirteen letters of the alphabet without any result. I began to see myself having midmorning coffee with my neighbors and once again giving them demonstrations on how I wrap the six yards of fabric around me when I get dressed every morning.

After a few days of melancholy, I realized that the glass was still half full. I had covered thirteen letters of the alphabet. There were another thirteen to go. It was possible that the department of zoology had an opening waiting for me. I had to be patient. I started again.

I came to the letter *P*. I did not call the department of pharmacy, for that is where my husband worked. I went straight to pharmacology.

I dialed. I gave my background information to the secretary in a monotonous ramble. I had done it so many times in the past weeks. "I'll let you talk to Dr. Carr," she said, and she put me on hold. My heart took a tumble with excitement. I was going to talk to the professor himself, the director of Upjohn Center for Clinical Pharmacology, Dr. E. A. Carr.

"I understand you are looking for a job," he said.

"Yes, yes, sir," I managed to say, trying to stay composed.

"Well, our lab tech is leaving next week, and I need to fill that position. I am not sure whether you would want that job. My secretary tells me you are a medical doctor."

"Yes, sir, but I think I can learn whatever needs to be done. I have worked in labs before, and so I do have the basic knowledge."

"Oh, I was not thinking on those lines. I have no question in my mind that you can do the job. The question is that you will be overqualified and underpaid."

"I do not think that would be an issue, sir," I said. "As long as I am learning something new and my salary covers the cost of babysitters, I will be fine." There was a prolonged silence. *Here we go again. I have not said the right words.* I quickly added, "My husband makes enough money for us to live on, and I am sure it will be all right by him, as well."

Whatever I said, I must have sounded convincing. I was given a time to appear at his office for an interview.

♦♦♦♦♦♦

I tossed and turned restlessly in bed that night, wondering what kind of questions I would be asked. My knowledge of pharmacology was pretty rusty. Next morning, I arranged for my neighbor Debbie to take care of the children. Taking the university bus, I found my way to the department of clinical pharmacology.

I walked through the maze of dimly lit corridors, being greeted by calls of various laboratory animals—guinea pigs, rats, and mice on one side of the corridor and dogs, monkeys, and other larger animals on the other. Going up to the fifth floor, I finally came to the door with Dr. Carr's name on it. I knocked. He was expecting me, for he came to the door immediately. He greeted me, and we introduced ourselves. He had a warm handshake, deep, small eyes, and a gentle look. There was something in his appearance that made me feel comfortable instantly. I handed him my résumé and took a seat. He browsed through the pages, and we began to talk. He did not ask me any complicated questions in chemistry or pharmacology. He described briefly what my job would entail, and I nodded to indicate that I understood.

There was no job offer. He continued to make small talk for what seemed to me a very long time. *Now what?* I wondered. The interview had gone well. The laboratory procedures he had described seemed pretty simple and straightforward. He had already complimented me on my command of the English language. Yet there was no job offer.

I waited.

"I don't think this job will work out for you," he said finally.

Why, why, why? I wanted to scream. Instead, I just looked at him.

"The obstacles are not major. Nonetheless, they are there," he said.

There was an awkward silence again. Then he said, "The attire you Indian women wear is elegant, but it is not congenial for working in a lab."

I did not understand what he meant. I was wearing a simple light-blue sari with small white motifs. I was not wearing anything flashy. That is how I would have dressed for any job interview, and that is how I used to dress for my employments in India. I looked at him, perplexed. He continued, "We work with a lot of radioactive materials in our labs. The floor could be contaminated, and you could carry that hazardous material on the hem of your sari. That will be harmful not just for you and your family but also to the public."

I gave a quick response. "I can buy some skirts. That would not be a problem."

There was a pause again.

Then he said, "I have never allowed a technician with long hair in the lab. The hair can get tangled in the centrifuge or other machinery and can cause dangerous accidents, you see."

I smiled inwardly at the way he presented his reasons for not offering me the job. I found myself awkwardly twirling strands of my hair that hung loosely down to my waist. This was the time when the hippies were coming out of the woodwork and making a statement in the society with their ponytails and tie-dye ruffled skirts—the late sixties. He waited for my response.

"I can take care of that as well," I said.

He offered me the position. I was hired as a laboratory technician at a salary of $5,400 a year for a forty-hour workweek. I was to start the following Monday. This gave me four days' lead time.

♦♦♦♦♦♦

I bade Dr. Carr farewell and retraced my way home. The bus service that made monotonous, circuitous drives from the university to the married student housing stopped again in front of the pharmacology building. I hopped in and took my seat, the same window seat, third row on the right. The bus began to fill up. A young woman about my age walked in and sat in the aisle seat across from me. Her golden silky hair fell to her shoulders in soft waves. She was wearing high heels, and the rays of sunlight filtering through the clear glass window gave her legs—her ankles, calves, thighs, everything—a smooth and sleek appearance. I stared at her legs. *These American women look so pretty with their golden hair and beautiful, almost flawless legs,* I thought.

I looked away from her and concentrated on my own list—the things I would need to attend to in the upcoming days. I would have to get used to wearing skirts, exposing my hairy legs to the public. I would have to shed my identity. Cut my beautiful long hair. First, I'd have to convince my husband of these needs. I could always start by telling him the good news. *I have a job in academia,* I'd say. Then I could trickle in the details.

Dinner was served early in Michigan. Kris was home at four-thirty, and we ate by five. "Never discuss serious matters with your husband without first feeding him," my mum had always said. I waited until we ate and the dishes were done.

"I have a job," I said.

"You must be kidding."

"No, I am serious," I said. "But it has come at a price. I have to fulfill some conditions."

I narrated my interview with Dr. Carr and told Kris what little I had understood about the nature of the experiments I would be performing.

"That is great. Pharmacology is my favorite subject, you know."

Kris was more interested in the work I would be doing than the other details. He did not ask me about the conditions I would have to fulfill in order to start work. So I volunteered to talk about them.

"I will have to wear skirts and cut my hair short. That was a part of the job package. Dr. Carr thinks my sari and my hair could be hazardous in the laboratory." I said it all in one long breath.

Kris's response was immediate. "It makes sense," he said. "Go shopping, and get yourself some new clothes."

"And what about my hair?"

Early in our marriage, I had asked Kris if he would like to see me with short hair. "I love your hair just the way it is," he had commented. "Why would you ever want to cut that beautiful hair?"

"You don't mind if I cut my hair?" I asked.

"We have taken the plunge to come to America for good," he said. "The sooner we blend in with the society here, the better. It will give the children an identity, as well. They need to feel that sense of belonging. They need to feel American." After a pause, he continued, "Remember, it is we who brought them here."

"That's true," I said. "They did not make this choice; we did."

"Now we must do everything we can to help them assimilate. This will be your start."

Chapter 33

A girl named Fortune worked in Kris's department. She was from Tel Aviv and had been in Ann Arbor for several months. Kris invited her home for dinner. I embraced her friendship right away. She was not Indian, but she shared my feelings of isolation in a foreign country.

"Go shopping with Fortune," Kris said. "She knows the shops around here and will help you buy everything you need."

The following Saturday, Fortune and I went to a small boutique in the strip of shops in downtown Ann Arbor where the university students shopped. I had a slim and girlish figure, so picking out a skirt that fit was not difficult. Skirts were short in those days, well above the knees. I bought two skirts, two blouses, and a sweater. A tweed wool coat was on sale. I bought that as well.

As we walked along the sidewalk toward our next destination, all I saw was legs—legs in pairs of twos and threes, always shimmering, always perfect.

"How come their legs are so perfect? They all have such a silky sheen and never seem to have a scar or a blemish," I asked Fortune, deeply concerned about my own legs.

"No, they have shaved their legs and are wearing pantyhose. That covers all blemishes."

I confessed my ignorance to Fortune.

"The more you pay, the better the sheen of the pantyhose, and the better it stretches to cover your defects." Then she informed me that no matter what I paid, pantyhose were always disposable. As soon as they got a rip, they had to be thrown away.

"You mean you cannot darn them?" I asked.

"No."

"What a waste."

We turned the corner and reached Woolworth's. We walked in and went to the end of the aisle that displayed the lingerie items. Standing at that remote corner, Fortune spoke softly and went over the items on display. "These are the knee-highs." She took one off from its hook and let me handle it. "Then these, the thigh-high, will need a garter to keep them in place. They are very uncomfortable. You don't want to get them. What you will need are these, the pantyhose." I carefully studied the packages. There were color choices. She picked up the one labeled Beige and put it against my skin. "This seems to be your color," she said. There was a lighter color called Wheat, and then there was Taupe. I quickly jotted down the name of her selection for future purchase.

Next, I learned that my American counterparts wore something called tummy-tucking panties. I had read about corsets in some British magazines. "Is that what these are?" I asked.

"No one wears corsets anymore." Fortune laughed. "What you will need are these stretch panties." We picked up two. Sheepishly, I asked another question. "Will I wear panties if I am wearing pantyhose, and if so, which one goes on first?" We discussed all this standing at the secluded corner of Woolworth's. I was glad to have a friend in Fortune.

That day, I had learned all about American legs.

Our final stop was at a hair salon. I had never been to one before. I stared at the row of women sitting and reading magazines, their heads under a bubble. Some held cigarettes in their hands, flicking the ashes on to the floor periodically.

Fortune and the hairdresser exchanged a few words. Next, I was sitting in a barber's chair. The hairdresser swiveled the chair back and forth and got herself positioned. My hair had been braided in two plaits. Without an apology, she lopped off my braids, first the one and then the other. Each braid fell to the ground with a gentle thud. Thirty years of pampering those braids with homemade *shika-kai* shampoo, massaging the roots with coconut oil and keeping them louse-free by meticulous combing fell to the floor and lay lifeless. I had often been frustrated with my long hair that was so tedious to wash, dry, and braid and had yearned to cut it, and yet today I was sorry to let it go. It was the essence of my childhood, my India. I picked up the braids from the floor and brought them home. I kept them as souvenirs for a long time. Like most material things, they did not make it through various moves, but that vision of their falling on the linoleum floor is still vivid in my memory.

By the time we returned from our shopping spree, I had added an electric shaver, a hair dryer, and dozens of hair clips and rollers.

It all happened so fast, faster than a chicken hatches out of its shell. In one afternoon, I switched from saris to skirts. I shed my Indian identity and was ready to embark on my American dream.

♦♦♦♦♦♦

All I had to do now was to find a good home where I could leave my children so that I could dedicate myself to my work without worries. This was not a difficult task. I had already made some connections, scouting for reliable babysitters. There were many women eager to take the job. They were living on campus, because their husbands were in graduate school. If they were foreigners, they often did not have a visa that permitted them to work outside their homes, and if they were Americans, they were stay-at-home-moms with young children. They appreciated the extra income.

A lady named Mrs. Bothe lived in an apartment diagonally across from mine. She and I had struck up a friendship when we had met at the clothesline hanging our laundry. I learned that she was from Germany. She complimented me for letting my children play outdoors in the cold. "Coming from the tropics, it is quite remarkable that you send your children outdoors in this kind of weather," she said. "The reason American children are always sick with a cold and a runny nose is because they do not expose themselves to the elements." Her daughter, Caroline, was a beautiful, blue-eyed blonde, a year or two older than Rajiv. She and my children enjoyed playing together on the playground located at the far end of our quad. From my kitchen window, I had often seen the miniature figures of Caroline and Rajiv boosting little Ravi onto the seat of the swing and taking turns pushing. A minute or two later, they were all climbing up the ladder of the slide. Down they came, one behind the other, giggling as they landed at the bottom in one great heap.

I decided to ask Mrs. Bothe if she would like to take my children while I worked.

"Your boys are a delight," she said. "Caroline has no siblings, and it will be wonderful for her to be in the company of other children, especially boys."

Thus, a deal was struck, and I was comforted that my children were in good company while I pursued my career. They would spend their day with a *white family*. They would learn *white culture*. This would be their first step at blending in.

Mrs. Bothe's goal was to give the children an outdoor exposure for several hours each day. She had already helped me procure the proper winter gear for them—snowsuits, snow boots, double-knit mittens—items quite alien to me. Once the children were dressed for the weather, they enjoyed being outdoors, coming in only when their boots were filled with snow and their fingers chilled and wet. Mrs. Bothe helped them warm up by rubbing their hands and feet and rewarded them with warm milk and home-baked cookies.

Mrs. Bothe also had strict and stringent mealtime rules. She insisted on a hot lunch and served it with proper silverware and cloth napkins. She found it frustrating that my children did not eat their food with a fork. "Even if I cut a piece of meat and leave it on a fork, they peel it off the fork and eat it with their fingers," she said. I felt embarrassed to admit that our family came from a backward third-world country whose culture I myself was attempting in vain to leave behind. We Indians were accustomed to eating most of our food with our fingers, thus engaging all our senses, including that of touch. And the truth was that my cooking did indeed taste better if I hand minced the hot and spicy curried chicken and delicately mixed it with exact amounts of the toning-down flavors of white rice and cucumber *raita* to suit the whims of my palate. I promised Mrs. Bothe that I would encourage the use of a fork and knife at home.

Chapter 34

Having met all the requirements—my hair cut short, my legs shaved, my children in a safe place—I was ready to join the working women of America.

I started as a laboratory technician in the department of pharmacology. Learning new techniques fascinated me, and I enjoyed performing the experiments. The key was accuracy in pipetting the chemicals and avoiding cross contamination by cleaning the equipment thoroughly before and after each use. Blood samples had to be handled in a centrifuge at -4°C. I felt as if I were in a kitchen and made sure that I followed the recipe precisely. My results were always dependable, and the research progressed well. To Dr. Carr's surprise, I finished analyzing the day's samples in just three or four hours. The technician I was replacing had worked an eight-hour day.

Seeing my progress, Dr. Carr offered me a new position. He suggested that I sign up for a master's degree in clinical pharmacology and use the data from my experiments toward my thesis. I could work in the lab in the morning and take a class or two in the afternoon. I could study in the library for the balance of my time. He pointed out that if I accepted this offer, my salary would go up to $6,200 per year.

I could not believe all this was happening to me. I was unable to take the entrance exam for foreign medical graduates—the ECFMG—until fall. Awaiting the exam and its results, I could have another degree, a master's in clinical pharmacology, under my belt. Plus, I would not be stuck in the position of a lab tech. I would be a fellow.

I came home ecstatic. I said to Kris, "Guess what! I have been offered more money for less work and am actually being paid to study. I have been offered the position of a fellow in clinical pharmacology, and Dr. Carr wants me to enroll in his master's program. He says I could work in the lab in the mornings and do whatever I wished with my time in the afternoons. Do you think I should go for it?"

"You couldn't beat that," Kris said. "Go for it. Who knows? You may like pharmacology well enough that you may never want to return to clinical work." He loved research and was hopeful that I might just get converted. He would have loved to see me become a research scientist. I personally knew this was merely a bridge toward my goal. Moreover, I was getting the opportunity of being a student in America. I wanted that experience.

I accepted Dr. Carr's offer and embarked on a master's degree in pharmacology.

♦♦♦♦♦♦

I loved being a student again, and all went well for several weeks. Then, as reality hit, my ecstasy faded. I had no idea what I had got myself into. The classroom load was not much, two or three lectures a week at the most. The exams, however, were brutal. They were "take-home, open-book exams" and were due in two weeks. Initially, the concept intrigued me and sounded easy. In India, exams were given annually and consisted of five or six questions to which I had to write essay-style answers in a classroom setting. I had to memorize material from textbooks and from the professor's lectures. The more accurately I regurgitated the material, particularly from the professor's notes, the better my grades. Here, I was given two puzzling questions and two full weeks to consult all the books and journals in the library, extract the pertinent data, and prepare a report. I read my textbooks. I read every article I could lay my hands on and prepared what I thought was a decent report. It was very disheartening and almost shocking to me that after all the hard work, my grades never went beyond B or B+. My ego was deflated. Kris tried to comfort me. "B, especially a B+, is considered a very good grade in America," he said. I shrugged my shoulders and looked at him skeptically. I wanted to see that pink report card with an A written all over it that I used to bring home in my school days.

I began to work harder. I utilized every available minute to improve my grades. After a full day at the university, I came home, served dinner, spent a small amount of time with the children, and returned to the library. While the family slept, I sat in my little cubicle in the library where I had left stacks of books and journals marked DO NOT FILE. WILL RETURN. I worked on my paper until the library closed at midnight, taking the last bus home. The grades never improved. However, the reward was that I finished my course work and dissertation in just fifteen months rather than the two years Dr. Carr had assigned to me.

In order to get a license to practice medicine in Michigan, in addition to the ECFMG certification, I was required to pass an exam in each of the basic science subjects that are taught in medical school. These were offered quarterly. While I was studying for my master's in pharmacology, I continued to sign up for one or two of these each quarter. They were multiple-choice and did not seem as difficult as the take-home, open-book tests that had haunted me. Once I recognized the pattern in which the choices were arranged, marking off the right answers was not too difficult.

By the time I completed the requirements for my master's degree, I had also cleared the ECFMG and all the exams in basic sciences—anatomy, physiology, bacteriology, chemistry, and pathology. I had become a bona-fide exam junkie. It was a compressed torture, and, moving forward, I was glad that I could finally dream about the joys of clinical medicine.

♦♦♦♦♦♦

Both my children were to start school in fall. I considered this a perfect time for me to begin the final grind—two years of pediatric residency in an accredited hospital. With that, I would become eligible to take the pediatric boards. I prepared myself for this ultimate drudgery.

I applied for my residency via the exchange placement program, wherein I identified the University of Michigan Medical School as my first and only choice. In a few weeks, I got a call from the school's pediatric department for an interview. I was to meet with the department chairman, Dr. Oliver. I was brimming with joy. In two short years, I would be a recognized pediatrician in America. Finally, my dreams were taking shape.

That morning, I took extra care to dress neatly for my interview. I wore a pleated gray wool skirt, a pink cashmere sweater, and knee-high boots—the only decent outfit I had. I arrived at Dr. Oliver's office well ahead of the appointed time. I sat in the waiting room, listening to the thumping of the receptionist's typewriter and nervously thumbing through the magazines on the table. Finally, the receptionist's phone buzzed. "He can see you now," she said, and she opened the door that led to Dr. Oliver's office.

The room was brightly lit and had a large executive desk. Dr. Oliver was seated in a leather chair behind the desk, his eyes focused on an open folder. I recognized some of the papers in that folder and knew that it was my application. I bowed in respect out of habit and greeted him with a "Good morning, sir." He did not look up, so I waited. Finally, he glanced at me and asked me to take a seat. I collected myself and sat on the edge of the chair. I shut my eyes for a moment and braced myself for the interview. I was beginning to feel a stiffness developing in my spine.

The interview started with the usual introductions and small talk. Dr. Oliver continued to thumb through the folder in front of him as we kept up our conversation. Besides my résumé, I had included several letters of recommendation from previous employers, including one from Dr. Carr. He reiterated some of the facts stated in my application. I nodded in affirmation. We talked about my past experience in pediatrics in India and recent studies with Dr. Carr.

He shuffled the papers some more. I waited anxiously in anticipation of more academically oriented questions. Looking straight at me, he said, "You interview well and appear very intelligent. I see that you come with strong recommendations."

Smiling meekly in a humble acknowledgment of his compliments, I relaxed. There was no reason for me to be so nervous about this interview. I rested my arms in my lap and leaned forward, keen to hear what he would say next. He continued, "However, I can tell you right now that when your application surfaces against the graduates from our school who have applied for residency"—he tapped on the pile of applications on the right side of his desk—"I don't believe you have a chance of getting into our program."

My jaw fell, and my mind went blank. I couldn't quite comprehend what he meant. I thought I had heard him say that I was intelligent and had interviewed well. I looked at him and said nothing. There was a pause. It seemed like a very long pause. Then he spoke and began to enumerate the odds against me. With his elbow planted firmly on the desk, he began to count the odds on his fingers, starting with his thumb. "One, you are a woman. Two, you are married and have children. If you were divorced and had a family to support, that would be a consideration, you see."

My thoughts swerved for a moment to my contented family life, which was seemingly a bar to my progress in America.

He continued, "Third, you have been out of clinical work for almost seven years. Science has changed a lot, you know. You will never be at par with the knowledge of our fresh graduates."

With every count, there was an emphatic movement of his wrist, and his fingers seemed to come closer and closer toward me. I pulled back and receded into my shell.

He counted the fourth setback. "You are a foreigner, an *Indian*." There was a special emphasis on *Indian*. I looked at the brown color of my hands as they lay limp in my lap.

He concluded, "You desire to join our program not because of the merits of our university but because of convenience, your husband being on staff here." He tapped the table with his forefinger. "You see what I mean?"

He leaned back in his chair and was now looking right at me. I was having difficulty meeting his eye. I kept my gaze on the large authoritative hand that had made the counts against my chances of success and then had tapped the table to make the final blow.

As if all this were not enough, he continued, "Did you know we are now giving phenobarbital to our neonates to prevent the complications of hyperbilirubinemia?"

In my course work in pharmacology, I had not only studied about this new use of an old drug but had also read several articles hypothesizing its mechanism of action.

I nodded ever so slightly.

I don't believe he was seeking an answer from me. He concluded bluntly, "Just think about it. Do you have a chance?"

I did not have anything more to say. Our interview was over.

I thanked him for taking the time to see me and stepped out of his office, shutting the door behind me. Tears that I had courageously held back came streaming down my cheeks. His secretary offered me a Kleenex.

On my way home, I joggled my thoughts this way and that. I looked at my bleak future. "Just think about it. Do you have a chance?" I thought about it. He had a point. I was brown. I was a woman. What chance did I have? Which American parent would like brown hands touching the tender white tummies of their precious babies? Maybe I should return to pharmacology. I should stick to mice and guinea pigs and rabbits.

♦♦♦♦♦♦

In the privacy of my home, I could let it all out. I threw a sobbing fit and told Kris all about my interview.

"What would you expect?" he asked, calming me. "Isn't it the same the world over? Do you think a Punjabi in Chandigarh would hire a Gujarati over his own brethren? I know only two solid rules. Either you prove that you are better than all the others applying for that position, or you go to a place where no one else wants to go. We are new immigrants and have to pay our dues."

My sobs continued. "So tell me, what do I do? What can I do?"

"Just don't despair. The difference between India and America is that this is a country of opportunities. Some other door will open. Take life as it comes."

It was a comforting philosophy. Tomorrow will be a brighter day. I went upstairs, rinsed my tears off in the sink, and changed my clothes.

Chapter 35

Not long after my interview with Dr. Oliver, Kris was browsing through some medical journals, the ones that start arriving free of charge as soon as the drug companies learn that you are an MD. It was a Sunday afternoon. I slumped next to Kris, doing nothing, just finding comfort in his warmth and letting my thoughts wander through the pessimistic world around me.

"Here is your opportunity," he said, sliding a *Journal of Internal Medicine* toward me. There it was: a half-page ad for an immediate opening for an intern in Toledo, Ohio. I bolted upright and looked at the advertisement.

"But it is in Ohio. I cannot leave you and the children and move to another state," I said. In the seven years of our marriage, I had always given up my job and moved wherever Kris had found opportunities. I had never lived away from him. My narrow tunnel vision could not see past that.

"Don't just brush it off. Give it some thought. It's not that far," he said.

We brought out a map and checked the distance … sixty miles.

"Go ahead and arrange an interview. I can commute. It won't be too bad," he said.

The following morning, I rang the number given in the journal. I introduced myself and took a brief phone interview.

"What is your visa status?" the voice at the other end asked.

"I am a permanent resident. I have a green card."

"Good," the voice said. "Have you cleared your ECFMG?"

"Yes, sir, I have," I answered.

"When are you available?"

"I can join as soon as I can make the necessary arrangements. My husband works for the University of Michigan, and I have two small children," I said.

The voice was that of Dr. John F. Brunner, director of medical education at Mercy Saint Vincent Medical Center in Toledo, Ohio. He gave me an appointment for a meeting.

♦♦♦♦♦♦

I met Dr. Brunner on September 12, 1970. He greeted me casually, and I handed him my résumé. He browsed through it and asked me a few more questions. I grasped very quickly that the opening was for a rotating internship, not a residency. I told him that I had a degree in pediatrics from India, and in order to pursue my interests in America, I needed two years of pediatrics in an accredited program. He offered me the position of an intern in general medicine with the assurance of a smooth transition to their pediatric residency program after I completed the year of internship. As an added bonus, he promised me a six-month rotation in pediatrics during my internship.

Without hesitancy, I accepted his offer. I submitted myself to three years of toil instead of the required two. I had done a similar training in India after graduating from medical school. I was a young twenty-two then and not married. I knew the willpower and endurance it would take to repeat the whole thing. At this point, I did not care. If the family could endure the hardships for two years, they could do so for three. I needed to get my foot in the door. I wanted to be a pediatrician in America. Here was my opportunity. I was going to grab it.

Kris had driven me for the interview. I met him in the reception area of the hospital and shared the news. I had just committed myself to three years of eighty- to eighty-five-hour workweeks, sixty miles away from home, and we had just about two weeks to make all our arrangements. His face flushed. I could not tell whether this was because of the triumph he felt in being instrumental in locating the door to my medical world or because of the sudden realization of the obstacles that lay ahead. I did not ask.

Chapter 36

Dr. Brunner's secretary gave me a map of the hospital and vicinity. "A lot of our young residents live here," she said as she ran the yellow highlighter over some of the streets and then placed an *X* over areas where these young doctors lived. "You may be lucky; you may find something to your liking right here, a walking distance from our hospital."

Maps in hand, we drove through the residential blocks between Cherry, Walnut, and Locust Streets. We wove through the cross streets of Moore, Yates, Noble, and a few others, slowing down in front of the apartments with For Rent signs. All we saw everywhere was peeling paint, small curtainless windows, and streets speckled with empty beer cans and stray plastic. Children in threadbare clothes were riding about on their bicycles, recklessly demonstrating their stunts. Kris and I exchanged frequent glances and checked that our car doors were locked. Surely, this was not the America we had envisioned for our children, not even on a temporary basis. We came away disappointed and discouraged. The idea of our finding a place where I could walk to work was clearly not plausible.

On our return journey, we stopped briefly in Temperance, a small town at the Michigan-Ohio border. Homes here looked romantic, complete with dogs, silos, and barns. For a few moments, we nurtured the idea of living in Temperance, a midpoint for the two of us, neglecting to think through the details. With two living parents driving off in two different directions in order to pursue their careers, the children would be like orphans in Temperance.

"It was just a thought," we chuckled as we left the dreamlike country town.

♦♦♦♦♦♦

We drove homeward in silence, listening to the clank and rattle of our 1965 Volkswagen. I had a lot to think about, and so did Kris. The drive on US 23 between Ann Arbor and Toledo was straight and flat. Our problems, however, were much more complex and serpentine.

I broke the silence. "You know what? The easiest thing will be for me to take courage and take on the driving. That way, the family stays rooted. The children can continue in the same school and have the stability of their friends and babysitters. I will have the VW, and you can take the university bus."

I could have been talking to the hollows of our car. I got no response from Kris. I was aware of one of his biggest fears—that of losing me in a fatal accident on the highway. When we had come to Ann Arbor and I had asked him to enroll me in a driver's ed class, he had come up with every excuse possible to negate the idea.

"Why do you need a license?" he had argued. "When we go out, we always go together, and when you go to work, you take the bus."

"Maybe I can occasionally run small errands without taking up your time to drive me around," I'd said.

"Driving in America is too dangerous—so many fatal accidents."

"You drive, don't you?"

"That's different. I am a man. Men have to drive."

When I looked at him in disbelief, he dug through his brain for another reason. "Those classes are so expensive. Where is the money going to come from?"

I knew I could not dispute that. If we did not have the money, I could not ask for it.

I, however, did not give up my desire to get a license. I looked for alternatives. I learned the basics by getting behind the wheel with one of my colleagues, a graduate student from Poland. After a few sessions with him, I went for my road test on a Thursday.

Taking the test on a Thursday was by no means something dictated by a palm reader or by a mythical voodoo belief. It was a solid scientific approach, a well-kept secret in Ann Arbor, shared by many a foreign student. I had learned about it accidentally. One day, I was having lunch with a bunch of students in the cafeteria, a good place for exchanging this kind of scientific gossip. We were from various parts of the world, facing similar obstacles.

"Everyone in the world drives on the left side of the road. To make things difficult for us, America decides to drive on the right," I said as I placed my lunch tray on the table and took a sip of Coke. I had just come from one of my behind-the-wheel sessions, frustrated with understanding all the rules of taking a left on green.

"Go for your road test on a Thursday," the girl sitting across from me suggested immediately. "That is how I got my license. You will be met by this short, stubby, square-looking officer. He works only on Thursdays. He is very nice. He takes you on the street for a minute or two and hands you your license. No need to learn parallel parking, none of that nonsense. He never asks for any of that."

I followed her advice. I obtained my license by going for my road test on a Thursday. That little piece of plastic with my very own photo on it was there to cherish and to teasingly show off to Kris. It bore no testimony to my skills of controlling the wheel.

Now, with no on-the-road experience whatsoever, I was proposing that I would take the commute.

After a long pause, Kris said, "What a brilliant idea, something worth considering."

"It is just an option," I said. And then, to comfort him, I added, "I will not be driving every day, anyway, because I will be on call every third night."

The thought of my taking on the commute jelled more and more as we kept driving and discussing all the alternatives.

♦♦♦♦♦♦

With my meager skills in driving, I was faced with a sixty-mile commute on highways, byways, and city roads. I needed a crash course. Kris would have to be my coach. Over the next few days, I took several dry runs with him, reading and interpreting road signs and learning to yield to the oncoming traffic when taking a left on green.

Whereas most exits on US 23 were on the right, the one I needed to take in order to get to my hospital was on the left. As instructed by Kris, I was driving in the right lane.

"How the hell am I supposed to know that my exit is on the left?" I said, clutching the steering wheel tighter and shifting lanes hastily.

"Read the signs," Kris said in a voice louder than mine. "And for heaven's sakes, slow down."

"How can I read signs and drive at the same time? Slow down? You just said that I could be ticketed for driving too slow on a highway."

"Just do as I tell you."

I pulled the car to the shoulder, got out of the driver's seat, and handed him the keys.

I had had enough. I declared myself ready.

♦♦♦♦♦♦

While I needed to practice my driving, Kris had to learn the art of being the sole parent. In the upcoming years, there would be many nights when I would be on call and he would have to play this role. He brought it down to a science. He learned to bathe the kids, read stories to them, and put them to bed. He also learned the morning routine of getting them dressed, fed, and packed off to school. After a while, the kids actually preferred him and resented my interference because I brought in harder disciplines. It was perfectly all right for Ravi to go to school with one green and one blue sock under Dad's guardianship, but not mine.

Dad read them bedtime stories every night. They demanded the monotonous reading of the *Three Little Pigs* night after night. Kris was no child psychologist. He did not want to find out why his children wanted the tedium of the same story over and over, every night. He was a scientist and a problem solver. He went to S. S. Kresge Company and spent five whole dollars on a tape player. He recorded the story of the three pigs in his own voice. The kids enjoyed taking turns in pushing the on/off buttons on their new toy. Kris enjoyed reading his journals while his voice told the story night after night after night.

Chapter 37

When I started my internship, Rajiv and Ravi were in school during the day. However, I needed to find after-school child care. This was generally not difficult, though at times it presented its own problems. Graduate students completed their terms and left. New families moved in to fill their spots. Though someone was always looking for a job, I worried about the frequent changes the children would have to endure. They, however, were resilient and adapted readily. The fact that they always returned to our stable home in the evenings must have helped.

I remember Julie in particular. She took my children into her home and mimicked a mininursery school, preparing their activities in advance. She had two children of her own. The four of them had their routines laid out: coloring, making collages, telling stories, reading, and writing. Naps and outdoor playtime were all regimented. I certainly could not have matched her skills.

And then there was Etsu, an enigma.

Etsu Raymond was a good friend, a very sweet, petite little Japanese girl. Like many Japanese, she had trouble pronouncing the letter *R*. Why she had married a man with the last name Raymond beats me. She introduced herself to me as Etsu Laymond. When I repeated her last name, she corrected me, "No, no, it is not Laymond; it is *Lll-r-aymond*," until I got the idea. She knew my children as Lajiv and Lavi.

I had known Etsu from my pharmacology days; I had met her in my neighborhood during one of my evening walks. Gradually, our friendship grew. Then one day, we pledged to become study partners and give each other moral support to get through the rigors of our respective class assignments. She would ring me with a wakeup call at four in the morning. By the time I got my books together and walked across the cold, dark quad to her apartment, a fragrant pot of tea was ready and waiting. I could smell the jasmine halfway across the yard. I poured myself a steamy cup and sat across from her at her kitchen table and studied. We both thought what we were doing was crazy, yet we both enjoyed the experience. Together, we could find merriment in the worst adversities of student life.

It was the first summer after I had embarked upon my medical career that I had to find a full-time babysitter while my regular babysitter was away. I casually mentioned to Etsu that I would be talking to some women in our neighborhood to see if they could help me out. Summer help was a bit harder to find. Women were hesitant to commit just in case they might have an opportunity to get away with their families for a week or two.

"Would you mind if I took your children in for the summer? I am not going anywhere," Etsu said. She was in the midst of her master's in child psychology. "As you know, I have no hands-on experience with children. I need it for my thesis. This will work nicely for me. I will not charge you, because I will actually be gathering data for my own use."

"You are sure you want to do this?" I asked.

She was sure.

"That would be fantastic," I said. "At least let me pay you something for their meals."

"Oh, no, no. You don't pay me anything. I am doing this for my own benefit."

As we were talking about the drop-off and pick-up timings, she asked, "Oh, you won't mind if I give them some psychological tests for practice, would you?"

"Not at all. Tell me if they check out normal." I laughed. She did not reciprocate.

I decided to trust my instincts and Etsu's Japanese hospitality. I felt that this was a godsend that had fallen my way. I put all other possible interviews on hold.

I don't think my children were too happy when I told them about this arrangement. Since Etsu had no children, they would have no friends to play with. She lived in an area of the student housing that was set aside for singles or young couples like herself. Of course, they were not given a choice. "You won't know till you try. She will have lots of games that she herself will play with you, and she will take you for field trips where you can catch frogs and collect pretty stones," I told them.

So the arrangement came about.

On Friday evening, the end of the first week of our new arrangement, I walked over to pick up the children. I stood at the steps that led to Etsu's apartment and rang the bell. She came to the door and announced abruptly, "I cannot take your children anymore, not even for one day."

She stood at the partially open door. Her face was very close to mine. I took a step back to position myself and looked for the hospitality that I had always received from her in the past. She appeared distraught and forlorn, her disheveled hair encircling her round face.

"Is everything all right?" I asked, and I steered my way into her kitchen. Sitting down, I prepared myself to listen.

"I think studying child psychology in the classroom is one thing, and living with it quite another. I just cannot stand children for eight hours a day—their demands, their noise. I get so exhausted." Having said the worst, she got a grip on herself. I also relaxed. I had imagined that something more sinister had gone amiss, maybe something in her marriage. She offered me tea and continued more calmly, "I do apologize, but I don't think I can do this anymore, not even for one more day. My husband has always said, 'No children for us, Etsu,' and now I understand."

Her decision was firm. That Friday was to be her last day. For me, it was just the first of many trials and tribulations yet to come. I walked back to my apartment, my two children in tow.

Knowing the strict regime of my residency, I knew that I could not take any kind of family leave. Kris was also in the midst of some important work and could not take time off. I felt stranded.

I put on my thinking cap.

I called my Indian friend Lalita. Her son and my children often played together while we the parents clung to each other for the sake of that Indianness that we had all left behind. I knew that she would never agree to babysit on a paid basis. Babysitting was like being an ayah. However, she was my dear friend. I could approach her for a favor. "Could you please take them for a couple of weeks? I am in a terrible bind," I explained my situation to her.

She took them, making clear that it was temporary and it was just one friend's favor to another. I started a search again. I could not find anybody for that summer from the married students' pool. However, if I remember right, I made arrangements with some high school girls, a sort of job share. It was not perfect, but it got us through.

The children survived that summer, and so did I. My residency and the dense days are behind me now, and I can only reminisce about the good, the bad, and the indifferent.

♦♦♦♦♦♦

The domestic arrangements were also solved amicably. The model I had used for that three-year period would be difficult to reproduce today. It worked beautifully in Ann Arbor in the early seventies.

I met a girl named Sharon. She was a senior at Huron High School, not far from where we lived. Vibrant and bright eyed, she was seeking part-time work that would also be stimulating to her. I explained my needs to her and asked if she could work five afternoons a week, offering her twenty-five dollars per week. This was excellent money considering the going rate of fifty cents an hour for babysitting. She accepted my offer.

Every afternoon, after her classes, Sharon walked to my apartment. With the house still peaceful and quiet, she made herself a snack and settled down at the kitchen table to finish her homework. That done, she started on her assigned job. She looked up her notes, her menus, and her recipes and carefully prepared the evening meal. By the time Kris picked up the kids from the sitter's and I drove back from Toledo, a delightful hot meal was ready. We all settled at the table and ate a leisurely meal together. After the meal, she stayed awhile playing with the children and socializing with us. The children adored her, comparing her culinary skills to my futile efforts at putting American meals on the table. They thought she was fantastic.

Home economics was much emphasized in schools in those days, and Sharon took her job as an extension of her schoolwork. Her teacher found this a great opportunity for her to put into practice the lessons she was being taught in class. Occasionally, Sharon took the weekly menu that she had prepared for us to her teacher and got her affirmation that she was preparing healthy, balanced meals. She always had her favorite cookbooks with her, and when she was unsure of something in a recipe, she called her mother for advice. Her mother was also very supportive of her job. She thought it was a wonderful opportunity for her to mingle with us, two professionals, and think of new horizons for her future. She did not want her to be a full-time homemaker like herself. Becoming a teacher, a nurse, or a secretary were the commonly offered options to women in those days. Her mother wanted her to look beyond that. Our coming from a different culture was an added bonus. India was hardly on the map in American schools at the time. Sharon asked us many questions and took the stories back to her school and family.

I also learned a lot from Sharon. I observed how she put our menus together. In Indian cooking, we take for granted that our meals are balanced just because they have worked for generations. Now I learned that in order to make a good American menu, I had to identify the three macronutrients—protein, carbohydrate, and fat—and incorporate each group in the meal in proper proportions. Then I was to add fruits and vegetables and finally a dessert. Sharon taught me all this. She taught me the difference between beef and pork. One of her cookbooks had a diagram of a cow with labels of the different cuts of meat. Thus, I learned the origin of butt roast, rump roast, spare ribs, and the like.

We were living on a budget of forty dollars a week for groceries. Sharon did the weekly shopping and learned to stay within that allowance. At the end of the month, she used the savings to serve us dinners that were more sophisticated. Sometimes we had steak for dinner. Once she served filet mignon and said that it was the ultimate in American cuisine.

I have often reconstructed Sharon's menus in my memory. They were so novel to me at the time.

Monday: Cheeseburgers, french fries, a green salad

Tuesday: Pigs in a blanket, mashed potatoes, steamed peas

Wednesday: Sloppy Joes on buns, green beans, carrots cut as finger food

Thursday: Parmesan chicken, corn on the cob, mixed vegetables

Friday: Broiled fish, Uncle Ben's rice, seasonal fresh vegetables

I also remember her varying the meals by including pork chops, meat loaf, macaroni and cheese, and tuna casserole. She always served a dessert after supper. It could be custard, tapioca pudding, or ice cream. Sometimes she baked a cake from scratch. Meals that I grew up on incorporated a dessert on special occasions only. No wonder my children favored Sharon in the kitchen.

Sharon could work for just about a year. When she was ready to graduate from high school, she took it upon herself to bring in a substitute, another dependable senior from her school. I did not have to involve myself in the screening or long drawn-out interviews or in the training of the new person. Thus, the faces and personalities of the girls changed, but the model remained intact for the three years of my residency. Except for a minor glitch when one of the girls proved to be somewhat dishonest with her accounting, the system churned along beautifully. This girl was also not fired, sparing me the time and energy for locating a new person. "We must talk to her before we make such a decision," Kris said to me, and he worked with her as a mentor, teaching her the importance of reliability and honesty. As we got to know her, she proved to be a very pleasant person and an excellent cook.

These vivacious teenagers who worked with us brought buoyancy into our otherwise strict schedules, and they played an important role in our lives. Not having to think about doing the dishes or the burden of planning menus and going grocery shopping was indeed very helpful to me during the arduous years of my residency.

Chapter 38

I started my medical career in America on October 1, 1970. As I stood in the corridor of the medical wing of Mercy in Toledo along with other residents that day, I knew I was home. The seven years I had been away from clinical medicine seemed to evaporate, and the memories of hospital routines and patient care resurfaced. I floated around in the hospital corridors as though I had always been there. I was assigned six or at the most eight beds. I examined these patients, took their histories, and documented their physical findings in their charts. As I worked, I could not help but compare my present life to that of my residency in India. There, though I was a fresh graduate, I was in charge of fifteen or twenty cases at any given time. Whereas that had given me an abundance of clinical exposure, I enjoyed the thoroughness with which I could work up my patients here. I cherished the time I could spend with each patient.

In spite of the long work hours, I was very happy. This wonderful opportunity of reentering the medical field had spared me the drudgery of spending a lifetime in research. I regained the weight I had lost while I was doing my master's in pharmacology. When I was working with mice and rabbits, my experiments went smoothly, and the data was accurate and reproducible, but I never felt that sense of ecstasy or exhilaration that a scientist is supposed to experience. There was never a novel breakthrough in my work. I felt like a lonely pseudoscientist working like a robot. I had resented that career path. Now it was all behind me. Working with humans was far more rewarding. Every case was different and presented its own challenges in diagnosis and care. I saw the fruits of my intervention. Patients came in sick and left feeling grateful for what I had been able to contribute toward their wellness.

Being sixty miles from the hospital and literally a state away actually helped my morale. When I was off duty, I was far enough from the hospital that I could tune out that busy routine and transplant myself to the laid-back life typical of a university setting. Then, relaxed and rejuvenated, when I returned to the hospital and heard the familiar voice on the overhead paging system anxiously locating one doctor or another, I could immediately tune out the world I had left behind and immerse into the fast-paced clinical world.

The clock changed by an hour somewhere between Michigan and Ohio. Since I had to report on duty at 7:30 a.m. in Ohio, I had to leave home at 5:30 a.m. Michigan time for the hour's commute—a minor inconvenience. Kris made it easier for me by warming up the car and scraping snow off the windshield on those chilly mornings. In the evenings, the hour's difference between Ohio and Michigan time worked in my favor. I left the hospital at 5:00 p.m., and somewhere during the drive, the time changed, and when I arrived home, the clock struck five again.

Chapter 39

Some setbacks had to be swallowed silently.

As previously mentioned, my driving skills were good only for the famous chub-chub officer who had given me my road test on a Thursday. When it came to real life and real roads, I did not do too well. The old stick-shift station wagon was not the best companion either. At least two or three times a year, I dealt with one calamity or another, and it is no coincidence that most of these occurred when I was on my journey home, sleep deprived and tired after a challenging night on call.

Once, the car battery died. Another time, I found myself out of gas on the highway. Without any kind of insurance for roadside assistance or a cell phone, even these were no easy tasks to resolve. Most common and most treacherous, however, were the winter catastrophes. I would go off the road, find myself in the middle of a snow-covered field, or just get stuck in a rut, unable to move forward or backward. I learned from experience what I needed to do immediately—turn on my blinkers. What next, I had no idea. If I pushed on the gas pedal, the wheels just turned and dug deeper into the snow. Helpless, I sat back, took a deep breath, and waited. Sometimes the tranquility of the snow around me relaxed me. The white expanse looked ethereal. I sat in the car with a towel over my knees to keep me warm and watched the rays of the late-afternoon sun create diamond-like glitters on the snow all around me, and if a gust of wind came along, it created delicate wavelike patterns. I watched the beauty and waited.

A Good Samaritan invariably appeared from somewhere and tapped on my window.

"Looks like you could use some help."

I rolled the pane down and looked at him expectantly.

He took over, settled in the driver's seat, and did exactly what I had attempted to do. It seemed so easy when he performed the same maneuvers that I had tried repeatedly and had failed. He would get me out of the rut and back on the road.

The first time I went off the road, I was puzzled, startled, and afraid. After a few such incidents, I became quite complacent. The flat terrain along US 23 was my savior. No matter how far I hydroplaned, I was never seriously hurt.

One snowy day, however, my car skidded, crossed the median, spun around, and rested in the field several yards from the highway. It all happened so fast, faster than the time it has taken me to describe it. Shaken and upset, I took count of my body parts. Nothing hurt, nothing broken. However, my ego was badly hurt, and my confidence was certainly shattered. At this rate, would I ever get through my residency? I had just started on that long journey.

I waited.

A Good Samaritan walked over. He asked if he could be of any help. I got out of the car and let him take the driver's seat. He turned on the ignition, rocked the car back and forth, and then, with a final acceleration, brought the car back on the road.

The car was idling, and I was standing beside the Good Samaritan.

"But I am going home to Ann Arbor. I need to be there." I pointed to the lanes across the median. The car was presently facing Toledo.

"Then just get into the car, go a few hundred yards, and take the next exit." He pointed to an exit visible in the far distance. "At the end of the ramp, take a left, go over the bridge, and take the ramp back onto US 23 going north," he explained.

Although I could see the bridge and the ramps, it was too much information for my tired and sleep-deprived brain to absorb. Mr. Chub-Chub had not trained me for such complex situations. The words *ramp* and *cloverleaf* and *highway going north-south* all muddied in my shaken brain.

Seeing the expression on my face, he repeated his instructions, now describing each step slowly, using hand gestures for clarity.

"What if I miss the turn? I will never find my way back. I'll never get home," I said.

The Good Samaritan smiled, shook his head in despair, and returned to the driver's seat. He drove me up and over the cloverleaf and got me back to the place where I had lost control of my car. As soon as the car was back on the road heading home, I regained my confidence. I thanked the Good Samaritan and took over. *I will do this as many times as necessary, but I will not quit my residency,* I told myself. This beautiful world is full of Good Samaritans. Someone will always be there to help me. I turned on the radio and let the music drown my misery.

When I reached home, I kept a straight and pleasant face. Such information must never reach Kris. He has always had a mortal fear of his wife getting into a fatal car accident. It took him a lot of courage to let me take on the commute. If he found out about these driving mishaps, my residency would have certainly come to a halt. I kept my secret. The roadside fiascos stayed buried in the innermost crypts of my brain. I willed myself not to dream about them lest I spill my secret in a garbled nightmare. I continued the commute.

♦♦♦♦♦♦

I began to enumerate all the advantages of my long commute. When the weather was good, that hour on the road was my personal time for reflection. Highway 23 was never very busy, and I had the road to myself. I could let my thoughts float at will with the music as a backdrop. The popular tune "Raindrops Keep Fallin' On My Head" always put me in a romantic mood.

I live a life of luxury, I contemplated, and I allowed myself to play with some of my fondest memories. When other working mothers come home, they have to kick off their shoes and immediately go to the kitchen so that they can get a meal on the table. My supper cooks while I drive. Arriving in Ann Arbor, when I turn the corner from Plymouth onto Beal, I smell the aroma of Sharon's cooking, and as I pull into my parking space, I see her movements behind the sliding glass door. She is just bringing out the sizzling hamburgers. Rajiv, Ravi, and Kris are already in their seats. I unbutton my drab white coat, throw it on the couch, and join the family, ignoring the blotchy stains of Betadine and mercurochrome on my skirt.

After being away for such long hours, every time I returned home, it felt like a reunion all over again. We ate together, talking, telling. Sharon kept a certain sense of calm as we all tried to talk simultaneously, trying to get our stories told. After dinner, Kris and I took walks through the neighborhood and chatted with friends. They eagerly asked about my residency, and the women were proud of me as a representative of their race trotting into male-oriented territories.

Rajiv and Ravi also adapted well to my long absences. If they asked me why I had not been with them for supper the previous night, I reminded them of the hospital tour we had taken together. I had shown them the bed in the residents' room. "Mummy will be sleeping here sometimes so she can be close to the sick children. If they are hurting too much, she will be able to get to them quickly and help them." This simple explanation had been enough for them to understand that I had left them for a purpose and would return. In this way, I also reinforced the fact that I was a doctor and had certain responsibilities that kept me away from home for long hours.

Chapter 40

As Dr. Brunner had promised, he transferred me to pediatrics after six months in internal medicine. He introduced me to the chief of pediatric department, Dr. Marion Rejent, who would be my new boss. She must have already browsed through my résumé, because she began to ask me questions about my training and experience in pediatrics in India as we were walking to the children's ward. Here I met Dr. Brookfield, the attending physician to whom I would be reporting on a day-to-day basis. She informed him that I was the new intern. I worked closely with Dr. Brookfield and saw very little of Dr. Rejent after that. She showed up for grand rounds occasionally, sat in the front row, and contributed little to our discussions.

Although I was an intern, I was given the responsibilities of a resident from the day I joined the department. The two residents, Dr. Luke and Dr. Naidu, were taking calls every other night. I came in as the third person to share calls. After the morning rounds, the chief resident assigned me my beds. He also handed me a copy of the on-call schedule for the month. I felt proud to see my name printed alongside of the two residents. I was moving upward in my career rapidly.

After a week or two of my posting in pediatrics, I was allowed to perform procedures that were generally performed by residents. I did lumbar punctures and bone marrow aspirations as necessary, and loved the trust and responsibilities given to me. I was on call every third night.

When on call, I had to work thirty hours straight, taking catnaps as time permitted. Sleep became a rare commodity, and yet I did not seem to mind it. Loving what I was doing, I exalted in my stamina. Weekends when I was on call, I worked from Saturday morning until the following Monday afternoon. My workweek averaged eighty to eighty-five hours.

Six months passed, and I merged imperceptibly into the residency status. I do not recall it as a special day. My paycheck went up slightly, and I was now referred to as PL-1 (pediatric resident—level one).

♦♦♦♦♦♦

I was lying on the couch and reading a letter from my father-in-law. In spite of a busy night at the hospital, I was unable to fall asleep. It was a sunny fall afternoon. Among other things, my father-in-law had written, "I don't stay well these days, and I do not know how much longer I have on this earth. I wonder whether I will see you again. I yearn to see you and the grandchildren." Kris was in the kitchen, probably making tea, and the children were playing in the sandbox just outside our apartment. Kris broke the silence. "Maybe we should go back home and visit our families this Christmas."

"You mean, go to India?" I perked up at the thought. We still referred to India as home.

"Why not?"

I considered the idea with interest. My thoughts jumped from the anticipated snowy December in Michigan to the invigorating warm climate in India. It had been four years since I had immersed myself in the sounds and smells that I called home. Letters from everyone in my family had been trickling in with patchy bits of news, always leaving me in partial void. *How sick is my father-in-law? How much have my parents changed? What do they look like?* I felt a deep desire to go back and fill in the blanks.

"Do you think we can afford it?" I asked.

"We might get lucky and get a decent price on tickets," he said. "All we will need is money for four tickets. Expenses in India will be minimal; the dollar is so strong."

My life at the hospital had fallen into a good groove. I had been working under Dr. Rejent for nine months. With twenty-one months of hard work, I would accomplish the goal I had set for myself—that of being a recognized pediatrician in America. Life was gratifying, but it was also quite exhausting. I could use a break.

"I will check if I can get leave," I said.

The next day, after I had presented my case at a clinicopath meeting and we were walking out of the auditorium, Dr. Rejent complimented me on my presentation. "Well done," she said. That was the most a resident could expect from her in appreciation of our work. I took advantage of her good mood and broached the subject.

"I was wondering if I could take my annual vacation in December. I would like to visit my family in India. Of course, I will go only if my husband can find tickets at a reasonable price since it is peak season for travel to India."

She considered my request. "Normally, we do not sanction leave to residents until they have worked for at least six months, but your case is special," she said.

Although I had worked under her as a resident for only three months, she was considering the fact that I had worked for an additional six months in the capacity of an intern where I was performing all the duties of a resident. "Just let me know when you have your dates confirmed, and we can work something out," she said.

Delighted with this positive note, I asked Kris to go ahead and find us tickets for a two-week trip.

While we were planning our trip, unrest erupted between India and Pakistan. Amritsar, Kris's hometown, being close to the Pakistan border, was always vulnerable to the effects of such disturbances, even if the turmoil did not culminate into a full-blown war. Riots had kindled between the Hindus and Muslims in Amritsar. With the fragmented communication between India and America, every bit of news that came to me became exaggerated in my mind's eye. I envisioned bombs and bloodshed just as I had seen during the 1947 partition. Flights were being cancelled and rescheduled every day. I wanted to get home before travel became totally disrupted. Dates of my departure and return—or whether I would be able to go at all—depended on the availability of tickets.

Finally, Kris was able to find confirmed two-way tickets. However, these required a minimum stay of three weeks in India. I went to Dr. Rejent's office to firm up my plans and ask for an extra week off. I learned from her secretary that she was out on a month's vacation, leaving Dr. Brookfield, the director of pediatric residency, in charge.

I talked with Dr. Brookfield. "That should not be a problem as long as the other two residents are willing to cover for you in your absence," he said. My coresidents, Dr. Luke and Dr. Naidu, were agreeable. We had been a friendly and cooperative trio from the time I had met them. We had exchanged calls readily to suit one another's needs. I promised to pay off my time by taking extra calls before I went to India. I took fifteen nights that month.

Chapter 41

With an extra week of vacation, we made a new itinerary. In addition to visiting family, we incorporated some sightseeing. A Fodor's travel guide about India gave us helpful tips on how to travel efficiently for five dollars a day or less.

We rented a private taxi in New Delhi. The driver, a knowledgeable Sikh dedicated to his profession, stayed with us for several days and was available to us at any time of the day or night. He knew the best eateries and where the locals shopped. For forty dollars a day, this worked out to be the safest and most efficient way to travel. We shopped at Connaught Circle, the market I had frequented in preparation for my wedding, and drove through 10 Windsor Place where we were married. It all seemed so long ago.

From New Delhi, we drove to Jaipur, where Shadi-lal, Kris's brother, was posted. On our way, we took an overnight halt in Agra to see the Taj Mahal. Unlike what a visitor might face today, we did not have to deal with any bureaucratic paperwork of getting a permit, choosing a time slot for our visit, or a tight scrutiny for security checks. For a small fee, we walked in, hiring a personal guide. Our guide, a boy who did not look older than thirteen or fourteen, had memorized the history of the Taj in great detail and recited it in a melodious way as we roamed around the tombs of the Mughal Emperor Shah Jahan and his wife Nur Jahan. After wandering through the beautiful marble structures and admiring the workmanship of the intricate inlay in so many pleasing hues, we walked leisurely in the surrounding gardens. Later that night, our guide returned to show us the mausoleum by moonlight. Its silvery silhouette against a full moon and an inky blue sky was magical. The traffic had died down, and we could hear the sound of the Yamuna River gurgling in the back. We could not have planned the timing of our trip any better.

In Jaipur, the Pink City, Shadi-lal arranged to show us around. We visited many old forts and palaces. The buildings in the main corridor of the city were painted in shades of pink, and the street was bustling with local Rajasthani women dressed in colorful long skirts, heavy silver anklets, large ear hoops, and nose rings. Rows of shops lining the street were crowded with hagglers looking for bargains, almost all of them non-Indians.

When we arrived in Amritsar, Kris's large extended family greeted us with flower garlands. My father-in-law, who had not been well for several days, perked up when he heard our voices echo through the thick stucco walls of the old house. He fumbled around to find his cane, got dressed in a clean, well-ironed Nehru shirt, cap, and vest, and joined us on the porch. His voice was feeble, but reassuring. "I am so happy to see you and my American grandchildren," he said, kissing Rajiv and Ravi over and over again. "I thought I would never get to see you all." The image, as he straightened his back and stood upright to pose for the 15 mm camcorder film, has stayed with me forever. That was the last time I saw him.

We spent a week with my parents and Pramilla in Durg. The nearest airport was just an isolated little building with a single runway where planes landed only on certain days of the week. Pita-ji and Mother met us with garlands of marigold and roses as we came down the stairs of the small plane. Once again, we were being treated as if we were celebrities.

As we breezed through so many places, meeting family, taking pictures, and storing memories, my heart was not at ease, always asking one question. *Am I an Indian, or am I now an American?* I had left India to become an American citizen. I was proud of my decision. And yet, as I immersed myself into the colorful life of India, my heart vacillated between the two worlds like the pendulum on Pita-ji's clock. *Do I want to leave my beautiful land and settle in a foreign country?* I asked myself repeatedly. I had gone to America on a permanent resident visa with the hope that someday I would be granted full citizenship. I was going through a labor-intensive residency program so that I could have my degree recognized there. I had made all these decisions, and yet the dilemma haunted me like my own distorted shadow.

My parents and my father-in-law were looking at us differently too. Their eyes perceived the change. We were their children, but we were now non-Indian. We were American. Their grandchildren were certainly American. Rajiv and Ravi had forgotten their native language and were speaking English with an accent that was hard for them to understand.

♦♦♦♦♦♦

The morning after our arrival in Durg, an elephant was lumbering down our street. Pita-ji hailed at the *mahout,* the elephant's caretaker, and asked if he could take a short break. "My grandchildren have come from America. I would like you to give them a ride on your elephant," he told the mahout. The elephant and the mahout were on their way to lead a religious procession for some family in town. The mahout did not seem to be in a hurry. "Not a problem, sir. I can do that," he said. "Those people can wait. If I am not there by noon, they will understand. After all, who can prod an animal to go any faster than the stride he chooses?"

This relaxed pace of life in Durg was such a contrast to my life in Toledo where I had to account for every minute of my life. If I reported on duty just a couple of minutes after seven thirty in the morning, I had to answer to Dr. Rejent's embarrassing comment, "You are running late today, aren't you?"

We all gathered on the front porch and watched. Following the mahout's commands, the elephant went down slowly, first bending his forelegs and then gracefully folding the hind legs and lowering his back. He sprawled in front of our house, occupying most of the street. That stopped the traffic, but nobody seemed to mind. No one complained. A circle formed around the elephant as the two American boys, now six and seven years old, slowly approached the enormous animal, touching and feeling its rough, corrugated skin. Encouraged and helped by the mahout, they took courage and climbed the elephant's mountain-like body and onto its back. They and their cousins sat holding onto each other and laughing as the mahout took his position on the elephant's neck. He took them for a ride around the block. When he returned, Pita-ji thanked him and gave him a rupee for his service.

"Will you remember this day when you return to America? You must tell your American friends about it," Pita-ji said to Rajiv and Ravi. He was delighted to see his grandchildren having an experience that they could not dream of in America.

A couple of days later, Pita-ji said to me, "I don't know what kind of entertainment you have for your children in America. They probably have very fancy toys to play with, but I would like to show them what we have available in our little town. I would like to arrange for the *bandar-wala,* man who trains monkeys, to come and give them a performance. Do you think they will like that?"

"Oh, they will love it," I said. *And I would too,* I thought, not having seen a *bandar-bandari* dance performance since I was a child.

Next morning, the monkey-dance performer—a slim man in his forties—arrived at our doorstep with two skinny monkeys. He had brought with him two small wooden stools and a few bananas that he would use as rewards for the monkeys if they performed well. He set up his paraphernalia on the small open area in front of the house and settled down on his haunches with a *damaru,* a handheld drum, and a bamboo stick splintered at one end. He spoke to the monkeys as if he were talking to his own children, asking them to behave in the presence of Sahib-ji and the American guests. The monkeys, their faces and bottoms as black as charcoal, walked around like two-year-old kids, ignoring their trainer and continuing to play with the stools, turning them upside down and rolling them around. As a reprimand, the performer whipped the bamboo cane on the packed gravel, making a sharp, screechy sound. A firm voice of the master and the thud of the splintered cane was enough for the monkeys to come to attention.

While the monkey-dance performer set up his show, Pita-ji and Mother pulled up their armchairs to the edge of the veranda. Pramilla and I sat on the steps, and the children—Rajiv, Ravi, their cousins, and a few kids from the neighborhood—squatted all around.

The story line wove around the life of a *sansari*, an average worldly man—love, marriage, and ghar-grahasthi. This is how the play went:

Mr. Monkey woos Mrs. Monkey. They fall in love and marry. Then there is the grind of daily life. Mr. Monkey is gone all day, leaving Mrs. Monkey to clean house, cook, and wash his clothes. The Mrs. is disenchanted with life. She complains. "I don't think you love me," she gestures in response to the signals given to her by the beat of the damaru that the turbaned performer is maneuvering with contorted movements of his wrist. Simultaneously, he is reciting the story line in a singsong fashion for the benefit of the adults in the audience. "You married me because you needed a wife to cook for you and to run your home," Mrs. Monkey says. Mr. Monkey shakes his head from side to side. As the dance performer recites the story, Mr. Monkey picks up cues and performs as if he were a puppet being guided by a human hand. He dances around and around the Mrs., smiles coyly, and tries to charm her. Mrs. Monkey is not convinced with his gimmicks and decides to give up her marriage. She returns to her mother's home. Here she gets advice from her mother (role played by the performer himself), and she is asked to go back to her husband. "No, no," she says, and she keeps shaking her head. She fusses and pouts and refuses to move. Finally, Mr. Monkey returns to her. This time, he brings her a skirt and a necklace. We watch Mrs. Monkey wear her new skirt and Mr. Monkey place the necklace around her neck. After a few attempts, he is able to maneuver the clasp. As Mrs. Monkey walks upright on her hind legs in a poised, ladylike gait, we all clap in admiration. She is finally convinced of Mr. Monkey's love and returns to her life of ghar-grahasthi. They live happily ever after.

When the show was over, the two monkeys were rewarded with bananas. They sat on their stools, peeled the fruit, discarded the skin, and gracefully devoured the flesh. Pita-ji had placed his hand ever so gently over Mother's, his fingers intertwined with hers. I got into a pensive mood. I translated today's story line to my own: my arranged marriage, my ongoing desire to be a pediatrician in America, the role my karma had played in my life. I looked at Pita-ji. He appeared content. Although his hair was sparse and gray, his forehead was wrinkle-free. He smiled frequently. In the past years, he had taken the pilgrimages to holy places that he had dreamed of. Maybe he had achieved what he believed to be moksha—ultimate peace.

I looked at my husband, my children, and my accomplishments. I felt rejuvenated and ready to return to America and tackle the remaining years of my residency.

Chapter 42

When I returned to America, the Toledo I had left just three weeks earlier had changed. The familiar happy world that I was living in had evaporated, leaving in its wake an empty shell.

Among the Christmas cards and other mail that had collected over the weeks, there was a letter from Dr. Rejent. It caught my eye, because I was not expecting any correspondence from her. I opened it immediately. I was puzzled and bewildered. I read it and then read it again. *This cannot be,* I thought. *There must be a mistake.* But, there wasn't. The letter was signed by Dr. Rejent, addressed to me, and had been delivered by registered mail. It stated that I had been terminated from the residency program. Reason: I had left without my leave being sanctioned and had thereby behaved very irresponsibly.

With tears in my eyes, I handed the letter to Kris. He was more perplexed than I was. When we were planning our trip, I had casually commented to him that neither Dr. Rejent nor Dr. Brookfield had asked me to fill out lengthy forms for the approval of my leave as might have been the case in India. He had replied, "Not in this country. I have not filled out any forms. I have told my boss about our trip and have given him the dates I would be gone. If for any reason we are unable to return on our planned date, he will understand that the circumstances were unavoidable, and the secretary will adjust my paycheck. America honors the honor system, you know. That is what I like the most about America."

Toledo had not honored the honor system. Toledo had let me down. On that last day before leaving the hospital, I had made sure that I had finished all my work, taking time to complete my charts on the floor and in the record room. I had visited the patients that were assigned to me, briefing them about the resident who was taking over. Finally, I had taken that proverbial five minutes of quiet time to think if there was anything more that needed to be done before I took the long oversees trip where communication would be next to impossible. And now, I was told that I was irresponsible.

I set the envelope aside in disbelief. I tried to busy myself with unpacking the suitcases and taking care of laundry and other sundry chores. Jet lag or not, I was scheduled to report at the hospital the following morning.

Much as I tried, I could not ignore the letter. After a couple of hours, I picked it up again, hoping that I had misread its contents. Nothing had changed. It was clearly stated that I had been terminated. I finally acknowledged the facts and absorbed its implications. My hopes and dreams of practicing medicine in America had been shattered by the stroke of Dr. Rejent's pen.

I felt a trembling, stabbing sensation in my heart. What had gone wrong in my absence that made Dr. Rejent feel that I was irresponsible? I thought about my life in the hospital and all the members in my lovely Toledo family. I thought about Dr. Brookfield, about my coresidents, Dr. Naidu and Dr. Luke. I thought about all the other attending doctors who were involved in my training. I thought of the pleasant nurses on the floor who always greeted me with a smile. I thought about the record room staff.

Grim possibilities went through my mind. Someone must have a grudge against me to trigger this. Or could it be a disgruntled patient who was not happy with the services provided by the resident covering for me and had made a complaint? It could be one of the nurses. It could be anybody. I lost the trust that I had developed in my loving, caring Toledo family—and in fact, in humanity itself. Years earlier, when I was in medical school, some of my friends used to say, "You must trust *no one* in this world until they prove themselves." I questioned their philosophy. I had liked to walk through life trusting the world around me until it proved itself to the contrary. I had sailed through life most of the time. This time, I was wrong. I had trusted everyone in Toledo, and someone had betrayed me.

Dr. Rejent had never raised an eyebrow about my work in the past. In fact, in a male-dominated workplace, she always had a soft spot in her heart for me. I knew this because at times she had referred to me as "my favorite resident" when we were on rounds. So what had gone wrong? What had changed?

Each time my eye fell on the red seal of that envelope, I felt an extreme hatred for the woman who had shattered my dreams.

The feelings of loathing and disgust did not last long. *There must be a misunderstanding, some reason for this, a big mistake,* I told myself. *I must trust my instincts. Maybe Dr. Brookfield did not get a chance to communicate with her. He himself might have gone away on vacation when she returned. I will talk to her and sort it all out.* She had written in her letter, "I am asking you to please come to my office in an effort to straighten out the mass of confusion that seems to have erupted." I could clear everything in our meeting. All she would need to do would be to talk with Dr. Brookfield.

The following morning, I drove to Toledo. The air felt thick and heavy, and the snow had lost its luster. The drive was long and tedious. I turned the radio on and then turned it off. The same songs that had energized me in the past felt like poison to my ears. My thoughts wandered. Just three weeks earlier, I was driving these roads as a happy, jubilant resident, and now I had nothing to look forward to. This woman, someone I had always respected, had put an end to it all. *No matter,* I thought. *I am sure we will resolve the matter when I see her.*

I reached the hospital and pulled into the residents' parking lot. I parked my car at the usual spot and felt an irregular seam of guilt go up my spine—I was parking illegally. I was, after all, not a resident anymore. What I had wished was to run to the pediatric ward and greet my friends and coworkers and tell them about my exciting trip to India. Instead, I took slow, anxious steps toward the department of pediatrics. Ethyl, the secretary, welcomed me and then peeked into Dr. Rejent's office, announcing my arrival. "She will see you in a bit," she said to me, and she offered me a seat. I waited a long time. I recapitulated everything I was going to say to her.

The door opened, and I walked in. I saw a cold, steely figure in front of me, and I froze. My head went blank as I slumped in the chair across from her. The simple words that would have easily explained my situation, words that I had rehearsed, vanished from my head. I waited for her to say something. Then she spoke. It did not take but a minute for our dialogue to end. I had left without my leave being sanctioned and had behaved very irresponsibly, she repeated, just as she had written in her letter.

"But, Dr. Brookfield …" I started to say.

She interrupted. She said that Dr. Brookfield had no authority in the matter. She was the only one in the department who made these decisions. The one extra week of my absence was an unauthorized leave.

"But you were away …" I wanted to say. I knew it was futile. She had closed my file, set it aside, and was turning her attention to the other correspondence on her desk. I stood up to leave. She handed me a piece of paper, a copy of the note she had sent to the accounts department. My paychecks had been stopped.

Feeling weak and dizzy, I went to the residents' room so that I could lie down. I stared at the ceiling and then at the small piece of paper with her signature. *My residency has been terminated,* I repeated to myself. I agonized at the thought of this reality. Everything I had invested in my career had been taken away from me with one small stroke of the pen.

Once I composed myself, I approached my colleagues, Dr. Naidu and Dr. Luke. If they had slipped in taking the additional night calls that we had agreed upon, causing a disruption in patient care, that would explain her anger. They shook their heads. "Everything was quiet when you were away. The wards were practically empty. Holiday time is always quiet. Everyone wants to be home for Christmas," they said. "You should have known by now—that woman cannot be trusted."

Unfortunately, I did not know.

I met Dr. Brookfield and asked if he would speak to Dr. Rejent on my behalf. After all, it was he who had sanctioned my leave. He was brief. "She is the chief. Her word is final. I don't think I can do anything." From the way he spoke to me, I gathered he must have tried.

My career as a pediatrician had come to an end.

♦♦♦♦♦♦

I started my journey back to Ann Arbor worn out and exhausted. At some point during my drive, my anger eased and transformed into a deep sense of guilt. *Everyone in Toledo had always been nice to me in the past. Now everyone is avoiding me. By going to India, I have, in some way, inconvenienced them all. That is my curse, my going away to India where I could not be reached.*

I could not undo that curse.

Hate pulsed through my veins again. I felt victimized and helpless. There was a choking sensation at the base of my throat that would never go away. *I should not have listened to Kris. I should have asked for something in writing. I should have never gone to India. I should have …* everything gnawed at me and made no sense.

I spent days and months mourning my lost opportunity. I blamed myself constantly. No one could help me through my feelings. I tried to find peace from within and accept life just as it was being dealt. I was raised to believe that there was a good in every act of karma, no matter how sinister it seemed at the time. I could not locate the good. I had to surrender to blind faith. Internalizing my emotions, I settled into a new life, a life of joblessness.

I had signed up for taking the first part of the pediatric boards, a written exam. Normally, this was offered only when a resident was at the PL-2 level. Taking my past experience into consideration, the pediatric board authorities had given me permission to take it while I was a PL-1. This was my hidden benefit, I convinced myself. I was being given uninterrupted time to study for my boards. But what good would this exam do if I did not have the necessary residency? I could not get a license to practice medicine. I did not want to think of the future. I had paid for the exam, and I must study for it. I burned all my negative energy by returning to my favorite cubicle in the library.

Chapter 43

I decided to approach Dr. Rejent again after my heart had quieted down and my mind held no malice. With time, whatever had made her so upset would also have passed. There would be an opportunity for fresh dialogue. Perhaps I would finally understand the real reason for my termination. It would give me a sense of closure. Then I could move on. On the other hand, who knew—she may warm up to me again. I'll tell her that I had passed my boards. She will be delighted to hear the good news and will reinstate my residency.

With all the mixed emotions floating in my head, I called Dr. Rejent's office. Six months had gone by. June was the time for hiring new residents, a good time to call. Ethyl answered the phone.

"Do you think she will talk to me?" I asked. Secretaries can always forewarn you of the boss's moods.

"Oh, Dr. Rejent is not here anymore, thank goodness. Do you want to make an appointment with Dr. Torres? He is our new chief," she said.

A *male* chief. I cringed. "Think about it. Do you have a chance? You are a *woman*," Dr. Oliver had said to me, declining my application for a residency in the school of medicine in Ann Arbor. Was I ready to hear these words again? Whatever my identity, whatever my flaws, and whatever my fate, I had to accept them all. I made the appointment.

As I parked my car at the hospital, feelings of guilt resurfaced in my mind. I had proved to be irresponsible. I had gone to India without my leave being sanctioned. I felt like a dirty criminal who was there to make a confession and beg for pardon. As I walked up to the elevator and hurried to the department of pediatrics, I hoped I would not encounter a familiar face. How would I explain my disappearance to them? I walked close to the walls of the long corridor, my eyes following the splotchy pattern of the linoleum tiles. Unsure of what lay ahead, I proceeded straight to Dr. Torres's office.

My only desire at this point was that I be given a chance to tell my story. And my only hope was that I would find the right words to tell it. I wanted Dr. Torres to know that I had done no wrong, at least not intentionally. Yes, I was a female, and I was brown, and I was struggling to find a footing in the male-oriented world in America. If this was indeed a crime, I needed to be convinced of it. Maybe he would be the person to convince me, and I would seek another career.

When I walked into Dr. Torres's office, I saw no anger or malice in that room. He rose from his chair and greeted me with a courteous handshake, the color of his skin similar to mine. My file lay open on his desk. He thumbed through it, and I saw a faint smile build up on his face as he stopped to peruse some of the documents. He looked at me and waited for me to say something. My nerves suddenly relaxed, and I began to rearrange my thoughts. I should be brief and not take up a lot of his precious time. I must tell him my side of the story—all of my story. If there is an opportunity, I can also tell him about my past encounter with Dr. Oliver. Maybe he will mentor me, and together we will decide my future. Does a female from India with a brown skin have a chance in this country?

For a few moments, I sat mute, unable to speak. Then, looking at his gentle face, words began to tumble out of my mouth senselessly. I was in a hurry to tell him everything. He interrupted, "I have reviewed your file, and I don't see anything personal against you. Whatever it was, it was all internal, and you had nothing to do with it. It was between the two authorities, and you were caught in the middle." He was smiling. Then, in a more philosophical tone, he continued, "I was an immigrant once too. We come to this country trusting. Yes, we do come in trusting. New immigrants have it tough." His body language comforted me more than his words.

He reinstated my residency. I thanked him for his kindness, and uncontrollable tears rolled down my cheeks. I finally understood my crime. Dr. Rejent had been a newly appointed acting chief and was establishing her own identity at the time, and so was Dr. Brookfield. Without realizing it, I had circumvented the authority of a female boss and gone to her subordinate, a male, to sanction my leave. In the America of the seventies, that was a crime.

Once again, my karma was tracking my life. I returned to the residency program the following week. I rebuilt my trust in the world around me. It was the same pleasant world, my Toledo family, my coresidents, and my busy schedules. I did not see Dr. Rejent. I heard that she had left the department and returned to an office-based private practice somewhere. Mention of her name gave me goose bumps, and I had no desire to visit her. I immersed myself into my work, taking interest in everything new that I could learn. Dr. Torres gave me the opportunity of postings in upcoming fields such as learning disabilities and ADHD. We had been oblivious of these conditions in our training in India. New residents joined, and I made lasting friendships.

On March 7, 1974, I completed my residency. I had given up my job as a pediatrician in India when I had accepted the life of ghar-grahasthi in an arranged marriage. After almost eleven years, I was a pediatrician again—now a board-certified pediatrician in America.

Epilogue

My husband and I moved to Northern Virginia, and I set up my practice in the city of Fairfax. Years passed. My children grew, and so did my practice. I got engrossed in doing what I loved most—caring for sick children and, of course, in ghar-grahasthi. I did not have time to think about the grueling past, and even when I did, the role Dr. Rejent had played in my life appeared like a fading dot in my memory.

After I retired, a friend asked me to accompany her on a trip to Ann Arbor and Toledo. This gave me pause to look back. In Ann Arbor, I retraced my student days, painting those memories with nostalgia. I walked through the university campus and located the school of pharmacology and the library where I used to study. The familiar blue bus was still running from the student housing to the university campus—still free of charge. The sandbox just ten feet away from my apartment was unchanged—four- and six-year-old boys and girls at play.

In Toledo, I met Dr. Brookfield, now working part-time and doing what he loved best—teaching residents. He graciously showed me around the hospital, describing the physical changes in the layout of the buildings and talking about the politics that were keeping the place from growing into a great children's hospital. *Politics never go away,* I thought.

I began pondering about the politics that had almost ended my career as a pediatrician so long ago. I got an urge to meet Dr. Rejent and resolve that deep-down—though almost forgotten—wound that she had inflicted.

Just as I had been finding my place in a male-dominated world, Dr. Rejent might have been struggling with her own identity. I might have been at the wrong place at the wrong time.

I visited Dr. Rejent in her new home—an assisted-living facility. I learned that she was suffering from symptoms of Alzheimer's and Parkinson's disease.

"She loves to have visitors," the receptionist said as I checked in at the front desk. "Her door is always open."

When I walked into Dr. Rejent's studio apartment, she was sitting in her living room, staring into space with a blank expression. She turned to look at me, and I introduced myself as one of her past residents. Her masklike face brightened, although I am not sure how much she remembered about me. She asked me to sit down, and I took a seat beside her.

As we sat side by side on her sofa, I held her hand in mine. I felt her warmth. I felt a pulse of camaraderie. She picked up a photo from the end table. "When I was in medical school, we were just three women in a class of one hundred," she said in a slow, gentle voice, pointing to the three females seated in the front row, dressed in white skirt-and-jacket uniforms. "Life was hard for us women in those days, wasn't it?" she asked and repeated over and over again. "Yes, very hard," she said. She talked about her lonely life, never married, no children. I listened without a response.

She has her own stories to tell, I realized.

After forty minutes, I got up to leave, gave her a hug, and kissed her cheek.

"Come again," she said.

Glossary

alloo-paratha—Indian flatbread with potato stuffing

Amma-ji—Respectful way to address an elderly woman

angrezi-log—British people

anna—A coin equivalent to one-sixteenth of a rupee—now obsolete

arti—A clay lamp waved gently before an idol or person to expel darkness and infuse light; a ritual of profound spiritual sentiment

ashirwad—Blessings

ashramas—Spiritual resting places

aum—A symbol considered auspicious in all Hindu religions; when chanted, its sound represents the cosmic source of creation, sustenance, and destruction

badhi-behen—Older sister

bandar-bandari—Male and female monkey

bandar-wala—Man who trains monkeys

banjara—A gypsy race of India

barat—Group of attendees at a wedding from the groom's side

baratis—Individual members in the groom's group of attendees

beta or beti—Term of endearment for a child (son or daughter)

bhabhi—Sister-in-law

bhajiyas—Chickpea flour and vegetable fritters served as snack food

bhangra—Punjabi folk dance

bharat-natiyam—A classical Indian dance

bhrumadhya—Distinctive area of the brain between the eyebrows and just above the nose

bibi-ji—Respectful way of addressing a female

bidi—Tobacco flakes rolled in a leaf, a poor man's cigarette

bindi—A decorative mark in the center of forehead

bindu—A spot on the forehead between the eyebrows and just above the nose

bua-ji—Father's sister

chacha-jis—Paternal uncle (*s* added to indicate plural)

chachi-jis—Paternal uncle's wife (*s* added to indicate plural)

chai garma–garam—Freshly brewed hot tea

charpoy—Lightweight cot with a wood frame and cotton tape webbing

chatai—Area mat made with native grasses and reeds

chaukidar—Watchman

cholle-allo—Chickpea and potato curry

cholle-baturae—Chickpea curry served with deep-fried naan bread

choli—Tight-fitting blouse worn with a sari

choti—Small or little

dahi—Homemade yogurt

dal—Generic word for all lentils

damaru—A crudely made handheld drum

dhobi—Man who provides clothes-washing services

dholak—A double-headed drum played to give a beat for folk singing or dance

didi—Respectful way of addressing an older sister

dudh-wala—Man who delivers milk

dupatta—Modesty wrap

gandi naalis—Above-ground channels that carry wastewater

Ganesha—Deity known for removing all obstacles

ganga-snaan—Ceremonious bath in the River Ganges

garam masala—Special blend of Indian spices

ghar-grahasthi—Stage that encompasses marriage, family life, and career—see the appendix for the four stages of human life

gobhi-paratha—Indian flatbread stuffed with cauliflower

gol-matol—Roly-poly

gul-mohar—A flowering tree

homa—Metal grill used for lighting the sacred fire

hoshiar—Alert and courageous

jai-mala—Ceremony where garlands are exchanged by bride and groom

jamadarini—Untouchable woman who cleans latrines

janam-patri—Astrological scroll prepared by a priest at a child's birth

janana—For women only

jhopar-patties—Slum living quarters

ji—Gender-neutral suffix that denotes a mark of respect

kal-yug—Stage of downfall of the human race in the earth's timeline measured in yugas

karma—Fate or destiny (as used in this manuscript)

kanya-dan—Ceremony of giving away the bride to the groom; performed by father or father surrogate

karela—Indian bitter melon

katoris—Small metal bowls

khansama—Chef

khatia—Lightweight cot with a wood frame and hemp webbing, lighter and more versatile than charpoy

koftas—Vegetable balls simmered in curry sauce

kuan-wali-gulli—Street identified by its well

kum-kum—A red powder used decoratively in women's makeup

Laxmi—Goddess of wealth

maasar-ji—Mother's sister's husband

mahout—Elephant's caretaker

mama-ji—Mother's brother

mami-ji—Mother's brother's wife

mandala—A symbol that represents the balance of the universe

mandapam—Wedding canopy

masi—Mother's sister

matar-paneer—Curried peas and Indian cheese

mem-sahib—Term originally coined for addressing the wife of an Englishman—now commonly used to address any respectful woman

moksha—Deliverance of the soul from rebirth and restless transmigration

motichoor-ke-laddoo—Sweet balls made with chickpea flour, ghee, sugar, and cardamom

muh-dikhai—Presenting the bride to groom's guests

mundoo—Boy servant available for odd jobs

namaste—Form of salutation with palms placed together at the chest and a slight bow: "I bow to the divine in you."

naan—Leavened flatbread

paisa—Indian coin, one hundredth of a rupee

palak-paneer—Curried spinach and Indian cheese

palloo—Sari segment that drapes over shoulder and can be used as head cover paneer—Indian cheese

papum—Wrongdoing, transgressing from the truth

paratha—Flaky flatbread

pati-vrata-patni—Wife who devotes herself entirely to her husband

peedhi—A low stool used for seating

phooffer-ji—Paternal aunt's husband

pita-ji—Father

poori-aloo—Deep-fried puffed bread served with potato curry

poories—Deep-fried puffed bread

pundit-ji—Priest

Punjabi-dal—Lentils made Punjabi-style

purohit-ji—Priest educated in scriptures as well as astrology

raita—A yogurt side dish

rickshaw—A small three-wheeled, hooded passenger cart, pedaled by a laborer

rickshaw-wala—Man who pedals a rickshaw

rotis—Indian flatbread (chapatti)

s—Suffix added to many Hindi words to indicate plural

sadhus—Ascetics dedicated to achieving moksha

Sahib-ji—Master, originally used by natives of colonial India when addressing a European of status samaj—Society

samosas—Pastry stuffed with spicy potato

sansari—Average worldly person

shamiana—Colorful canvas enclosure

shika-kai—Shampoo made by boiling the bark, leaves, and pods of a special plant

Shiv-Parvati—God and Goddess of protection

shloka—Sanskrit verse

sindoor—A ritual in Hindu weddings where the bridegroom colors the parting of the bride's hair with kum-kum

stotrum—Hymn or prayer in Sanskrit

surai—Terra-cotta potbellied container with a narrow spout used for storing drinking water

tandoor—A clay oven

tandoori-rotis—Flatbread baked in a tandoor

thali—Stainless-steel plate

tiffin—Snack

tilak—Colored powder or paste placed on the forehead as a spiritual or religious symbol

tonga-wala—Man who drives a two-wheeled horse-drawn carriage

toor-dal—A fragrant Indian yellow lentil

wala—Suffix added to a person or object to connote profession or ownership

Appendix

Stages of Life in Hindu Philosophy

In Hinduism, the human life span is divided into four stages, often referred to as *ashramas*. The first stage, *brahmachari,* is the early life—that of studentship. The second, *ghar-grahasthi*, encompasses the span of marriage, career, and family life. The third stage, *vannaprastha,* requires that we slowly begin to give up the active pursuit of worldly gains and the ties that bind us to this earth and start a life of introspection. The last stage, *sanyasa*, takes us to a deeper introspection, that of looking inward, preparing for the next journey, seeking moksha, rejecting anything that constrains liberation and thus exiting this body peacefully. The division is arbitrary, and there is often an overlap as we merge from one stage to the next.

Boundaries of the Wind

Photos

Image layout: Courtesy of GRC Direct

Urmilla (left) and Pramilla
1958

When our life was unencumbered by men, marriages, and babies

Our home (1961-1963) in Bhilai, Madhya Pradesh, India

Mother

Pita-ji

Family Priest

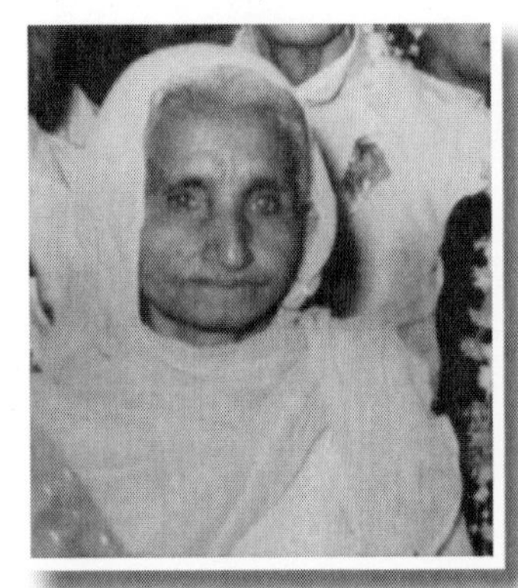

Grandma

Wedding Photos
1963

Urmilla

Kris

Kris as I remember him

College Photos - Urmilla
1951-61

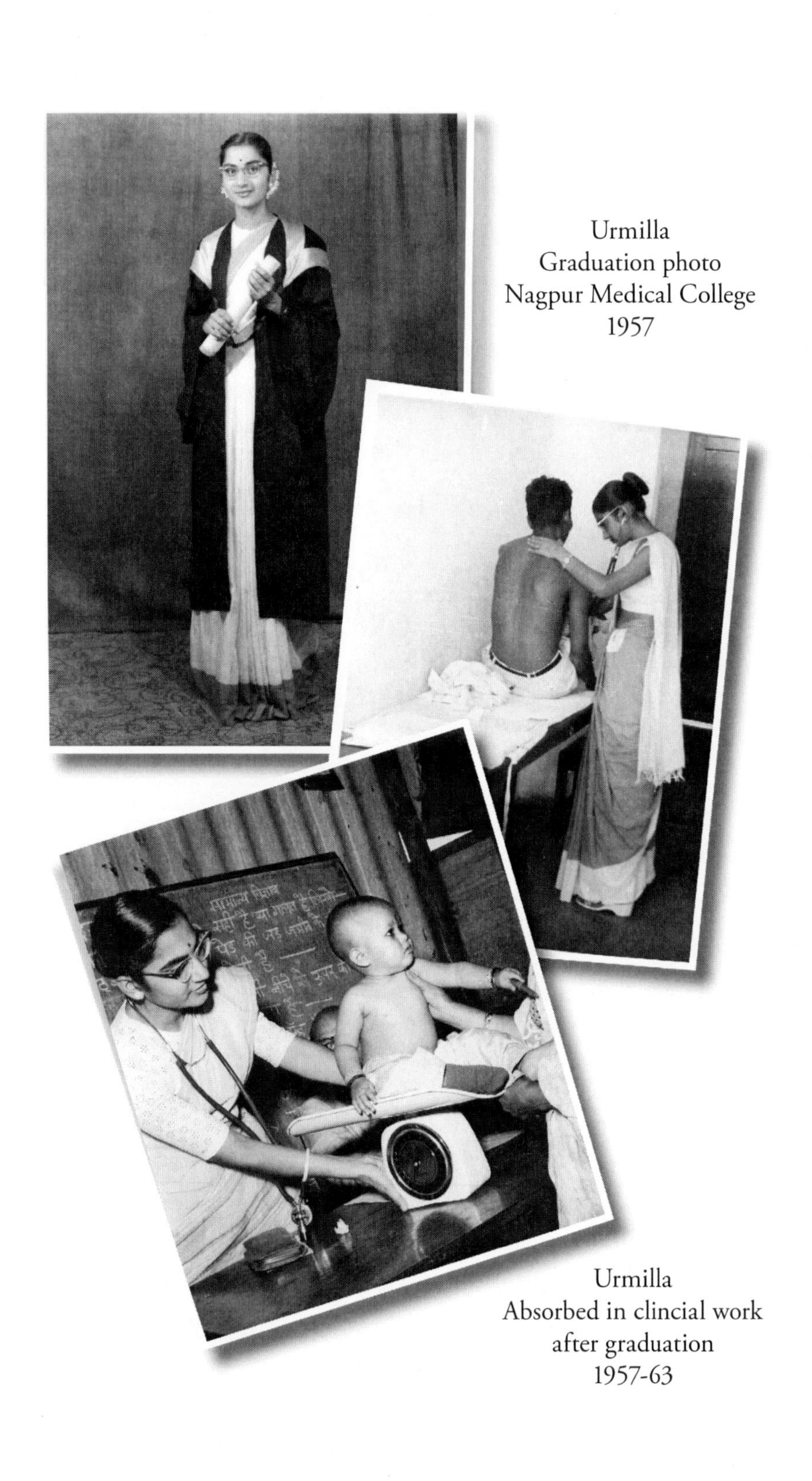

Urmilla
Graduation photo
Nagpur Medical College
1957

Urmilla
Absorbed in clincial work
after graduation
1957-63

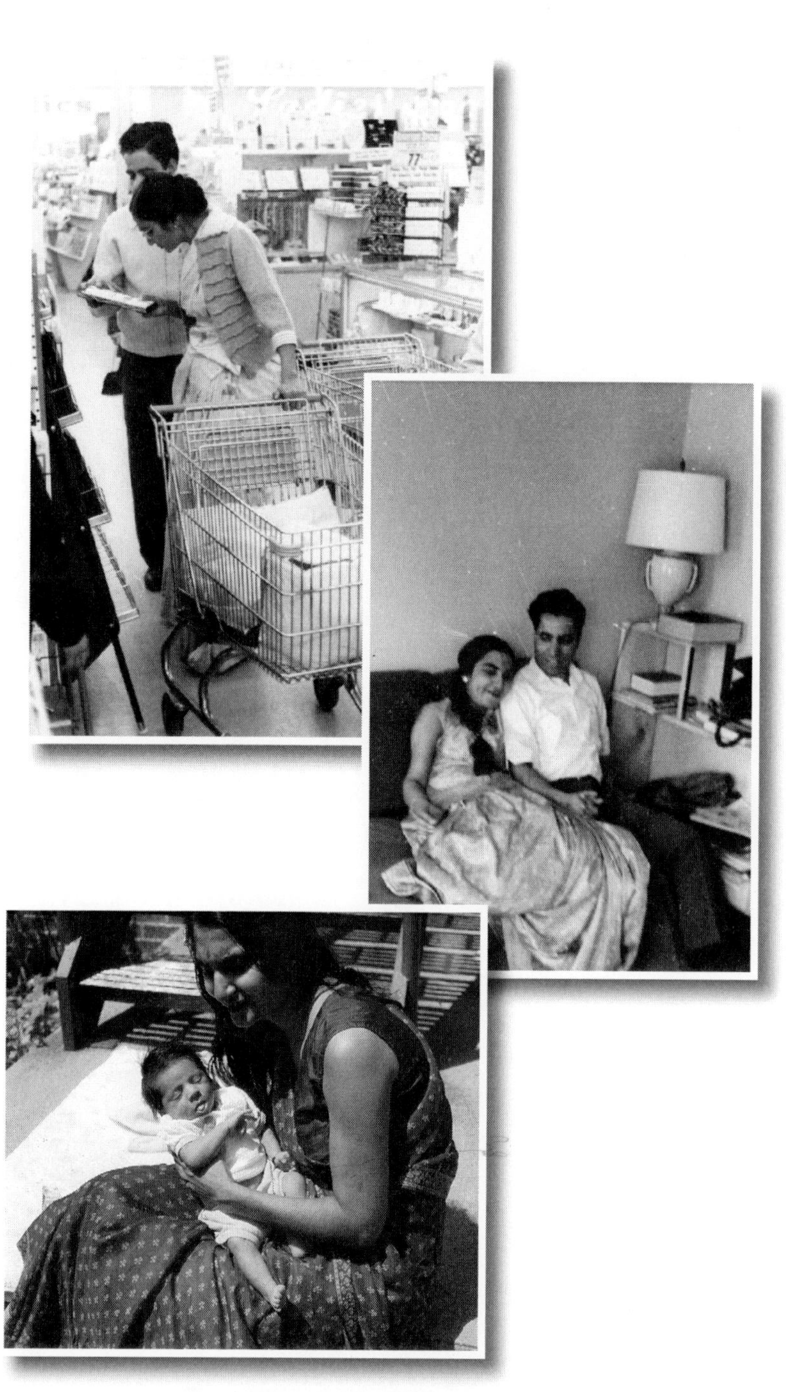

Storrs, Connecticut, U.S.A.
1963-64

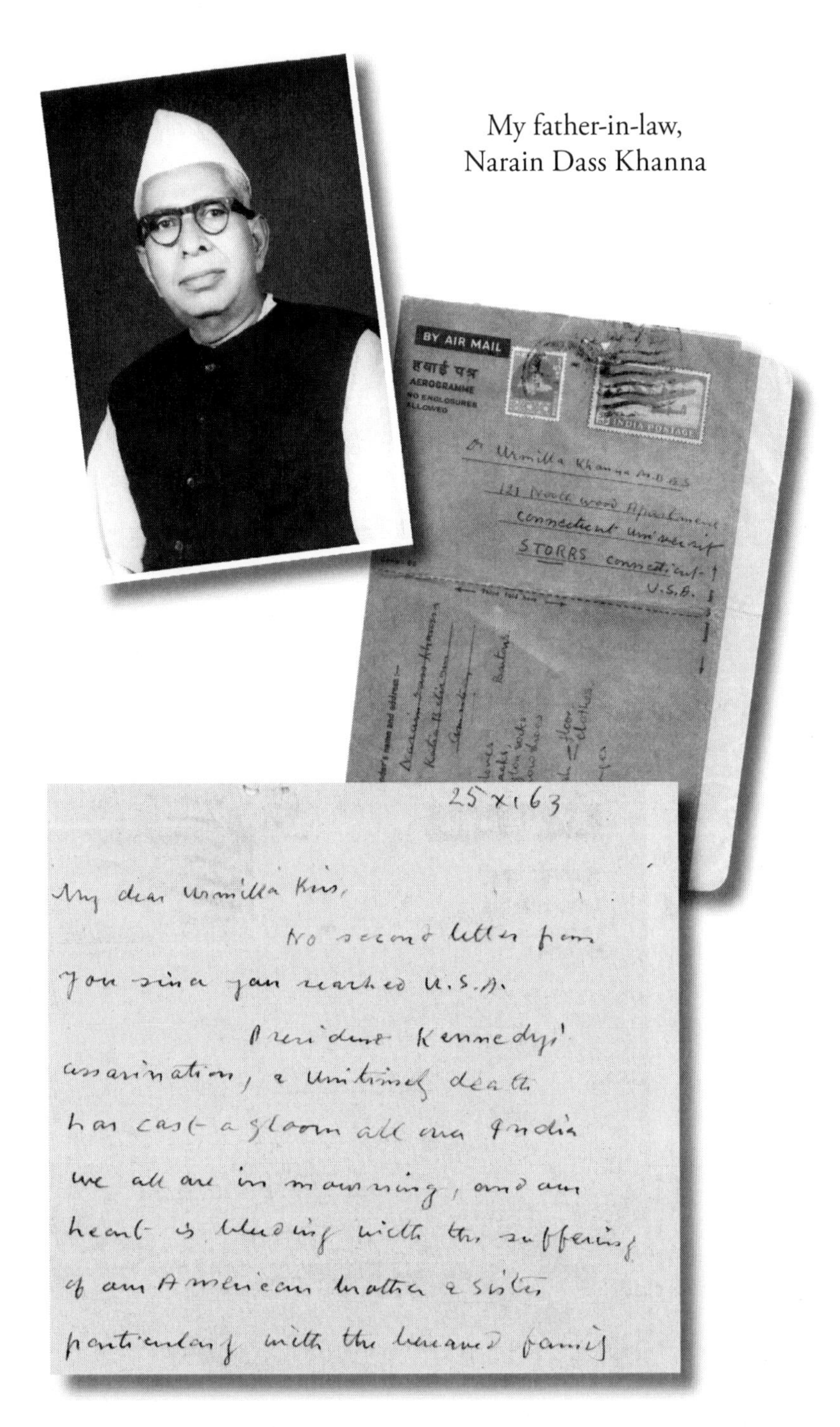

25 xi 63

My dear Urmilla Kis,

No second letter from you since you reached U.S.A.

President Kennedy's assassination, a untimely death has cast a gloom all over India we all are in mourning, and our heart is bleeding with the suffering of our American brother & sisters particularly with the bereaved family

My father-in-law,
Narain Dass Khanna

His stream of letters helped brighten the bleak Connecticut winter.

November 25, 1963

My dear Urmilla, Kris,

No second letter from you since you reached U.S.A.

President Kennedy's assassination and untimely death has cast a gloom all over India. We all are in mourning, and our heart is bleeding with the suffering of our American brothers and sisters particularly with the bereaved family of President Kennedy. May the departed soul rest in peace. May Almighty grant strength enough to all of us to bear this irreparable loss. Please convey of our sad feelings and heartfelt sympathy to our brothers and sisters of America in their sad plight. We are drowned in the ocean of sadness, it is all the more pity that the death of this assassin of President Kennedy has covered the crime and its background, the conspirators behind it as it is not one man's job.

The motive and cause of this crime ought to have been known by intelligent department of U.S.A. at any time in future, if not now.

Please send U.S.A. news paper to throw light as we are keen, very unhappy over this affair.

With love and greetings

Affectionately yours,

Narain Dass Khanna

He wrote further: India declared a holiday on that day in mourning of the death of our President.

The untimely death of the President has caused a stir in political as well as social circles here. All govt. offices are closed here today in his memory.

Saris to Skirts
Fulfilling the American dream
1968

After long nights at the hospital, there were cherished moments of bliss.1970-74

Durg
Madhya Pradesh
India
1971-72

Ann Arbor Apartment

University Shuttle Bus

Urmilla (left) and Dr. Brook

Dr. Rejent

Thirty five years later - a visit to
Ann Arbor, Michigan and Toledo, Ohio
2010

About the Author

Urmilla Khanna came to United Sates as a young bride in 1963. She became a board-certified pediatrician in 1974, had a successful career in pediatrics in Fairfax, Virginia and retired in 2000. She began writing as a hobby after the death of her husband in 2003. Since then, she has been writing with a passion. Some of her short stories have been published. Others are waiting to find their space in the literary world. This is her first book. She lives in Northern Virginia.

Edwards Brothers Malloy
Thorofare, NJ USA
May 3, 2016